Praise for *SOLO MUM BY CHOICE*

'Exuberant and tender-hearted, *Solo Mum by Choice* is a memoir of choosing the bravest love and pursuing it to the ends of every IVF procedure. In her debut memoir, Lorena Otes brings humour and warmth to the most dire experiences of her life, crafting a story that is immersive, touching and, ultimately, joyful.'
—*Ashley Kalagian Blunt, author of 'How to Be Australian' and 'Dark Mode'*

'Thank you to Lorena for writing the book that all solo mums and solo-mums-to-be need! The real story is in her sense of fulfilment, contentment and joy. The power of what is possible. She addresses the fears we all experience; she doesn't shy away from the hard bits. And anyone reading this book will feel seen, validated, and either empowered and excited about the future, or like they've found a soul sister.' —*Alisha Burns, founder, Solo Mum Society*

'Deciding to become a solo mother is one of the most difficult and confronting decisions a woman can make. The fear of telling your family and the possibility of rejection can be overwhelming. What I loved most about this book was the beautiful way Lorena's parents embraced her decision. Their support was deeply moving and gives hope to so many women standing at similar crossroads. A must-read for anyone contemplating becoming a solo mother by choice.'
—*Michelle Galea, founder, Australian Solo Mothers by Choice (ASMBC), Assisted Reproductive Treatment Families Australia (ARTFam)*

'For anyone who's ever wished the quirky best friend could be the hero of her own story. A tale of love, longing, and determination, with a happily-ever-after like no other. Adorable, off-beat, deeply vulnerable, and laugh-out-loud funny – this honest account of one woman's brave journey towards solo motherhood will make the sisterhood cheer.' —*Anne Freeman, award-winning author*

Praise for *SOLO MUM BY CHOICE*

'Engaging, compelling and moving. Moments of darkness are balanced with moments of brevity and lightness that made me snort-laugh. Highly, highly recommend.'
—*Holly Cardamone, author of 'The Summer In Between'*

'The uncomfortable truth about being female is that the fertile window is brief. After studying, working, travelling, and establishing a career, it is easy for the opportunity to have babies to slip away, resulting in an increasing number of women turning to reproductive technologies to overcome medical or social infertility. For any woman determined to have a family on their own terms, *Solo Mum by Choice* is a compulsory read as it confronts the challenges of infertility, whatever the underlying cause.' —*Dr Jo Skinner, GP and author*

'The story of an uncommon path to motherhood, told with grace and humour. Before I knew it, my heart was breaking, and my ovaries were aching. An immense story of love and longing.'
—*Porscia Lam, author of 'The Unlocking'*

'How far would you go to become the mother you know you were meant to be? This unflinchingly honest memoir lays bare the emotional and physical toll of IVF with courage and wit. I laughed, I cried, and I came away with a reminder that it's love, not genetics, that truly makes a family.' —*Holly Brunnbauer, author of 'What Did I Miss?'*

'Through Lorena's eyes, readers experience the emotional highs and lows, the stigma, and the societal judgment that come with choosing to have a baby alone. Told with humour, self-deprecation, and staggering strength.' —*Camille Booker, author, literary judge*

SOLO MUM
BY
CHOICE

Lorena Otes

HAWKEYE
PUBLISHING

First published in Australia in 2026 by Hawkeye Publishing

Cover Design by Skye Martin

This book is based on real events. To protect the privacy of people included in this book, some names have been changed.

Hawkeye Publishing recognises the Traditional Custodians of the lands where we live and work. We pay our respects to Elders past and present and extend that respect to all Aboriginal and Torres Strait Islander peoples. We celebrate more than 60,000 years of storytelling, art, and culture that continue to shape and enrich our world.

A catalogue record of this book is available from the National Library of Australia.

ISBN 9781923105607

Proudly printed in Australia.

www.hawkeyebooks.com.au

For Mum and Dad,
who have always supported me,
no matter what.

Author's Note:

This is a memoir through my own lens. Sometimes, opinions and views are expressed, but this is purely based on my own experience. It is not meant as an example of how to do things, and it is not intended as a guide, or as general advice. There is no right or wrong way to make a baby. Views on the way it happens are purely the interpretation of the beholder. So too, is lifestyle choice. I love being a solo mum by choice. For me, it was destiny. It may not be that way for everyone. Please seek counselling or professional advice if you are unsure. Parts of this book may upset some people. Please go gently.

All names, places, physical descriptions, and some occupations have been changed to protect the identities of medical professionals, friends, and in some cases, family. Some characters in this book are amalgams of people to create a streamlined storytelling experience. The author and the publisher exclude all liability for any loss or claim arising directly or indirectly from the use or misuse of this book, or any information or material in it.

Beginning

I managed to faint without spilling a single drop of wine. My glass miraculously landed upright, intact beside me on the loungeroom rug. To this day, I have no idea how. I came to in a blurry haze, trying to figure out what the hell had just happened. Before the fainting spell, there had been a buzz behind my eyes slowly taking hold. Like someone was pressing a mutant wasp to the inside of my forehead, and I couldn't make it stop. Thinking quickly, I threw the needle into the sink and grabbed my wine glass. I'd only had one sip. For Dutch-courage.

The lights in the bathroom stung my eyes. Too bright. Squinting my way out through the door, I told myself, *Just get to the lounge. Then you can lie down.*

My shoulders trembled as beads of clammy sweat filled the worry lines across my forehead, snaking down my temples in trickly waterfalls. Shooting stars raced across my eyes, blurring my vision.

The buzz got louder. Stronger. I swiped at the invisible wasp.

One foot in front of the other. You're nearly there.

I tried calling for help, but there was no one around, I lived alone. I could feel myself going down.

No, no, not this! Then there was only—

Black.

I came to feeling frightened and confused, unaware of what

had just happened. Where was the mutant wasp? The first thing I noticed was the glass I'd been holding, on the floor beside me, standing to like a soldier.

Before the buzz had begun, I'd been administering my third ever IVF injection, and although I was becoming more confident with it, a flutter of nerves still hovered beneath the surface. I'd imagined myself as the quintessential, qualified expert. *You've got this, Girl*, my subconscious had assured. The sip of wine had certainly helped.

The reason I'd fainted was becoming less patchy. I probably hadn't had enough water that day. Nor had I given myself enough pre-needle rest time. I'd forgotten to have lunch too. All this foolish breeziness had landed me in a heap on the floor beside an unfazed goblet.

Things were going to have to change. I had to find a way to realign my priorities, put my well-being at number one. Continuing with life in the old familiar spontaneous way would no longer do.

Clawing my limp body up the couch to lie down, I felt my senses awakening to motherhood. Sounds crazy, but something was telling me I needed to start thinking like a mum, even though I wasn't yet one. I had to protect the baby I longed for. In order to do that, I had to take better care of my own body.

Everything else, *everything* else, was a distant second.

PART ONE

1

Unlucky in Love

Richie was his name. Richie Hayes. And he captured me instantly. We met at the climbing gym while I was dangling upside-down by a finger and four toes, trying to reach for a higher hold.

'Push with your left foot,' commanded a voice from below.

Following the voice's order, my body surged upwards. Yelling in exertion, 'Aaargh!' I managed to grip the higher hold with a shaky hand. I'd done it. I was at the top!

'Yes!' yelled the voice. 'You got it!'

My hands shook as I released the holds, allowing gravity to drop me onto the crashmat below. Lying there in a sweaty, euphoric heap of lactic acid and giggles, I could see a face peering over me.

'You've been working on that for weeks.' It was the voice.

'Yep,' I replied. 'And I couldn't have done it without your help just now. Thank you.'

I'd seen him there a few times. He was a great climber. One of the best; confident and skilled.

'The name's Richie,' he said, offering his hand. Before I knew it, he had swung me to my feet and we were eye-to-eye.

Those big brown eyes seemed to care. His wavy beach hair hinted at impending excitement, and his slightly rough around the edges look spoke to me of untold adventure. Not my usual type, granted, but it didn't matter. From that instant, to me, he was flawless. And the parts of him that weren't? I could easily fix. I knew I could be the one to *save* him.

I loved his name. It sounded oh-so-cool, like the lead guitarist in a band. Well, Richie hated it. Loathed it, like his parents had committed the crime of the century by assigning it to him. 'It's the name bogans use to describe people who are cashed up,' he told me over drinks one night after the climbing gym. '*Richies*.'

'Well, you could call yourself Richard! Or Dick? Ha-ha.'

He wasn't amused. A shot of sombre hostility flew from his eyes, piercing me in the gut. Those shots would eventually gather and compound into vacuous wounds, but this first time I barely noticed it, full of naïve infatuation.

We soon learned we had motorbikes in common. 'You'd be the perfect girlfriend,' he told me. 'You're fun, you love climbing, and you're obsessed with motorbikes. Some guy's going to be very lucky to have you on his arm.'

I assumed the *some guy* he was talking about was going to be him, and from that moment on I anxiously awaited his move.

Richie had the *motorbike effect*: a term coined by a friend of mine, Monica, to describe the instant sex-appeal of somebody riding a motorcycle. This effect can sometimes wear off at restaurant pit-stops when helmets come off, revealing faces underneath. But not Richie. He had my heart both on and off the bike. He walked, talked, and breathed motorcycles. And riding alongside him was my world for a blissful while.

I looked deep into my psyche as Richie began to polarise me more and more. What was happening to me? This was one of the few times in my life I'd been entirely spellbound by a man. An entranced, loved-up mess. I couldn't see any faults in him and my giddy head orbited his every word. How could it be that he wasn't already taken? *How was Richie still single?*

It wasn't long before we were riding regularly. Sometimes he would pull over and I'd follow suit. We'd take our helmets off and he would point to something on the road ahead that I was advised to look out for. I hung on his every instruction.

'See that corner up ahead, Lorena?'

'I think so. The first little turn, or the second bigger one?'

'The big one. There are jacarandas above it. See the sludge on the road? That's from the petals. Be careful, it's slippery.' Then he'd put his helmet back on and lead the way.

I wanted to absorb everything he knew. And believe me — he knew a lot. According to him, anyway. I drank him up and spent as much time with him as I could. It felt like I was in the company of a superstar.

After a while, it became obvious that my time wasn't his priority. His time, however, was a coveted trophy. Something I had to win, earn, and compete for. Always busy. Sometimes available. Work. Friends.

One night we were on a ride with friends. I was riding beside Richie hoping we'd stop at the upcoming red lights so we could flick up our visors and chat. Point something out and laugh about it. A crazy seagull, a cute puppy on a leash, a souped-up chameleon Mitsubishi. This was in the early days of his company. I often think back to those happy times when I see people on motorbikes at traffic lights, flicking their gears into neutral, having a natter.

Back then, I was more rapt in wonder as to whether Richie was thinking of me as his girlfriend yet. We hadn't talked about it, and I was way too scared to bring it up. I let it ride, so to speak.

Meanwhile, we'd pulled over and were heading into a huge beachside pub. 'For a feed,' Richie said.

I was so lovesick at the time, food was the last thing on my mind, but I made a good attempt at it. Mid-meal, he stood up — it was his turn to buy a round of drinks. He took me with him, leading me to a bar around the back near the poker machines. His hands on my shoulders, he planted me against a wall in the corner near an ATM. I could feel his lips on mine. It wasn't a romantic kiss. Or our first. He was making a private show of affection in a public place with a ferocious urgency: the thrill of being seen. The joy of being caught in the act. I was reeled in, absorbed by the rush of spontaneity and passion.

After exactly thirty seconds, and without a word, he stopped, grabbed my hand, and directed me to the bar. We split the round and headed back to the group table with a tray of beers. No one had an inkling of what had just happened. Richie always let go of my hand as soon as his mates were in sight. I could feel my body deflate every time he did it.

Even in those early days of euphoria, something was unravelling. Why did Richie never kiss me or hold my hand in front of his friends? I was also hoping the rumours I'd heard that he only dated blonde twenty-something women were not true.

On one occasion, after a particularly long motorbike ride, I walked into the familiarity of his bedroom. This was the part of our time together I cherished the most. Richie's walls would come down a little bit when we were alone. He'd treat me like I was the only person in the world. I sat on his bed flicking through a climbing magazine from his bedside table.

He was standing beside his corkboard, which was covered in a collage of photos, like teenagers do in high school.

'Look,' he said, 'You're on here now.'

I scanned the immense compilation of Richie's friends and family, following the direction of his pointed finger. Yep, there I was. A small cut-out of my face in a crowded sea that was Richie's social network. I'd finally been promoted to his photo collage.

I smiled, feeling closer to him than ever. 'That's so sweet, Richie.'

I put my head on his pillow. Squinting my eyes, I studied the beige fabric of his cheap polyester pillowcase. Then. *No!* A clash of horror surged through me as I focused harder, praying my imagination was playing tricks on me. There, on his bed, I could see countless strands of long golden hair. Strewn everywhere, from the sweat-stained pillowcase to the bottom corners of Richie's king single bed.

I ran my fingers through my own black tresses. I could taste the vomit in the back of my throat. Gathering the courage to speak, I caught my breath, swallowed my nerves, and blathered out the question, 'Gee, Richie, it looks like someone with blonde hair has been (cough) in here.'

'Oh, that's just my mate, Claudia.' He gulped, followed by an awkward sigh.

I managed to stay the night. I wanted to believe him. I tried. And I think for a few flickering moments, I actually convinced myself. But there was a deep fracture forming in the façade of our relationship. Relationship? Was it that? I honestly still didn't have a clue. I was crumbling, holding strong only on the outside.

A few weeks later, my biggest fears were confirmed when I *accidently* met the owner of those infamous blonde hairs. A tall, beautiful girl stood before me, her long locks tied neatly into a ponytail. She beamed a sunny, toothy, cover-girl, eyes-very-much-part-of the-deal smile.

'Hi, I'm Claudia.'

She was slim and graceful, wearing tight leather riding pants. Her legs went on forever – just Richie's type. I asked how she knew everyone.

'Oh, through Richie, the guy I'm seeing,' she replied.

Pardon? 'Richie Hayes?' I gasped. I couldn't believe I was having this conversation.

'Yes, you know him,' she replied, more as a statement than a question.

'I thought I was the one he was "seeing",' I croaked.

She didn't even hear me, or register, and I hated her with every fibre of my being.

Richie was conveniently absent that night. Off working or something. A few days later when I asked him about Claudia, he came up with an inventive story: 'Oh yes, Claudia. She's a bit crazy, that one.'

For the first time, I didn't believe him. 'Then why are you friends with her, Richie?' I needed to know it all.

'I've been trying to palm her off. She's just an obsessive idiot.' His eyes darted around his bedroom, scanning his bed.

I had previously scanned it, but there were no evidential tresses this time.

It took me nearly five years in total to get Richie out of my life. We were never an official couple. I was just a toy for his ego; the booster he needed when he was in the mood. I would come running, and he knew it. Gosh, was I naive, and gosh, have I changed since those days! I can barely believe that girl was me. How could I have been so entranced by such a moron?

I was a true mess when I finally let go – in my late thirties and tenuous about getting out there into the dating scene. I figured I didn't want to be alone forever, and probably wanted to find someone to love.

What I really wanted was to find someone who would love me.

And, I wanted to have babies.

There wasn't anyone after Richie. He well and truly ground me to a pulp, and when I eventually emerged I was a limping, overcautious mess. In a sordid, ungainly attempt at revenge, I had a bit of a thing with his mate for a while. They'd fallen out and I think he probably wanted a piece of revenge from the old Richie pie as well.

Hooking up with Richie's best buddy felt like the ultimate act of betrayal. He seemed like a nice enough bloke. Quite cute and funny. We'd ride motorbikes together, eat pizza, and smoke cigarettes in his bachelor pad, while he force-fed me movies from the horror-genre that he knew I hated. He loved to witness my terror.

'Don't breathe a word to Richie,' he made me swear, like we were ten-year-olds fighting to keep the Santa secret from a little brother.

In the end, he had my eyes covered too, and I learned my final lesson. A real gentleman, whose charming idea of consent was to go ahead anyway. Between him and the other, I was left in a horrendous jumble of assault and humiliation – the knife truly in and twisted. I didn't feel I could risk another relationship ever again.

Shattered physically and mentally, my inability to trust was so high I could barely breathe. Which meant I was also somewhat afraid of other men out there. Not all men. But how would I know the difference? How could I tell which men would pretend to like me and string me along? The ones who'd pull me into their world of empty promises.

I also became quite angry, rearing up, wondering how my life had ended up this way. Why had I let those meagre men take control and trample me? I assumed I'd get married one day like my parents. I wanted to find happiness with a good man. A man like my father or my brother – honest, caring, protective, and kind. I knew for sure I was in no state to continue that search as I was. I also knew the trepidation would pass. I just had to wait it out. Come out the other end stronger and more aware.

Yet still, there was an even bigger dilemma.

The *tick-tock* of passing time and the ever-louder call of my biological clock. After turning thirty-eight, I knew I desperately wanted to have a baby. I wasn't sure how that would work but I started to muck it out in my head.

There were a few options I could think of:

1. Don't have a baby. (Easy!)
2. Go out, get drunk and… (Not as easy, but an option, I guess.) It alarms me the number of friends who have suggested this to me over time. 'Just go down to the pub, find the best-looking guy and, well, he never even needs to know.' (Um, no! Absolutely not!)

3. Actually force myself to go out on dates, meet someone fast, shack up, and get pregnant. (A bit desperate, but still workable if I could just get myself to do it.)
4. Do IVF as a solo mum by choice.

Numbers one and two were not options for me. No way. But I really did want a baby. And I wasn't going to trick some drunken fool down the pub into fathering one for me. Number three could have had potential if it hadn't been for Richie and his 'mate'. I had some healing to do, which would take far longer than the time I had left on my biological clock.

I'm a happy hermit and love my own company. So, crawling into my shell was the best option for the time being. But you can't make babies that way.

Bring on option four: IVF. I'd heard of a couple of single women who'd done it; had donor-conceived babies and found their 'happy ever after'. This was a serious option, so I hit Google for information.

Google is notoriously dangerous, especially when seeking medical advice. We all know that. 'Don't do it,' they say. And the inevitable eyeroll of a GP when the word 'Google' comes out of a patient's mouth is undoubtedly involuntary.

But I sat down at my computer and Googled like the clappers. And I was horrified. Firstly, I learned how expensive IVF was. Terrifying in itself! I watched videos of women injecting themselves. I studied processes, timelines, and fertility facts. The more I Googled, the more frightened I became – but something else was happening too: excitement crept in. This was something I could do! I could grab the bull by the horns, be proactive, and have a baby. By myself. Solo. I could pour all my energy into it and really, really, do this!

Yes, it was going to cost a lot. Yes, it was going to hurt. The needles! It was going to be difficult on my own in an emotional sense too. What would my parents and friends say? Would they think I was mad? I tried not to let my imagination run with too much abandon.

One thing was crystal clear after those few days of decision-making: I was going to forsake everything in my life to become a mum. I was going to say no to potential relationships because I needed all my emotional energy for IVF. I was going to pool all my money into it. No more overseas holidays. No deposit for a house. This was going to take everything I had, and I was going to do it.

After a very long minute, I picked up my phone and called Mum and Dad. What would they say? What was the world going to think? I was nervous, but eager to find out.

2

And So, It Begins

January 2012, age 38

'Are you pregnant, Miss Lorena? Not that you look it.'

Sometimes those little comments stung the most. I knew I didn't look pregnant, but that didn't matter. At the time, I desperately wished I was. The innocent remark of a student in my Monday advanced contemporary dance class hit home like an earthquake.

I loved my work as a freelance dance teacher, lucky enough to be teaching in some of the most renowned studios in the state. Taking all kinds of students from just under ten-years-old through to full-time classical ballet kids training to make a career of it. My technique classes were a blend of fun, hard work, improvisation, and the best part was I could choose any music I liked. Sometimes I was in the mood for a bit of Lady Gaga, other times Prince, Alanis Morissette, or 90's Madonna. The only artist off-limits was Bonnie Tyler, my absolute favourite singer. Her music was far too high on the sacred scale to get lost in the cyclic playlists of my daily grind.

For me, choreography has always been a form of escape. A chance for my imagination to take my very capable students to a level of expertise that, in many cases, was easily of professional standard.

To transpose the images from my head onto my dance students is a gift and to this day, it helps me get through tough times. I put on music, creatively play, composing dances in the way I guess a child would. Like disappearing down an artistic rabbit-hole, hiding from the world for a while. A joy, a privilege, and very often my saviour.

'I have an announcement to make,' I was telling my students on this particular day while pulling up a chair. Huge mistake in hindsight. The gesture of taking a seat to make an announcement was all too much considering how insignificant the *announcement-ette* was: something about starting a new performance group.

The vacuous comment of a thirteen-year-old girl suggesting I might be pregnant totally floored me. I had only just decided I wanted to be a mother, and the coincidence was unsettling. But I had to get used to feeling rattled. It was about to become a constant in my life.

Meanwhile, my parents' reaction to my solo mum by choice plans floored me in the opposite way. I felt nervous telling them. My hands were clammy and my stomach fluttered as I dialled their number. Our conversation went like this:

Me: 'Hi, Folks, I have some news.'

Mum: 'Is everything okay, sweetie?'

Me: 'Yes. It's just that I've made a big decision to… er… have a baby, um, on my (cough) own.'

Mum: (no pause whatsoever) 'Woohoo! That's great, Lorena! Wow, what an enormous decision, sweetie.'

Dad: 'Brilliant! Congratulations, Lorena.'

(Pause. I start to breathe again.)

Dad: 'How will it work?'

With my heart still beating into my throat, I clumsily

explained everything I'd Googled thus far, accompanied by a host of 'oohs' and 'aahs', mostly from Mum. I was so relieved their response was positive. I needed their support, even in those early stages. If they hadn't approved (which I knew was unlikely, because they have stood by my adventurous decisions my whole life), I would have been lost.

After our chat I felt heard, seen, and validated.

Way to go, future grandparents.

Becoming a mum hadn't always been at the forefront of my mind. In fact, for most of my early life, I wasn't maternal. Nor was I particularly interested in being in a relationship. Those things just didn't come naturally. As a teenager, I watched friends go crazy about boys, but I couldn't muster up any enthusiasm. Just wasn't interested. I wondered if perhaps I was gay, but that didn't seem to fit. Trying not to worry about it, I concentrated on my biggest loves: ballet, Madonna, and whether or not the legendary Jim Steinman would be the producer of Bonnie Tyler's next studio album.

As I grew older things didn't seem to change. I wanted to be in the ballet studio every day, perfecting my technique. I aspired to being a superstar like Madonna, singing into my hairbrush to a stadium audience of meticulously lined-up dolls and stuffed toys. The thought of dating made me ill, so I never dared to go there. I don't know why – some kind of yet-to-be-identified anxiety, perhaps? Regardless, I must have subconsciously sensed, even back then, that I was destined for the solo life.

By the time I reached my late twenties, I'd given relationships a bit of an awkward attempt. But none of them lasted. I would run the minute someone was truly interested, and somehow ended up chasing the *bad* guys I knew I wouldn't end up with. I'm sure a psychologist would have a field day rustling through my head to figure out why, but as I didn't feel like anything was *wrong* with me, I never considered seeing one.

I didn't want marriage – that would mean someone being there all the time, and *no way* to that! As Whoopi Goldberg famously said on being single: 'I don't want somebody in my house.' I wholeheartedly concur. I guess I could pull out the *never say never* line, but I have a feeling it's not relevant.

There can be an air of desperation around women dating in their late thirties – a stereotypical 'snagging him in quick' kind of approach, in order to get on with the business of bringing on the pitter-patter of tiny feet.

'Let's get married and have four (thousand) kids,' she shrieks after the first date. Cue immediate exit of said man.

Guys know about this. They'll sniff out a procreatively-challenged woman with a time-poor biological clock in a second. Then they'll run. Fast! They'll spring off quicker than you can say off-spring.

I'm not saying I wasn't that woman. I had my moments. And I don't want to suggest that all single women in their late thirties are like that. In the end, I was way too self-conscious to go down that road. Just couldn't do it.

In truth, I always found it tricky to be wholly open with the man I was dating, afraid to lose him. Some people can sit there on date number one, asking all the big questions: 'Do you believe in marriage? Do you want kids? How many?' Personally, I'd die asking that stuff, even on the fiftieth date. Too worried I'd scare the guy off! I couldn't even muster the courage to ask Richie if we were a couple.

I'll ask. I will. Next time. I just don't want to ruin such a perfect evening by getting heavy, I'd say to myself, unconvincingly. *Yeah, Lorena. Next time.* But relief would always wash over me the minute I'd let myself off the hook. I could breathe again.

It was so liberating, and a *coming out* of sorts when I finally took the pressure off, realising I could just remain single. There were subtle swathes of judgement from certain people in my life. Just a little lift of an eyebrow when absorbing the notion that I could possibly be happy alone. What? But surely you need a partner in life! A partner in *crime* as people like to put it. Those furrowed foreheads got to me in the beginning. I recall waves of embarrassment when put to trial over my own choices. Choices that really had zero to do with anyone else.

Well-meaning friends would gather. 'We have a friend you should meet. He's single, and he's great. Shall we give him your number?'

'No thanks, I'm fine.' I would smile. They would look confused or disbelieving. Nobody got it. Nobody seemed to get me.

'But you're never going to meet anyone if you don't try.'

'I have tried. And I hate it. I feel awkward and uncomfortable. Blind dates make me anxious, and I actually prefer spending time on my own.'

My friends eventually got the message. They learned not to worry about me, turning their focus to their own versions of settling down, having 2.4 kids, and doing the family thing. In the end, with the pressure lifted, it felt great that I could just be me.

As I got older, watching my friends have children made me ache. I submerged myself in the dream of motherhood. What it must be like to hold and care for a baby of your own. The unconditional love! I didn't want my life to go by without that experience.

My thoughts became grim as I leaped into the future, flying deep into my subconscious, imagining the last thoughts of my dying moments. Would I have any regrets? And if so, what would they be?

The answer was clear: the grief I'd suffer if I didn't have children, it would tear me apart, leaving me in a void of unfulfillment and aching longingness. I at least had to try to become a mother. I had to find a way while I could. It felt right. Something I didn't question. Something I had to make happen.

I never intended to tell many people of my solo mum plans. But the ones I did tell were the ones I could truly count on. My parents and friends were, and are, my cheerleaders. I am extremely lucky that although I did not win the lottery of good men, I certainly won the friends and family draw. Critical for someone embarking on something that was going to be not only difficult, but somewhat controversial too. How blessed I was to be so engulfed in love and support.

Oh, and I *did* need a man. A sperm donor. Now I just had to find one.

3

What Happens Now?

Winter 2012, age 38

The sheer number of women without partners walking through the doors of IVF clinics around the globe is truly staggering. Much higher than I ever imagined. I dove further and further into the realms of the solo mum by choice world, finding it astounding and amazing that this way of having children is fast becoming more and more common.

There's a whole solo mum by choice movement on the rise, growing exponentially by the day. I didn't realise at the time, but I was going to be part of a revolution. I was excited, to say the least!

IVF is no longer just about female infertility through lack of eggs or inability to conceive the natural way. Not having a male partner is also considered a form of infertility known as *social infertility*. Somehow, I found that term hilarious. It's so sterile. And yet there it was. I imagined being told, 'You're *socially infertile*, Lorena. You're going to require donor sperm.' Quite confronting, really. And though this form of infertility has existed for some time, to me it still seemed 'out there'.

Lifestyle choice has begun to overlap science. Even ten years before my decision, the chances of trying for a baby as a single woman would not only have been much less likely in terms of availability of treatment, but also almost impossible to finance. Not to mention socially far less acceptable. Go back to the 90s or before and it was unheard of, even illegal in some parts of the world.

Gay couples would have a few problems conceiving without IVF too. You don't have to stretch your imagination too far to work that one out. IVF has entered the building for all. Not just for infertile *couples*. Women can freeze their eggs as a safety net for having kids later in life. There are cancer patients and other terminally ill people, who still desperately want to procreate with their partner, who have the option of freezing their eggs or sperm. There are women who conceive using a deceased partner's sperm retrieved *after* he has died. Wonderful, and unimaginable, at the same time.

I had to get the ball rolling with my baby-making plans, but didn't have a clue how to begin. Googling was one thing. Stepping off the edge of the cliff was something else entirely. Decision made, it was time to draw on some serious gumption to get moving.

A friend of mine knew of another single woman seeing a fertility specialist at a boutique clinic in the city. This appealed to me for several reasons, but mainly because they specialised in treating women who needed donor sperm. I quizzed her and got the details of the clinic. First step, done. Easy!

As a socially infertile woman, I thought I'd be a somewhat unique IVF candidate, but not at this clinic. Just one of many. It wouldn't be awkward, I hoped. I'd be in similar company with specialists who knew the score, which gave me a sense of ease. Though in all honesty, I really didn't have much of a clue. I was just going on the recommendation I'd been given, and a bit of instinct. So, off I went to an information night.

My friend Nicole came with me. Now Nicole is a bit of a walking cliché, because to describe her as 'beautiful inside and out' would be an understatement. With strawberry blond hair and an abnormal love for butterflies, she is well-renowned for having the generosity of a saint. An *actual* saint. Meeting for coffee, I have often watched her stagger toward me, dragging huge gift bags of presents. 'It's nothing, just a tiny birthday gift,' she'd gasp with exertion, heaving an extortionate deluge of perfectly wrapped offerings onto the table.

Nicole is a friend who has always been there for me. I struggle to match her in that regard, try as I might. She was never going to say 'No' when I invited her to the clinic information evening. The fact that she's also an IVF nurse, an insider, clinched the deal. She'd be able to tell me if things seemed right in the way a mystery shopper might. I revelled in the cloak-and-dagger aspect.

We did have to be careful though, because we tended to get the giggles in *audience* situations. Once, at a contemporary dance performance, I could feel the seat next to me shaking. In my periphery, Nicole trying to suppress hysterics as we witnessed a man 'performing'; lying on stage, jolting and flopping about like a newly landed jellyfish. She snorted as we both leaped from our seats, running to the safety of the foyer, unleashing torrents of laughter. This kind of thing could *not* happen at the IVF talk, so we grabbed each other by the shoulders and gave ourselves a mock pep-talk. 'We can do this.'

Wits gathered, we took the lift to level twenty-two, proceeding through the glass doors of the relatively conservative waiting room. Little did I know how much time I would end up spending in this place.

I don't know what I expected the waiting room to be. Pink with blue striped walls? A velvet maroon chaise longue? There were plastic chairs set in rows, everything camouflaged against beige walls. It smelled bleachy: a good sign I supposed, because it was a clinic after all. The usual women's gossip magazines were piled on a corner table and a bloom of pungent lilies balanced precariously on a shelf behind the reception desk. I wondered whether it was wise to trust people unable to safely shelve a bunch of flowers with the business of making my baby.

On the wall at the other end of the room hung a huge artwork, an abstract impression of sperm/oocyte surrealism. But apart from that, we could have been in any doctor's waiting room.

We took our seats at the front. I didn't want to miss a thing. The place was bulging with potential parents: all alert, fervent, and ready to take in the waves of pending information. A few couples raced in late, rushing from work, needing to cram into limited standing room at the back. So many people needed IVF, it seemed.

This particular information night wasn't really aimed at single women like me. There were other nights for that. It was more a general infertility talk about the options available. Clearly anyone could attend, but the place had a *Noah's Ark* feel to it: two-by-two. Something I hadn't expected, and it threw me a bit. I guess, in my head, I'd built up a level of comfort, assuming the main clientele would be single women. I swallowed hard, put on a tough façade, and blinked at the marvellous man who had just stood to begin his presentation: Doctor Robert Hopkins.

I really liked Dr Hopkins from the get-go. He had a father-figure way about him. Confident and knowledgeable, he exuded a kind, approachable demeanour. Towering above everyone else in the room, he looked us all in the eye as he spoke, immediately earning the trust of the crowd. His calm reassuring blue eyes and down-to-earth way made me feel I could readily name my firstborn after him.

Nicole nudged me in the ribs, letting me know she had worked with him before. 'He's great!' she mouthed. I instantly knew he would be my specialist fertility doctor.

During the talk, I learned that if a woman is fit and healthy, with regular periods, even despite her age, there was no reason to believe becoming pregnant was an impossible dream. Much of the night's information consisted of raw basics. Such as ovulation tracking – where a woman finds out *when* during her monthly cycle she is most fertile.

That was all fine. But I was eager to learn about other components. Such as the essential thing missing from my life: the male contingent: sperm.

After the talk was over, I approached a nurse at the desk to arrange my first appointment with Dr Hopkins. I was shakily excited. The nurse was clearly not; a surly, unempathetic woman, whose snappy air of efficiency shivered away any elation I dared to express. Never taking her eyes off the papers on her desk, she snorted loudly, asking my age.

'Thirty-eight.'

I flinched as she sighed heavily, pursing her lips until they disappeared into the vacuum of her mouth, her focus remaining intent on that ever-important paperwork. Finally, with a lethargy normally exhibited by sloths in the zoo, her gaze shifted to my neck, past my mouth, nose, then zeroed in on my pupils. She raised an indifferent eyebrow and commanded, 'Well, you'd better get on with it.' Then? Silence.

Yikes! I hadn't expected that. I seriously didn't know whether to laugh or cry. Or both. Nicole snorted, subduing her laughter, despite the seriousness of the matter. We had only just seen *Matilda, The Musical*, a few weeks before, and this woman was giving off *Trunchbull* vibes.

Well, lovely nurse *Trunchbull*, I may be thirty-eight, but I don't *look* a day over twenty-five. And that had to count for something, right? I was going to find my answer to that one soon enough. And I wasn't going to like it.

Ovulation tracking.

There's a lovely technical pair of words. Ovulation is when an egg (also called an ovum or oocyte) is released from an ovary. It happens every month, or should do. This is optimum pregnancy conception time. After it's released, the egg heads down the fallopian tube. It stays there for around a day, just floating around, so sperm, should they find themselves in the vicinity, don't need an immense adventure to find it.

Ovulation tracking is a series of blood tests telling a woman if, and when, her monthly egg is going to set sail.

I decided I should do this as my next step, mainly to keep proactive while waiting for my appointment with Dr Hopkins. Little did I know, ovulation tracking was mostly what couples did to start their treatment. Not solo women like me. It's all about timing. And if you don't have sex at the right time, your chances of getting pregnant are pretty slim. Especially if you and your partner are having fertility troubles to begin with.

My circumstances were vastly different. In some ways, not

getting to have sex to get pregnant seemed like a bit of a downer. Even as I say that I realise how weird it sounds, because having sex is the way you make babies, right? I'd be missing out on the fun part. My way would be excessively scientific and clinical, so I figured I should start by getting to know my body and my cycles.

Easier said than done. I went to the clinic on day one of my period for a blood test. Back up to level twenty-two, where nurse *Trunchbull* summonsed me to the blood extraction room. Then I had to go back every day or so for the same so the nurses could track my hormone levels. I was instructed to phone the clinic on the afternoon of each test to find out what my levels were.

Through this process, the nurses were able tell me almost exactly when I was going to ovulate. I had to keep reminding them I wasn't trying to get pregnant – I was simply tracking my cycle to make sure all was in order. It felt good to be having tests and communicating with the clinic, acting like a woman who was planning on having a baby. I was in the pre-conception club.

On day thirteen of the tests, I was teaching ballet to a class of indifferent teenagers on a Friday afternoon. These kids were hip-hop obsessed. Most of them hated ballet and weren't afraid to show it. I was taking them for their compulsory weekly hour of technical torture when my mobile rang. It was the clinic.

'Is that Lorena Otes?' I immediately recognised the voice of surly nurse *Trunchbull.*

'Yes, that's me,' I said, looking at the room full of students glaring back at me.

'Can you tell me your date of birth please?' This was a security procedure to ensure she had the right person.

'Fourth of the eighth, seventy-three,' I muttered. I didn't

really want the kids knowing how old I was.

'YOU CAN HAVE SEX TONIGHT,' nurse *Trunchbull* blared down the receiver. 'YOU'RE OVULAAAATINNNNG!'

Faaaark! Could she have been any louder? How could someone so gruff be so enchanted by my ovulation success? And that matronly voice of hers really carried. I was sure the kids heard it.

Waving my hands at my students to keep working on their pirouettes, I winced my way out of the studio. Then quietly reminded the nurse that I wasn't trying to conceive during this cycle. She gave me the polite and expected responses, and the phone call ended.

I sighed. Damn, I could've been having marvellous sex that evening making babies with the (imaginary) man of my dreams (Liam Hemsworth). But as I say, I didn't know what I was doing at that point. Just going with the flow and getting on with things. Keeping busy. That's a part of my personality that was really magnified during my endless IVF shenanigans.

Back at the studio I gathered my wits, cringed my way inside, regained the students' attention, and continued teaching the pirouette exercise that had been so unceremoniously interrupted.

The good news was that I had ovulated. My body was functioning as it should. In other words, my hopes of having a baby were one step closer to reality. It's an interesting realisation to have while telling a room full of bored dance students to point their feet. I felt calm, cool as a cucumber on the outside. But boy, was I jumping for joy underneath. With correctly pointed feet, of course.

My first appointment with Dr Hopkins was three weeks after the ovulation tracking debacle. I was forced to wait that long because he was booked out, which gave me a sense of relief. You've got to be a bit suspicious when specialists have too much appointment availability.

But Dr Hopkins was busy, busy, busy! A regular walking, talking, baby-making machine. And I was nervous, nervous, nervous! I clumsily sat down at his desk, nearly missing the chair entirely. I couldn't take my eyes off him. All I could think of was, *this man is going to create my baby*, utterly hypnotised. The deep, full tone of his greeting, 'Welcome, Lorena. Take a seat,' was a warm hug.

There were baby photos on the wall and sideboard. Good! Evidence of success. He obviously loved kids and was keen to get more of them into the world. More plusses, in my book. He began to gather pieces of paper, firing countless questions at me. All run-of-the-mill stuff.

'What's your plan, Lorena?'

'To have a baby using IVF and donor sperm before my ever-aging ovaries sign off for life.'

There, I'd said it out loud for the first time. *Donor sperm*. The elephant in the room of a single woman's IVF journey.

Actually, there are many elephants, but I giggled a little bit when I first encountered the term *donor sperm*. I think it's the word 'sperm' that causes the immature response. It's hard to name the species 'sperm whale' without having a little chuckle. Or maybe that's just me? *Grow up, Lorena!* My infantile level of humour was about to hit crisis-mode, because little did I know at the time, I was soon going to have an appointment with a nurse whose title was *Sperm Coordinator*. What kind of person chose to deal with 'coordinating' donor sperm as a profession? But, where babies are going to be created in tubes, sperm has to be sourced – and sometimes eggs too. These then need to be labelled, filed, correctly stored, matched up to the correct recipient, and so on. A huge job!

I felt like someone needed to come up with a nickname for sperm. Something less awkward, less embarrassing. Along the lines of *pregnancy assistance serum*. Hmm, maybe a bit cringey? *Seed for conception* is good – says what it is. Although I'm not a big fan of sperm being referred to as 'seed'. I quite like *vials of life*. Simple and to the point.

I soon found out that my *Sperm Coordinator* was extremely confident in her profession, not at all embarrassed to say the word 'sperm' over and over (and over) again. I was to get used to it too – pretty quickly, let me tell you.

So, there we go. Some squirmy cats of IVF awkwardness are out of the bag, and there are plenty more on the way, so hold on tight. I was still cringing a bit at this appointment with Dr Hopkins, but at least I was beginning to be able to use the lingo.

Dr Hopkins sniffed. 'Do you have a donor in mind?'

'Not yet. I was hoping you would help me out with that. I mean, not YOU, you. Sorry. No. Um…' (So much for not being awkward.) 'I mean perhaps you could help me *find* a donor?'

'Yes, yes, Lorena, I can do that. Do you have regular periods?'

I breathed a sigh of relief. 'Yes, doctor. Clockwork.'

He asked a few desultory questions about my family history. Plus a few other bits and pieces. He then booked me in for every blood test on the planet. Not so much the testing of hormones, this time, more to detect viruses, diseases, genetic issues, and anything else possibly lying in wait.

'Do you also want the extra testing?' Dr Hopkins asked.

Everyone who did IVF at the time had to have tests for cystic fibrosis, but you could also get a super-test that checked for over a hundred diseases that may be lying dormant in your chromosomes. It cost quite a bit, which is why not everyone did it. I didn't think twice – my attitude was if I was going to do this, I'd do it properly. 'Yes, please. All the tests.'

The rest of my visit with Dr Hopkins was uneventful. We did the, 'It was nice to meet you,' departure pleasantries along with sentiments of, 'We'll get you there, Lorena.' I felt better now I had the ball rolling. *Really* rolling in a 'Holy shit I'm doing this' kind of way.

I walked out the door feeling overwhelmed but excited. I rubbed the replica Salvador Dali egg sculpture by the door for luck on the way out. That would become my ritual.

4

Blood, Spit, and Fears

Summer 2013, age 39

It was crunch time. I needed to organise the tests I'd committed to, and it was overwhelming. Blood tests, phlegm tests, and a scary internal test I didn't even want to think about. I kept reminding myself that the more information I had, the better equipped I'd be to face future hurdles.

The blood tests came first. No big deal, really. Funny that the man taking my blood looked a bit like a vampire. Pale, sunken eyes, dark red lips. Protruding canine-teeth. It was a bit disconcerting at the start. Then he told me he needed nine vials of blood. NINE??? A couple of spares for the road perhaps, Count Dracula, sir?

'Let me know if you start feeling a-queasy…' he whispered, feeling my inner arm for a juicy vein. *(A-queasy? What's that?)*

'—Because there is so much a-blood to be taken, you might a-faint,' he continued.

Gosh, how much did he need? I buckled myself in as The Count commenced his withdrawal. He'd obviously done it a time or two, because I didn't even feel the needle go in. Nor was I faint or queasy, walking out very pleased with myself for ticking the first box in this marathon of tests.

Cocky, brave, and a little smug. What a puerile moment,

revelling in this miniscule achievement. At the time, every little step felt ground-breaking, so I allowed myself the occasional feeling of valour.

Most of the test results came back a week later – all normal. I still had to wait for a couple more, but wasn't at all worried.

Next was the *Counsyl Foresight Carrier Screen* test that checks for genetic disorders such as cystic fibrosis. The purpose is to minimise the risk of having a baby with an incurable genetic disease. My question was, how on earth do you test for genetic diseases? I assumed I'd be in for more blood tests? Nope: saliva. Not very elegant.

A kit was sent by courier from the United States to my home. Of course, my kit was accidentally delivered to Eve, an elderly neighbour living in the apartment above. She'd mistakenly opened the package thinking it was for her. At eighty-five years-old, her eyesight wasn't all it could be, and no doubt she spun into a frenzy of panic thinking the US government was trying to genetically morph her into an alien. Confused and flabbergasted, she assigned our neighbour, Diane, to the case. Diane happened to be the resident busybody.

I ended up with a half-opened parcel on my doorstep with Diane updating me in inordinate detail a few days later.

'Eve gets confused you know. She thought the parcel was for her. Well, it came from the United States. She doesn't even know anybody there.' She quizzed me on what the package was.

My bumbling, 'I'm not actually sure,' narrative bought me enough time to back through my door, slam it shut, and catch my breath.

I was sure my neighbours would all soon know about the strange genetic test kit delivered to apartment twelve. I could hear it now: 'Perhaps she's one of those volunteers going on a one-way trip to Mars?' Or 'Maybe it's to do with the CIA? FBI? CSIRO? Do we have a dangerous international criminal living in our building???' To think a simple package delivery could cause such a fuss.

After that, the test itself was straightforward. I had to fill what is very civilly called a *collection tube* with my saliva. Not as easy as it sounds. I needed to get it to the level of a marked line, and then tap some bubbles away. It wasn't fun, but I got it done, popping the evidence into a courier bag and posting it back to the United States for analysis.

Tick. Another task complete.

The wait for results took several weeks. And sitting in Dr Hopkins' office, I was probably a bit too relaxed.

There's a big difference between being the carrier of a disease and actually having it. There are complex scientific explanations to it but here's the gist: if you're a carrier of something, you don't have it yourself. But you *can* pass it to your children.

Dr Hopkins concluded that I didn't *have* any genetic diseases. Woohoo! I'm a perfect specimen! Just as I was starting to relax into my chair with a complacent sigh, I noticed the doctor pause. Then he leant forward.

'But…'

Aah shit, here we go.

He continued, 'You are the carrier of a genetic condition.' The doctor peered over his reading glasses. 'There are issues with your GJB2 gene.' (Sounds like a fighter plane.) 'This relates to congenital hearing loss. The official term is Non-Syndromic

Hearing Loss and Deafness.'

There was a spectrum of how much this could affect my offspring: from totally deaf to partial hearing loss. It would be more of a problem if the sperm donor (or partner) had the same genetic issue. Then, the odds would stack against me, and though it wouldn't be a definite, the chance of passing this disorder on would be much higher. I started jumping to conclusions, assuming I had symptoms. Though my hearing can be a bit crap, apparently that has nothing to do with the condition I carry. Dr Hopkins assured me that I was asymptomatic. Any lack of hearing I had was either voluntary, coincidental, or from playing Madonna tapes too loudly on my Walkman in the 80s.

I felt disappointed with the test results, but also grateful they weren't worse. And they really could have been much, much worse. What a wake-up call! People have babies with genetic problems all the time. The chance of being a carrier and not knowing about it was huge. I felt like I'd had a sneak peek into a portal of information not everybody gets.

In a weird way, I felt like I was already protecting and mothering my unborn baby. Making sure my future little person had all the safeguards I could provide, even before coming into the world to meet me. I felt emotional. Doctor Hopkins snapped me out of it to discuss options. Firstly, I could ignore the results and risk passing on the hearing disorder. *Er, no.*

Next option was to find a sperm donor willing to have the *Counsyl* genetic test to check he wasn't carrying the same condition. If he was, I'd ditch him and find someone else.

I still had another can of worms to deal with: the karyotype test. This was the analysis of chromosomes via *another* blood test. It was different from the genetics test, being entirely about chromosomes. Humans have forty-six of them in twenty-three pairs.

Here's the science lesson: chromosomes are made of hundreds, perhaps thousands of genes. Each chromosome has two parts – one from each parent. Genes are made of deoxyribonucleic acid (DNA), which contains information and instructions that give living things their characteristics.

The karyotype test would look at my chromosomes to make sure they were all sitting correctly, doing the things they should, and looking right. Whereas the genetics test analysed what the chromosomes were actually made of and the information they carried. Science lesson over – along with flashbacks of trauma from year eight biology.

Dr Hopkins had been sitting there for a long time. His nostrils flared slightly every time he breathed in. He sighed, looking as though he was about to say something. I was poised and ready to hang on to his every word. It must have been quite a complex report because it felt like he was reading forever.

Eventually he looked up. 'You have an inverted chromosome.'

I didn't know what that meant.

'The official term is a pericentric inversion of chromosome seven, between breakpoints p11.2 and q21.1.'

Questions danced around the left side of my baffled brain as I tried to envisage a chromosome doing an upside-down handstand. *But chromosomes don't have hands*, the right side of my brain argued, overriding the picture with an image of what an inverted chromosome might look like in a textbook diagram.

It turned out that every single cell in my body contains this inverted chromosome. Whatever that meant. I subconsciously scanned myself for abnormalities. I had no idea what I was looking for, but I was on the hunt. Ten fingers, ten toes? *Check.* Two arms, two legs? *Check.*

I looked at Dr Hopkins. 'But what about me? Am I… is there anything…?'

The doctor recognised my confusion. 'It won't affect you,' he said. 'But you are at risk of passing on a much more debilitating chromosomal problem to your child.'

Oh. Again. Another thing. I'd gone from assuming I was a healthy superwoman (albeit slightly over the hill fertility-wise) to being genetically and chromosomally inept. The news hit me like a smack in the face. I knew it wasn't terminal. I didn't have a death sentence. But the idea of being chromosomally imperfect seemed impossible. I hadn't even considered it. I'm a dancer. I strive for perfection in myself and in the way I teach. How could every cell in my body be so blatantly imperfect? And how could I *fix* it? No control. Can't be done. This was me, and I had to accept it.

These karyotype results U-turned everything. A pivotal point where I realised my IVF experience was going to be much more of a *fight* than a *journey*. I needed to arm myself like a boxer in the ring, because nothing was going to be straightforward or easy from that moment. I had to be very clear I *really* wanted this. Especially as I was going solo. These karyotype results were in a long line of challenges testing my determination and desire.

I couldn't stop thinking about my inverted chromosome. Dr Hopkins explained that it was probably passed down from previous generations. The further it's passed down, the weaker the chromosome gets, creating a greater chance of the chromosome breaking and not reattaching properly. This is where trouble strikes. If any part of that chromosome doesn't reattach properly there could be missing information resulting in all kinds of potential problems.

Down Syndrome is the result of an extra copy of chromosome 21, and one of the most widely recognised chromosomal disorders. Williams Syndrome is one I hadn't heard of before. It's a less-known disability, but one that affects around one in ten thousand people worldwide. It is a developmental disorder where people are intellectually challenged, have heart problems, and certain physical and personality characteristics. Williams Syndrome is directly related to chromosome 7, caused by the deletion of some of the information it carries.

So, if I had a child and there was a weakness in the inversion of my seventh chromosome, it could break off in one, more, or all of my eggs, resulting in fertilisation of a disability such as Williams Syndrome. Or a miscarriage. Clearly heart-breaking scenarios.

As a future solo parent, I was already scared I wouldn't cope even at the best of times. Factoring in a child with a disability – well, I couldn't even think about it without a churning panic sweeping through my stomach. I knew I should do everything in my power to avoid it.

Yet another problem with my chromosomal inversion was that I could end up finding it difficult to fall pregnant at all – or worse, have a miscarriage. Our bodies have systems set up where they should naturally reject abnormal foetuses. If there was a chromosomal abnormality of any sort, my body would be unlikely to allow the embryo to implant. If it did somehow implant, it would typically be rejected. Sent out in what would be a miscarriage. Something that terrified me. Frightened by the thought, I desperately hoped I'd never have to go through it.

Furthermore, and yet another thing: a woman's eggs age in tandem with the woman herself. We're born with all of our eggs, and as we age they get weaker, becoming less functional and more prone to calamity. I was nearing forty by now, and my increasingly decrepit old eggs were starting to look decidedly iffy.

As nurse *Trunchbull* had indicated, I had no time to lose.

5

Smurfy Periods

Winter 2013, age 39

The last thing I needed to tick off my pre-IVF list was the Hystero-salpingo contrast sonograph. Quite a mouthful. It's usually shortened to HyCoSy, a medical test to ensure my downstairs area was functioning correctly. The fallopian tubes need to be clear, so a medical team runs blue liquid through them to check. Blue? That provides contrast so the ultrasound machine can see and record everything clearly.

It didn't sound like much fun, but I figured if all went to plan, I'd soon be squeezing out a watermelon-sized person. And nothing's as painful as that!

I went alone. I preferred this with most of my appointments, particularly the intrusive ones. I couldn't imagine going with a partner even if I had one. And certainly not a friend. Perhaps that's just me. Many of my friends and family didn't understand, offering to come along and hold my hand. My insistent, 'No, thanks, I'll be fine,' was met with uncertain eyes. Having a support person just wasn't a huge source of comfort for me. As a solo mum in the making, I was already fiercely independent, thriving on doing things alone. That way the only person I needed to focus on and worry about was myself – more than enough to contend with.

The clinic was in a freezing but beautiful heritage-listed building. The toothy receptionist was welcoming and chatty. She asked me to fill out some forms – mostly personal details – then go and wait in one of the back rooms.

I noticed all kinds of equipment in there. Like the sonography room from an *E.R.* episode with stark white walls. My eyes scanned to the back of the room where a huge scary robotic probe device sat on a trolley. I hoped it wasn't going to be part of my procedure but feared the worst. I was nervous, my hands fidgety and clammy as I breathed in an aromatic mixture of old-building smell and eau de disinfectant.

A friendly nurse came in and introduced herself. She looked a bit hippy-esque with dreadlocks encased in a black hairnet, a blue band aid over her nose-piercing, and a smile that put me straight at ease. I had to remove my clothing from the waist down and lie on a chair-bed thing. She wheeled the scary probe machine over. *Oh no!* That feeling of being at ease all but vanished.

The procedure began the same way a pap smear does: small talk. Subjects like: 'How has your day been so far?' (Translation: *It's about to get a LOT worse.*) 'Did you see how sunny it is out there? How could this be winter?' (*You will not care about the summery winter weather once we're finished with you.*)

The nurse inserted a cold metal contraption down below. A catheter was then guided through, and a tiny little balloon was blown up at the top of my uterus. I gasped, as that was the most painful part. I didn't feel the balloon as such, but my body hurt in the same way as intense period-pain-times-a-trillion. I'd been told to take painkillers before the procedure to 'lessen discomfort', so I suppose that helped. The purpose of the balloon was to prevent the blue contrast solution from leaking out. I winced as the nurse pumped it up using the smallest bike pump in the world.

The dreaded ultrasound scanning probe was then inserted. I flinched and settled. There's an awful lot going on at that point. Did I mention that a doctor had arrived? Not my Dr Hopkins, but an in-house ultrasound doctor. Another lovely person who was comforting and sweet. She kept me calm by letting me know what was going on, even though I was squirmy and uncomfortable.

'It'll be over in a second,' she said, smiling. Her gentle demeanour made everything okay. 'If you look at the screen above, you can see the balloon in there.' It was an ultrasound screen and yes, I could see movement. The image on the screen appeared almost voyeuristically artistic, full of black and white swirls and blurs with just a hint of agony. The nurse took screenshots of the images as they went along.

Back at the business end, the catheter somehow let out some blue saline solution which would hopefully wash through my fallopian tubes. The solution flew through – they were clear. Yes!

It was over. I could breathe again.

'Textbook,' the doctor told me afterward. 'Nothing interesting to report at all.' I heaved a sigh of relief. One of the few times in my life I was glad to be average. 'Now, you'll notice some blue spotting in your undies over the next few hours,' my now favourite doctor added. 'Much like a Smurf having a period,' she continued with a grin.

Leakage, I guess. But I had to laugh. I really love Smurfs. My BP collection is still in a box at home from when I was a kid. As the doctor bade me farewell she told me, 'Next time you're here, we'll be doing an ultrasound of your baby.' Then she smiled and left the room.

Tears began to run down my cheeks as I pulled on my clothes. Imagining what it would be like to see my baby up there on the ultrasound monitor. I felt a pang of urgency and intense longing. The feeling was so physical I could sense my arms reaching toward the monitor, wanting to jump in and hold my future child.

Normally, I busy myself with the task at hand, saving the emotional response for later. But the rawness of that moment took over; I was just so relieved and thankful all was well.

As I exited into the blustery winter air, it suddenly hit me that I'd been so consumed by getting on with things, I hadn't paused in a long time to consider the bigger picture of this mission. My baby! This was the first time such a potent image of my future child had flashed into my head. It felt so tangible I was shaking.

A couple of days later, at another appointment with Dr Hopkins, I received the official version of my HyCoSy results. 'Uneventful and usual,' he told me. Then we moved on to more serious things.

Because of my inverted chromosome, Dr Hopkins suggested I do some sort of embryo genetic testing. But before any crucial steps were taken, I had to speak to an actual geneticist who could assess me to help make proper informed decisions. I was given the phone number of Doctor Neal Peters, one of the leading geneticists in Australia. So cutting edge he couldn't fit me in for an appointment. His receptionist suggested either a phone call or Zoom consultation.

I hate Zoom. I'm not a big fan of the phone either, but on Zoom I become vain and acutely conscious of the sudden and disturbing appearance of excessive double-chins. I wasn't particularly worried Dr Peters would think I resembled an anguished turkey. It was more about being nervous speaking to a scholarly stranger face-to-face on a computer screen.

So, I opted for the more favourable good ol' landline. Yep, I still had one. A dying breed, holding on to anything with a retro vibe. My green dial-up phone was from the 60s. Positively vintage! It rang in that familiar good old-fashioned 'brrring-brrring' way. Dr Peters' assistant answered in two rings, putting me through to the man himself.

His voice was quite ordinary. Nothing scholarly about it at all. I don't know if I was expecting a British accent, or a deep commanding Morgan Freeman reverberation? Dr Peters sounded distinctly friendly and approachable: 'Lorena, good morning. We have a few things to discuss.'

Our chat went for almost an hour. He is clearly a thinker because he covered everything. Out of the blue: 'Are you taking folate, Lorena?'

'Yes, doctor. A multi, and magnesium too.'

'It's the folate that is essential. Are you aware of the results of your DNA test?'

'I am.'

'So, you understand there's a risk your eggs may carry a chromosomal abnormality? That, and your age.'

'My age? Yes. Thirty-nine. Too close to forty for comfort. Ha-ha.' And just over a year since my decision to do IVF.

'The older you get, the less likely you are to have chromosomally healthy eggs. But there are things we can do to test your embryos, Lorena. I recommend those tests. Dr Hopkins will go through that with you.'

The conversation went on. He threw a few hard-hitting facts at me and asked loads of questions. As for me, it was 7am. Not being a morning person, my boggled brain struggled. I managed to comprehend most of the information, responding with reasonable levels of intelligence, scribbling notes as he went, just in case.

The genetic testing he mentioned is called Pre-implantation Genetic Diagnosis (PGD). That means my embryos would be genetically tested before they were implanted for pregnancy.

Dr Peters explained, 'So, Lorena, your eggs will be removed and fertilised in the clinic using donor sperm. They then form embryos. The cells multiply each day until around day three when they are technically sturdy enough to withstand the removal of a single cell. That cell gets sent off for testing.'

Phew! Big news. And another pivotal moment in my baby expedition.

I thanked Dr Peters and hung up, revelling in the tell-tale 'ding' that happens when you hang up those old phones. A familiar comfort amid new and overwhelming information.

I was awake enough to hit Google by that stage. Never a good idea. I learned that PGD was not a new technology; but not yet common, either. Why? Because it was hideously expensive! It was going to cost me thousands. I would have to sell my first-born to pay for it – around eight-thousand dollars!

Nausea washed over me as I entered the pits of panic once again. How was I going to fund such an enormous amount? I didn't have many facts or figures on PGD, but I knew then and there that the long and winding road to motherhood was going to be a painful and expensive route. On the other hand, I also knew I needed to maximise my chances of having a healthy baby, so if that meant spending thousands of extra dollars to get there, well, so be it. I mean, that's something I really *had* to do. Non-negotiable.

Sometimes though, I wondered. Is ignorance bliss? Is having extra knowledge really such a good thing? I was glad I knew about my inverted chromosome. I was also glad I'd been made aware of my dormant hearing-loss gene. And relieved to know I didn't carry any genes that caused inherent disease. Technology was now my angst-inducing friend.

I realised how damn lucky I was to be doing any of this at all. I mean, having a baby by myself is insane when I really paused to think about it. The extra information was a big, juicy cherry on top!

There's more I'll say about PGD later. But for now, the frustrating news was that this technology was not only crazy expensive, it also wasn't yet available in Dr Hopkins' clinic. Urghh! They were kidding, right? Nope. *Another* hurdle.

Of course, it was all very complicated. If my treatment had been in a more conventional clinic, I could get the PGD testing done easily. But my clinic wasn't like that. I went there *specifically* because they specialised in IVF for single women. Other IVF clinics had a very different focus. Their advertising campaigns were heavy-handed, clearly aimed at 'couples'. Every. Single. Ad. No mention of single/solo women, excluding me entirely.

Through Google, I learned of a big-name IVF company in my clinic's building that offered PGD. For a millisecond I considered switching, and I'm sure they would have happily treated me. But I couldn't just swap clinics. Not that easily. I'd have to start again from scratch. Nor could I just pop in and *borrow* their PGD facilities. The two clinics were competitors.

The nearest clinic with a PGD facility affiliated with Dr Hopkins was two-hundred kilometres away. This meant travelling for three-plus hours, having my eggs harvested there, after which they would perform the PGD procedure in their high-tech science labs. That seemed like my only option.

Again, how much did I really want to be a mum? How much did I want a child? *Did* I want a child? DID I?

Yes: the short answer.

Abso-fucking-lutely: the longer one.

And although I'd asked myself that question over and over again after each hurdle, my answer never faltered. It was always a resounding, 'Yes'.

After all the tests, science, endless information, and obsessive organisation, I still just wanted that warm bundle of beautifulness in my arms. The baby smell, the soft breathing, the unconditional love, my own squishy baby that I could just gobble up. Everything else was merely an unavoidable distraction until the moment my aching dream came true.

It looked like I'd be heading out of town, at hideous expense, to have my embryos genetically given the thumbs-up before being transplanted. That's assuming there would be embryos to test. And eggs to make embryos out of. I asked again, one more time. Did I really want to put myself through all that to have a baby?

Abso-bleeding-fucking-lutely yes, yes, yes!

6

From Pretty Awful
to Pretty Handsome

Spring 2013, age 40

Going through costings was one of the parts of IVF I dreaded. It swept me into a nightmare of paperwork, making ends meet, and general financial terror. Because I had to factor in the extortionate expense of genetic testing, I'd managed to whack another eight-grand onto the final bill, which increased the trepidation tenfold. Medicare rebates didn't stretch to PGD either – a double-whammy. It's worth noting that these are 'time of writing' costings, and that things have since changed.

PGD technology was still very new at this point. Two embryologists at the affiliated clinic had been specifically trained in the procedure. It had taken years to get to the point they could offer it to patients.

One of the main reasons to do PGD was to help minimise my chance of a miscarriage. I was having regular recurring nightmares that I'd get pregnant and lose it, so I needed to do everything in my power to avoid that from happening in real life. The chances of going full-term with a healthy baby are so much greater when the chromosomes of the embryo are correct and accounted for.

The doctors had a repeat mantra: 'We only need one good egg.' Then Dr Hopkins would relax into a smile, adding, 'And at forty, you still have a few. We just need to find them.' Hearing that certainly helped. But panic still bubbled below the surface.

Dr Hopkins shuffled around in his seat, handing me a pamphlet about costings and reading aloud. I listened, light-headed with disbelief. In 2013, IVF cost around $7,300 (Aussie dollars, not pesos!) – with a $3,600 Medicare rebate. The surgery for the egg retrieval ('pick-up') was $1,200 (no rebate). Anaesthetic for the pick-up was $400 (30% rebate), and if I was lucky enough to have spare embryos, it would be $700 a year to store them. PGD was another $8,000 on top of that. Plus, I needed to find around $3,000 for sperm, as well as thousands for tests, and specialists' appointments. The stab of those figures hit me right between the shoulder blades.

I couldn't bring myself to add it all up. Just too high for a humble dance teacher. I had no idea where I was going to find the money and I could feel a sweaty anxiety beading on my forehead.

Anyone want to buy a kidney? I have two, so won't miss one very much. A very healthy kidney up for grabs. Not completely pink due to occasional wine consumption, but perfectly functional and willing to find a new home.

No, I wasn't at that stage yet. But sheesh, my mind reeled wondering where I was going to find that kind of dosh. Dr Hopkins could tell I was starting to freak out. He paused clumsily after giving me the figures. Then he got back to the business of being my doctor. 'I'll give you a few days for this to all sink in,' he said. 'Then we'll get on with it.'

So many harsh realities. And the worst part was risking paying all that money but ending up with no baby. What if I had to do it all over again? To find the money twice? Or three times, even. Or (horror) more?

I drove home in a trance. Once in the safety of my haven, I let the tears flow. Couldn't stop them. I cried for the lack of control. Cried because I was worried it wouldn't work, applying extra lashings of worry for that! I cried because it was going to take all my savings and more to afford everything. I cried for losses I hadn't even had yet, and for the anticipation of everything miserably failing.

I needed that low point. Sitting on the lounge, looking out the window, bawling my eyes out. But once I'd had this big cry, it was done. I decided then and there I had no more time for tears. I needed to keep fighting my way forward. The mantra of my quest.

In the grand scheme of things, there was no risk at all. If I wanted it enough and there was a way forward? I had to give it a go. I *had* to. Failure was always lurking. But success beckoned. That's what I kept telling myself, like a favourite song on repeat over and over and over again, 'Success will prevail!'

I phoned Mum not long after my cry. She gently reminded me, 'Just stay positive.'

That helped. Thanks, Mum. And all being said, the coming hurdles would only make me more determined.

Straight after my epiphany, I had to go to the fertility clinic to see Sabine-of-the-sperm. She's officially known as *Sperm Coordinator*, but I preferred the former. I never used it in her company, of course. She didn't seem to have my appalling sense of humour, so I doubted she would appreciate it.

Sabine was a leathery, salt-and-pepper-haired, pre-retiree

with a gentle soul and a very *clean* humour. She never made sperm jokes like I secretly hoped she would. She had been working in the fertility industry for seven-thousand years, so was about ready for her next phase in life.

'I'll work here a couple more years,' she told me. 'Then hubby and I are moving to the Gold Coast. Live in a retirement village and see our days out lying on a beach.'

'Sounds perfect,' I replied, trying to engage.

My mind was swarming. We were about to enter the mysterious realms of the donor room where the sperm-donor files were kept, and I was nervously excited. Certain I'd find the perfect donor. But what if I didn't? Maybe I wouldn't connect with any of them. Truth is, I had no idea what to expect.

I tried to lighten the mood. 'So, how many donors do you reckon you have?'

Sabine didn't answer. I thought she may have laughed, telling me there were hundreds queueing out the door waiting to help women like me. But she didn't. She was busy filling out part of a form I would have to sign later (always so many forms). She led me down a corridor into the guts of the clinic. We went through a door aptly labelled *Donor Room*. Seeing Sabine for an appointment was like getting your aunty to set you up on an internet date. Except the sperm donor profiles were on paper.

The room was a tiny box with a window overlooking the city. I stared out at the Harbour Bridge which felt comforting, like an ever-present friend.

Sabine placed a pile of manilla folders onto a small round table. The donor files. I took a deep breath. One of the guys in those files could end up my future donor! I selected a random file from the middle to begin with, like choosing a card in a magic trick. I ran my hand over the dog-eared cream folder. It had been handled a lot. Did that mean it had also been rejected a lot? With a sudden urgency I opened it, wondering, *What's in a sperm donor profile, anyway?*

Well, there were local Australian donors, and American ones too. If it was American, it was likely to be a bulging folder of at least thirty printed pages. The first part was usually basic information: age, eye colour, skin colour, ethnic origin, and all that stuff. Then the next few pages were more in-depth, and those American guys were not afraid to elaborate. Favourite colour? *'Well, in my childhood I dreamed of a black cat called Snowy. Snowy stumbled upon a grey fox, only the fox was really a brown squirrel in the dream. I don't know, you just know. You know? And for that reason, my favourite colour has always been: aqua.'* Huh?

So much information! The detail soon exploded to mega-overload in my head.

I wasn't sure how much of it was relevant to my search. I didn't need to hear about the dream. Nor was I too concerned about my donor's favourite colour. Favourite food? Yes, maybe. Favourite books? Absolutely vital, yes! Those things are personality insights, but things like 'best holiday' and 'favourite childhood memory' didn't give me what I was after. In the end I found it confusing.

There were over thirty profiles blurring into one. And a hell of a lot of medical background. Pages and pages about the health of aunties, great-uncles, and cousins. Some profiles had a small book worth of medical history covering every single extended family member of the donor.

It was all there for a reason, and useful to know, but a lot to take in. For me, the profiles that stood out were the shorter ones.

I felt I knew those people better because their profiles were brief, relevant, and easy to digest. It made their interests and personalities shine through with just *enough* medical info.

In the Australian files (the small ones), it was a requirement that the donors have the full genetic *Counsyl* test. Very good for me, because I needed to find a donor who wasn't carrying the same deafness gene.

Sabine picked out a donor she thought I'd like. His name was Gerard, and he was just right in many ways. Only problem was, he had a slightly weird childhood photo which disturbed me. The picture was poor quality and made him look like an evil devil child. The kind of child who pulls the wings off butterflies. I couldn't get past it.

There I was whinging about too much information on the profiles, yet I was about to reject a perfectly good donor because of a poor photo? I was going nuts! It reminded me of my brief time on 'RSVP' internet dating: *He's really nice, but could I live with a person who has lop-sided ears? I'd always be staring at them.* So superficial, but let's be real, most of us have done it.

There was also a 'notes' page at the end of each profile for additional information. Some were packed. One was filled with what could only be described as a list of commandments on how to bring up *his* child. Conditional, and intimidating. And also, not *his* child at all. That's the point of human tissue donation. You're donating it. Letting it go. I could feel his anger leaping off the page and tossed his profile straight to the 'no' pile.

I spent over an hour pouring through profiles. My eyes were beginning to cross. My head throbbed. None of them were quite right and I was beginning to think perhaps I'd need to settle. Then Sabine uncovered a newly arrived Aussie one.

The rest is history, my friends. I found the perfect donor! The minute I saw his profile, I knew. Like falling in love – you just know.

Listen to this: tall, brown hair, brown eyes. Divorced with a son he adored. He was a 33-year-old Hungarian rock climber working part-time in a climbing gym somewhere in the city. He loved motorbikes (yes!) and had a brain too, studying for a Psychology PHD. He was into modern art and loved to laugh and joke. I liked him so much I wanted to marry him!

It was weird to think, I could actually track him down if I wanted to. (I wouldn't.) But how many climbing gyms were there in the city? How many Hungarians worked in them? What if I went climbing and saw him there? It could happen. I liked the idea he was nearby. Sabine told me he'd been in the donor room only a few days ago, sitting in the same chair I was in. How fantastic! He probably made his donation in the *Donation Room* next door. Not something I really wanted to think about.

Tracy, the lovely sperm assistant lady (yep, Sabine-of-the-sperm had an assistant), retrieved my donor's master file containing more detailed information. As I waited for her return, I stared out the window in daydream mode. This donor was the one. THE ONE! I loved everything about him. He was going to help me have my child; help me become a mother. And he was somewhere out there in the city. What a feeling. Like I was floating above myself, watching my own story unfold with a dopey smile on my face.

My donor was someone I felt I could get along with, and it was nice to think I'd found qualities in this man that I'd look for in a partner. Almost too good to be true. In the Hollywood movie version of this, I'd have his babies, we'd eventually meet by total accident, fall in love, and the rest would be history.

Then, my life got even better!

Tracy returned and said she'd spent some time with my donor, preparing him and so on. He'd had counselling sessions, health checks, interviews, sperm analysis, and various other varieties of scrutiny. A lot! I always wondered what drove a man to donate sperm. In my guy's case, he'd read an article in *Time Magazine* about the shortage of sperm donors in Australia as a result of changed laws around banning anonymous sperm donation. That inspired him to step up. A lot of men don't like the lack of anonymity, understandably. So, the number of Aussie donors has drastically lessened.

Tracy looked at me. 'By the way, the donor you've chosen is insanely good looking.'

WHAT??? I gave her a stunned look.

'Your donor. He's… well, handsome,' she said, plonking my Hungarian hunk-of-a-donor's master file onto the table. I was ecstatic! Now I'd lowered myself to a whole new level of superficiality. But who cares? I was going to have a good-looking baby. Yee-hah! For the first time in my life, I had *finally* chosen the perfect man.

I toned my excitement down to a dull roar so Tracy wouldn't think I was a completely shallow fool. (While screaming 'hallelujahs' on the inside.)

Turns out my measured response wasn't necessary. Tracy was right on board telling me when he'd left the clinic a few weeks before, all heads in the waiting room swung in his direction. One couple pulled her aside to ask if he was a sperm donor, and if he was, could they please reserve him? Ha-ha, what a classic. I felt a magic spark in the air. So happy, giddily overjoyed something was finally going right.

I toddled off to reception and handed over $3,000 to secure five of his golden vials of life. They were now officially mine. Who'd have known I'd pick the handsome one. (Am I talking about that again?) And to think, it was his interests and personality that initially attracted me. Happy times, after an initially very unhappy day.

Just goes to show – ya gotta keep on keepin' on. Tables turn quickly, but the pathway is set and ready to be trodden. I floated home, not knowing what was ahead.

7

Hurdles

January 2014, age 40

It was late in the evening and I was knackered after a long and character-building workday. I'd just had a comforting warm shower and was pulling on my new, soft, bamboo blend pyjamas, when I had the sudden urge to check my emails before bed. My laptop was taking a lifetime to load as always, but I just had to check: my sixth sense in bad news detection mode.

Finally, the email screen popped up. Sabine-of-the-sperm had sent a short, but to-the-point message telling me the genetic testing could no longer happen. She instructed me to phone Dr Hopkins first thing in the morning to discuss options. *WHOA?*

My head dropped to the pit of my stomach. I doubled over, suffocated by sadness and unease yet again. The softness of my new PJs suddenly felt scratchy as my skin prickled against them. Why so many bloody obstacles? I'd hoped for plain sailing from this point, but it seemed I couldn't even have twenty-four hours off. Tiredness didn't help either. Contrary to my new 'no tears' policy, the familiar sting that heralded the revival of the waterworks erupted. This display of weakness pissed me off, which only made me cry more.

I was angry with Sabine for the brusque tone of her email. There was no soothing sugar-coating at all. My rage was, of course, unreasonable. How else would she have written it?

Pessimism washed over me, wave after wave, and I readied myself for the end of the road. At the very least, I'd probably have to start again. If I wanted a baby, I'd either have to do it without genetic testing, or without Dr Hopkins. All too much for my overworked fatigued brain to fathom.

Then I remembered: MY DONOR! My lovely donor. I'd have to abandon him if I went to another clinic. Shit! Shit! Even more shit! Everything was falling apart. Surely, I'd been tested enough.

Little did I know.

My mind revisited the option of changing clinics. But there wouldn't be a great selection of sperm donors, and red tape prevented me from taking my precious vials of life somewhere else. They were competing businesses. It'd be like trying to return a Coles branded item to Woolworths.

As for not doing genetic testing – well, I certainly didn't want to risk having a miscarriage, or to make impossible decisions about aborting a baby. I know, I know, that's worst-case scenario stuff. But that was where my mind insisted on taking me.

Future plans, dreams, and hopes flashed before me. Sadness suffocated me through to the morning, beyond sunrise, and into my workday. When I couldn't get through to Dr Hopkins' office, exasperation joined the party. I NEEDED more information. I dialed their number like a stalker. Nothing. In sheer desperation, I called Sabine's direct line, leaving a wobbly message imploring her to call back.

I waited and waited. Tick-tock, tick-bloody-tock. I could feel my egg quality deteriorating with each passing second. Sitting by the phone never ends well. Like in the old days, waiting for a boy to ring. Please never take me back there.

Sabine eventually called. Busy as she was, and given the tone of her email, her voice was warm and concerned. I listened in disbelief as she told me she didn't have any new information. Despite that, it was reassuring to chat to her. To let her know I was worried and anxious.

After a while, Dr Hopkins' receptionist finally called, offering the first available appointment the following week. The following week? Couldn't we just do this over the phone? I had no idea how I'd hold out that long, though having the appointment put me somewhat at ease. Still none the wiser, but at least I was moving forward. If only in uncertain, wobbly lollipop steps.

Glimmers of hope and optimism began to reappear over the weekend. Well, what else could I do? It was time to place faith in my doctor. I trusted he'd have the right options and answers for me. That said, I still felt sick every time I thought about it.

After all the worry, tears, and crazy churning butterflies in my stomach, all it took was two quick phone calls during my consultation with Dr Hopkins to get my genetic testing back in place. And that was it. Insanity!

Apparently, someone had put my case in the too-hard basket. *Er, what?* I didn't take any pot-shots at Doctor Hopkins. He was my magic fixer who I needed onside. I thanked him (probably too many times) and watched him get on with arranging my meds and egg collection. By the end of the appointment I was set to go, and very soon. Dr Hopkins didn't charge me for the appointment either, which really helped.

The after-effects of all that stress loomed over me like a black cloud. Another lesson learned: don't stress – it might not happen. Not so easy to do when you're buried alive in it and feel like you're headed for the abyss.

For the first time in over five years, I was going to start on the contraceptive pill. It seemed so strange. When Dr Hopkins told me I was perplexed.

With a huge chunk of red tape out of the way, I was at yet another appointment filling out more documents to proceed. It already felt like a saga of epic proportions, and I hadn't even seen a needle yet. Then Dr Hopkins hit me with a torpedo announcement: 'I don't want to waste another month. Let's get you on the pill today.'

Huh? The pill?

He went on to inform me that it's to do with timing. My period needed to happen on a particular day, and the hormones in the pill help to control that. This also needed to be coordinated with the PGD clinic.

I recalled from past experience that the pill meant complete emotional disarray for me. Goody! Couldn't wait for that to kick in. Last time I was on the pill I cried for three days straight. Perhaps I'll put on weight too. Couldn't wait!

Admittedly, last time I was on the pill, I was seeing Richie who had by this time deservingly earned the official nickname, 'Shithead'. There really was no other word to describe him. Actually, there was, but it isn't fit for publication. A friend of mine, Ellie, nicknamed him 'Shithead' in my mobile contacts list. When he texted or called, and 'Shithead' came up on the display, it made me laugh. Which made things better. When friends do little crazy things like that, I really know I'm in good hands. That is where I lean on others. Ellie absolutely knew what she was doing and how much it helped.

When I was on the pill, I think I may have actually broken the Guinness World Record for continuous crying. Mostly over Shithead. He was being a real arsehole at the time, and my tears were exacerbated by the pill's hormone-induced fluctuations. The irony was I was crying over him because of the pill; and taking the pill because of him. I'm probably not the only woman in history to have *that* happen.

I've mentioned before how I often found myself wanting to *help* the guys I was seeing. Shithead was no exception. For some reason, I wanted to be his saviour. Saviour from what? Arseholedom? I persisted through his mood swings, lack of commitment, and humourlessness, while offering acceptance and warmth in return. Desperate proof of my unlimited loyalty, none of it reciprocated.

Perhaps in the end it was me who needed to be *saved*?

Meanwhile, the following incident with Mum took me by surprise.

'Oh yes, Lorena's given up on men.'

I looked over at her, my jaw hitting the floor. I had never put it like *that*. Perhaps I'd hinted at it from time to time, but never said the actual words. Was that the vibe I was sending into the world?

But I knew Mum. Her eyes exuded a melancholy shine as she spoke on the phone to a lifelong friend, who is something of an aunty to me. I was at the other end of the room slumped on the couch sipping coffee. 'She just can't stand it anymore,' Mum continued, a forlorn edge to her voice. 'It's been so hard for her.'

I inadvertently gasped, bursts of coffee spurting out my nose. Like when you laugh, but I was in shock. Mum cares so much about me, and I never wanted to disappoint her. She also knew the reality of my situation better than most — the strangeness of putting off finding a partner in order to procreate. Certainly, a topsy-turvy scenario.

I'd paused my seemingly impossible quest to find the love of my life because it was way too complicated to explain to some *Tinder* date that, 'While I'd love to be in a relationship with you, I'll also be having a baby with an anonymous sperm donor.'

Putting off finding a life partner to become a solo mum by choice seemed a much more interesting story than simply 'giving up on men'. I mean, who stops looking for a man to get pregnant? Not many people. And anyway, I hadn't given up.

I've never found dating or finding a partner in any way enjoyable. Some folk love it. Meeting new people, going on dates. I found the whole thing stressful, depressing, and embarrassing. I particularly hate first dates. For me, they're an unbearable, anxiety-inducing, vomitus waste of time. And I've had plenty. I've been set up, rejected, stalked, and badgered; dated wolves in sheep's clothing and mistaken charm for kindness way more times than I care to recall. I've been forced to do things I hadn't consented to and have shed tears over more men than I care to remember. But I've also had some wonderful times. I truly love men, and still, perhaps, might find a good one someday.

My parents are an inspiration to me, having been married for nearly sixty years. How could anything compare to that? They're a very happy couple, growing old together. True partners for life. So, to hear Mum worrying about me 'giving up on men' hit hard.

Back to the pill. That was the first of an astounding and seemingly endless array of drugs I would soon be taking. I'd be sniffing, injecting, and ingesting more hormones than a body builder in training-mode.

I just had to remember, in the wise words of any woman who's gone a bit nuts the week before her period is due, 'It's just the hormones'. Shedding tears over the *All Things Bright and Beautiful* RSPCA ad is not normal behaviour. And *The Bachelorette* isn't that moving. It's not even real! Not that I ever watched it. A-hem.

It also helped that I didn't have any Shitheads to cry over.

Righty-oh. Three weeks had passed since I'd seen Dr Hopkins, and I hadn't heard from anybody. Time was creeping away, so I rang the nurses to ask what I was supposed to do next. I'd been waiting for their call, but it seemingly worked the other way. Bloody learning curves everywhere.

They handed me over to Dr Mapleton, one of the specialists there. He seemed pleasant and very efficient. Your stereotypical doctor. Serious, to-the-point, and resourceful. And when I say, 'to-the-point', I mean full of facts. Luckily, I had my notebook handy. He regaled me with all kinds of information including the possibility of the medication overstimulating my ovaries, which sounded crushingly painful. It conjured up images of two massive, glowing, sore ovaries jumping up and down at a rave party after dropping too many ecstasy tablets.

The reality wasn't too far from it. The drugs, if taken in excess, could cause my ovaries to overwork. Everybody's version of 'excess' is different, so the doctors can never really tell exactly when and whether it might happen.

My ovaries would be working hard enough as it was, preparing multiple eggs for ovulation inside little fluid filled sacs called follicles. Each has the potential to contain an egg. Usually, it's just one egg a month but the drugs I'd be given for IVF would potentially help many more to develop – somewhere between five and fifteen. Sometimes more, sometimes less. Sometimes, WAY more. Maybe up to forty! Sometimes zero.

Overstimulation could cause my ovaries to shut down with irreparable damage. I didn't ask too many questions at the time and resisted looking it up, which took strength! I could only hope none of those things would happen to me. If I was lucky enough to have any eggs, they'd be fertilised in a lab. The process is called ICSI (Intracytoplasmic Sperm Injection). The scientist injects a single sperm cell into the egg. I mean, my God – the egg is already microscopic. The sperm cell, even tinier.

So, if – and fingers firmly crossed here – I get any embryos, I'd go on to have the genetic testing I spoke about earlier. Then if, F that works, my best-looking embryo (yes – the Liam Hemsworth one) would be transferred back to me. That's called a 'fresh transfer' because it happens straight away. It's all pretty hectic, and from what Dr Mapleton said, I'd be lucky to even get to that stage.

Then, if, if, IF I have any remaining embryos, they'd be frozen for another time. But even the process of freezing and thawing embryos is risky. They don't always freeze. They don't always thaw.

There would be ebbs and flows when it came to doses of medication and the whole thing could get pulled at any time if my body reacted unfavourably. I earned a gold star from Dr Mapleton for understanding that particular aspect. I think a lot of women have very specific IVF expectations, often way too optimistic, bordering on fantasy.

I planned to keep my eyes on the prize, putting out positive but realistic vibes. It felt good knowing the possible hurdles, but I also had to find a way to keep fighting the good fight. Most of it was out of my control. Everything was a slalom of Olympic proportions.

And oh my God, at the end of our conversation, Dr Mapleton told me he had to once *again* double-check it could all still be done. Really? Holy crap, was he trying to kill me? He was making sure all the *i*'s were dotted and the *t*'s crossed, but he was really scaring me.

He said he'd call back later that week. Which probably meant the week after. But that was okay. Gave me some extra time to save my money. Lord knows I would need it!

8

Periods of Waiting

May 2014, age 40

I was on the pill for three months and absolutely hated it. Just didn't feel like myself. On top of that, the notion of the pill as a contraceptive bothered me. I couldn't get my brain to understand it was okay to use it while trying to make a baby.

Then, just as the doctor predicted, the minute I went off the pill my period arrived. My body was always like clockwork where cycles were concerned: on time, every time. I was relieved to pull it out of the bag on this occasion too. Really didn't need a *Murphy's Law* moment of failure, or performance anxiety which I presume would have created frustrating setbacks.

If I'm brutally honest, it felt great to have my period. I never thought I'd hear myself say that. As a teenager, I was *gutted* when my period first arrived and have intermittently struggled with it since. Back then, it meant I was 'fat' enough to be able to have a baby – a clear sign I needed to lose weight. A very complex phase of growing up for me, not helped by the wall of mirrors in my ballet studio. Our teachers were pretty vocal about our appearance back then, especially regarding weight, which didn't help either. No doubt, the main contributor.

These days, I love getting my period. Well, I don't LOVE it. Not the gory part. I love how it symbolises good health, that my

62

body is functioning as it should. Further proof that I'm capable of making a baby.

Meanwhile, the next step on the IVF ladder was to start the nasal spray. I was instructed to snuffle a squirt of it every morning and every night for three long weeks. The technical name for this medication is *Gonadotropin-releasing hormone (GnRH) Agonist*, but I'll just call it 'nasal spray'.

I'd wake in the morning, squirt it into my left nostril, then wait for the strange chemical taste to drip down to the back of my tongue. The rancid taste meant the dose was taken, and the meds would do their thing. I repeated the process into my right nostril twelve hours later.

The purpose of the medication was to delay ovulation. Plus, it helped grow multiple ovarian follicles which would, fingers-crossed, house eggs. I'm sure the spray did a lot of other little jobs, but I focused mostly on those parts.

I needed a blood test ten days later that told the nurses whether everything was going well enough to progress to the next stage of treatment (the scary bit; the injections).

I couldn't wait to inject myself. Weird, I know. Don't get me wrong, I was scared shitless, because, holy crap, nobody likes needles. It wasn't like I had a needle phobia or anything. It just seemed like a big deal. I was going to administer mine myself too. Eek! Whenever the jitters took hold, I reminded myself of all the people who have to regularly inject themselves. People with diabetes, for instance. Perhaps it becomes less of a thing the more you get used to it? To me, it seemed very brave. I was going to find out exactly how 'brave' soon enough.

I also made sure to remind myself that this was something I *chose* to do. I only had to do it for a couple of weeks, if that, so minimising the pity-party was essential. I hoped the blood test results would give me the green light to start the injections the following day.

I always hated phoning in for test results. So friggin' nerve-wracking. As time went on it never got any easier either, and I'm somewhat scarred for life. But on this occasion, the results were good. The nurse joyously announced, 'You're ready to go, Lorena.' Woohoo!

Here's what it's like to inject drugs into oneself: (Promise I won't get too graphic).

For this drug (called *Menopur*), I had to concoct a potion. Just like the witches in Macbeth, I pictured myself throwing in the toe of a frog and muttering 'boil and bubble'. Instead, I sat on the edge of the bath, used the (thoroughly disinfected and cleaned to within an inch of its life!) toilet seat as a table, and combined a couple of sterile ingredients.

There was a tiny bottle containing white powder, and another with distilled water. Squinting through my reading glasses to decipher the miniscule fairy writing in the written instruction booklet, I followed word for word. I began by injecting sterile water into the powder bottle. This felt a bit like rehearsing for the big event of injecting *myself*.

In a distinctly un-James-Bond way *(stirred, not shaken)*, I gently swirled the bottle. Then I was good to go. I put the needle into the bottle, sucking out 187.5IU of the clear liquid. (IU means 'International Units'.)

With trembling hands and pursed lips, I took a deep breath. I held the needle up to my eyeline, and straight from a scene out of *Zombie Nurse*, pushed the plunger just enough to let out the air bubbles until a bit of liquid squirted out. Nya-ha-ha – time to inject.

But I nearly forgot to swab my tummy with an alcohol wipe. Oops! Not necessary for zombies, but essential here. Next, I pulled out a chunk of tummy flesh and went for it. One of the nurses had explained how to do it using a demonstration kit when I'd picked up my meds earlier, so I felt like I knew what I was doing. Sort of.

I eased the needle in. It hurt a bit – especially when pressing the top thingy (technically known as a plunger) down to get the liquid moving through. That part stung more than expected. Like having those super stingy, very painful, tetanus injections as a kid. Those things smarted!

So, what exactly was I injecting? Well, the active ingredient in *Menopur* is a hormone extracted from the urine of menopausal women. Delicious! But it didn't make sense to me. The substance is called Human Menopausal Gonadotropin (HMG), and its purpose is to activate Follicle Stimulating Hormone (FSH) in the body. Stick with me here. FSH is a pituitary hormone that stimulates the growth of follicles in the ovaries that will, in turn, hopefully produce eggs.

There are other goodies in the injections too, but HMG is the big one. It also raises your progesterone level; a hormone that prepares the body for pregnancy by thickening the uterus lining (endometrium) so a fertilised egg can implant.

Phew! But I had to explain. The long and the short of it is I survived my first injection. It really wasn't that bad. I was grateful and relieved the first one was over. And proud too. Well, why not? It was a scary thing to do, and I did it reasonably effortlessly. Sometimes anticipation is the worst part. Don't get me wrong, I wouldn't want to do it every day; but it was fine and so was I. My tummy felt tender at the injection site, but the reality was it was easy-peasy.

I was content to do the injections myself. That way I didn't have to rely on anyone else, and there was no drama. Some women have to ask for help for various reasons, but luckily for me it was easier to just get on and do it alone, being in total control. If I had a needle phobia or something, I'd be in a spot of strife, I guess. Then I'd probably seek out a friend. But as things were, I could breathe easy going into future sessions knowing everything would be (fingers crossed) okay.

Having said that, I still had endless lessons to learn. I would eventually need to let people help me. Especially after my child was born. The saying is, 'it takes a village to raise a child'. It would be extremely challenging to do it fully on your own and asking for help is okay. I'd do well to tattoo that on my forehead as a reminder.

Sometimes those thoughts scared me. I'd become so focused on the immediate task I tended to forget there would be a noisy, demanding, all-consuming little dependent coming along, and life would never be the same. I *was* going to need help, at some stage. Not needing help with the needles was one thing, but raising a child alone?

Being a solo mum by choice is a complex notion because yes, I am categorising myself as an independent woman who is choosing to become a parent without a partner. But does that mean I'm not entitled to help? There are people out there who throw forth the phrase: 'Yes, but you chose this.' Particularly to solo mums by choice who dare to ask for help. Things like having the audacity to say that they're tired. Everyone's allowed to feel and experience these things, and mention or complain about them if that's where they're at. Motherhood is hard. And let's face it, not all partners are a wealth of assistance either. But that's not for me to discuss.

All was going well, until…

Injection number three. Cue *Jaws* music please, sound department.

It had been a busy Sunday catching up with a friend – coffee and brunch at a favourite local café. After that, I headed over to Mum and Dad's for a coffee. Funny, that morning at brunch I remember telling Nicole how 'easy' the injections were, 'not nearly as scary as I thought they'd be'.

Me and my bloody big mouth.

Even when catching up with my parents, I had boasted how the injections were 'no problem', blah, blah, blah. Famous last words. That afternoon I returned home with big plans to spring clean my flat and build a large piece of Ikea furniture.

I decided to do the injection a little earlier than usual – to get it over with. I poured a glass of wine and took a small sip, just to take the edge off a bit. Placing the wine glass on the bathroom vanity, I prepared the injection the same way I'd done before. My hands were trembling less this time. I pushed the needle into my stomach, noticing that it hurt a bit more than the previous two times. And there was a tiny bit of blood. Other than that, it was 'textbook'. Last time, I'd sat down for a while afterward. But why do that when there's furniture to build?

Suddenly a woozy rush filled my head. My eyes buzzed, which sounds wrong – but it's the only way I can describe it. Nausea washed over me. A little voice in my head kept saying,

Oh, no! over and over again. Something wasn't right.

Staggering out of the bathroom, I grabbed my wine and aimed intently on making it to the lounge. I needed to find the leaflet for the medication I'd injected to check it for side effects, also trying to assure myself that this was not an anaphylactic reaction. I made it as far as my bedroom, wine glass still in hand, my ears ringing so loudly it was all I could hear. Something. Was not. Right.

I couldn't see properly. The fuzziness in my head was now a black and white snowstorm. Then an avalanche came. Everything falling. I dreamed of walking toward the loungeroom.

A little later, my eyes opened, blinking away the bright daylight streaming in from the remnants of the afternoon. I was lying sideways on the loungeroom floor, unsure how I ended up there. My eyesight was hazy, and I could barely make out the upturned coffee table beside me. Stuff was everywhere – books, magazines, television remotes, a small, empty vase that had been a present from my parents last Christmas. My wine glass had somehow, astoundingly, landed upright on the rug. The last man standing in an action movie. The Bruce Willis of my predicament.

I didn't have a clue what the hell had happened. Perhaps I'd been robbed and knocked out by the intruder? Maybe I'd had an allergic reaction to the medication? My brain in overdrive, I was scared shitless.

I waited a little while unable to move. Eventually, the fog began to clear, and I gently rolled over, pulled myself up onto the couch where I rested for a while. From there, I managed to get up and wander around a bit.

Time-check: 6:19pm. So, I hadn't been out long. Maybe a

couple of minutes? A few seconds? More? I'd heard the start of the 6pm news from the bathroom before I began the injection, so it had probably been around fifteen minutes. I calmed down and lay on the couch again. Wow! What the fuck? Clearly I'd fainted, but why? What was different this time? I must have done something wrong.

I grabbed my mobile and called a twenty-four-hour medical hotline. I needed advice and reassurance. The nurse was great. She asked a gazillion questions before putting me through to a doctor. The doctor was very thorough. He ruled out allergic and anaphylactic reactions. 'You'd know about those if they had happened, especially the latter!' He seemed to think I'd had a reaction to the pain of the injection. Hmm, maybe. I hadn't eaten much that day, just a croissant at brunch. Nor had I had much water.

The doctor didn't know much about the medication I'd injected, but seemed certain it was just a fainting episode and that I'd be all right. I was already starting to feel much better. The plan? To relax! Eat something if I could, and call the clinic the following day to find out more. Cue sigh of relief – chances were I'd live through the night.

The doctor suggested I lie down for half an hour after future injections. That made sense. I took his advice from then on. It's all too easy to forget how vulnerable we can be – I mean, injecting drugs into my body with a hypodermic needle? That's no small thing. I needed to treat the process with the respect it deserved.

I knew I'd get through this. So what if I fainted a little here and there? Next time I'd be ready. In hindsight, I felt I'd become a little too cocky about the process. And from now on I really needed to calm down. Take things slower. I tipped my wine down the sink and had an early night, my last thought before falling asleep: *I hope I don't die*. Well, I still wasn't a hundred percent positive why I had fainted, and the question of whether I'd survive the night was still a bit of a worry.

9

All About the Follicles

Late May 2014, age 40

Thankfully, I did wake up the next morning. I felt a bit off-colour, but at least I was alive! Onwards and upwards, as they say.

I was still weirded out in the days after my fainting spell. Just couldn't stop thinking about the moment I came to, unable to move. And the upturned coffee table. It made me realise that taking medication on my own was a somewhat risky business. There wasn't much I could do about it though, apart from just pushing forward.

When I phoned the clinic, Nurse *Trunchbull* was quite underwhelmed by my tale.

'You should be okay,' she said, hard as a hammer. I was hoping one of the sweeter, more motherly nurses might have answered the phone. Someone who'd at least have given the illusion they cared. But *Trunchbull* cleared her throat with thunderous refrain. 'Just keep taking the meds as instructed. Goodbye.' Then she hung up the phone with a bang.

It's okay. I'm alright, I told myself, the post-hangup dial-tone still ringing in my ears. Naturally, I was shitting myself at the thought of doing the injections the following night. Being the independent, stubborn, refusing-to-ask-for-help person I was,

71

I'd kept this all to myself. I didn't need the extra concern of loved ones worrying about me.

I meticulously mapped out the next day from beginning to end. I'd eat plenty of healthy food and gear up mentally for the moment of truth. Driving home from work that afternoon knowing I had to do that wretched injection instilled panic in me. I could feel myself heating up, my skin prickling at the thought of it. Like a child being forced to do something they desperately didn't want to, like diving into the swimming pool after a previous water-up-the-nose calamity.

I really didn't want to dive back in. Water might go up my nose again, and that hurts!

Do it, Lorena. Dive in! Do it for the unborn child you so desperately want. Make sacrifices. There's no reason to get upset – you are not a child, and this is not a swimming lesson!

Poised by the bathroom sink, I prepared the injection the same way I'd done every other time. My hands shouldn't have been shaky, but they were. Anxiety was escaping my body, and half-hearted attempts at deep breathing were of little help. The injection went ahead. I paused. Waited. Looked down at my bare stomach. No blood. I wandered into the bedroom. No fuzziness. Phew! Then, I carefully lay down.

I must have been there around ten minutes wondering what was going to happen. Eventually, I got up slowly and walked out to the kitchen. Grabbed a half open box of Savoury Shapes and scoffed a few. All seemed well. Not only did I not pass out, but the injection was painless too. With a massive sigh of relief, I put some pasta on the stove, poured a glass of wine, and was back to myself again.

That evening, I had a mini celebration, because it was a

tangible turning point. I was going to do anything it took to make my baby. The injections were the tiniest part of the picture – I had to remember that!

NOTE TO SELF: In the future, do NOT attempt to subcutaneously inject old lady urine into lower torso unless fully fed, watered, and rested. One must always remember the power of these drugs, and I am but a humble structure of flesh and bone.

I'm not a big fan of the term 'rollercoaster' unless you're talking about a ride at a fun park. In the context of people's life experiences, it's a much-overused word. 'Literal' is another. Grossly overused, massively misused. Alanis Morrisette rendered the word 'ironic' entirely ineffectual after that song of hers. I won't even mention 'journey'…

I do understand why people keep using the word 'rollercoaster', though, to describe life's ups and downs. Its definition has become much more than just a fun ride at Disneyland.

In reality TV a rollercoaster is when a contestant forgets how to boil an egg one minute, but is miraculously able to concoct a consommé out of nothing but water and the eye of a newt the next. The following week, the same person must somehow bake scones, while harnessed to a flying fox hurling them across the Grand Canyon, wearing only their underpants. *That's* a rollercoaster.

I'm going to use the word just this once: making babies, IVF style, is a fucking rollercoaster! In every sense. My ups and downs thus far are obvious. Two days after the fainting episode, I had my first ultrasound scan. The one with the probe. I had to lie down, watch a nurse slip a condom over the probe, lube it up, and commence with the magic. Only not so magical this time.

'There just doesn't seem to be a lot going on,' she said, with a sympathetic tilt of the head. 'I don't know why. Have you been injecting the correct amount of medication?'

I sat there like a stunned mullet. This hadn't been the conversation I'd imagined. Wasn't she supposed to tell me I was doing great? And that I had more follicles than she'd ever seen before? I coughed. 'I check it about a thousand times each night, before I inject.' I was wondering what the hell was wrong with my body, feeling certain that this IVF round was going to fail before it even began. I looked up and read the stark laminated sign in the ultrasound room that said:

Follicle does not necessarily = egg.

Great. Each ovarian follicle should in theory contain an egg. But that doesn't always happen. Yet another thing to stress over.

The nurse moved the probe over to my left ovary. 'Ooh, now look what we have here,' she sang.

My eyes lit up. 'Follicles?'

'Lots of them,' she replied. 'At least five.' My heart did a jittery jig as dopamine flushed through my body. Finally, something positive. The good news I needed. Still, there was that familiar, relentless niggle in my brain reminding me, *Your right one had only two tiny follicles* that wouldn't shut off. I needed more follicles if there was any chance of getting more than one or two eggs.

The nurse put her hand on my shoulder, her auburn hair escaping a little at the side of her hairnet. 'You're still only in the early stages of your medication,' she said. 'Keep doing what you're doing, and let's hope there's better news in a day or two.'

I thanked her and walked out, past reception, nodding to

Trunchbull on the way to the exit. I was bitterly disappointed, unable to understand why both ovaries weren't kicking into gear like they should.

Then, in a moment of academic brilliance, I self-diagnosed the reason my right ovary wasn't playing ball: because I'd done most of the injections on the left side of my tummy. Ha-ha, that MUST be it. Genius. That night, I planned to start injecting more on the right side. To see if it made any difference, and to give that side a boost. I was determined to get that right ovary moving.

Despite all those things, I still had to get on with life and act normal. On an escalator in the shopping centre after my appointment, I started thinking, *Who the hell am I kidding? I'm now forty years old!* Asking the doctors and nurses to make my baby in a test tube with no father on the scene was pure madness. Injecting myself with drugs and possibly pushing my body to the brink of hyper-stimulation seemed nothing short of nuts!

Once again, I was in a movie. This time as the protagonist walking in slow motion through a crowd of oblivious shoppers. But really, who was I kidding? It had all been done before. I wasn't the first, or the oldest. Not knowing whether my body would cooperate was the hardest thing. I hated the total lack of control. And what if none of it worked? What then? My mind plunged into a downward spiral.

Somehow, I ended up in the car park unlocking my car. Turning on the ignition, my heart filled with warmth as the familiar piano riff of my favourite song came onto the radio: *Total Eclipse of the Heart* by Bonnie Tyler. My spine tingled. I sat there, surrendering to the serendipitous moment.

'*Once upon a time there was light in my life…*'

Everyone who knows me knows how much I love Bonnie. Once, as an adventurous twenty-something, I decided I was going to follow her tour bus around Denmark and see as many of her shows as I could. I'd met an Austrian guy, Hans, a complete stranger, at her Copenhagen gig. He offered to give me a ride in his gold VW beetle which was faithfully covered in pictures of our idol. Well, how could I resist?

I rode with him in that little car across Denmark. We went to multiple gigs, and even slept in that freezing, heater-less car to save money on accommodation. Shivering my way through the night with just a tiny square blanket for warmth, I reminded myself *I'm doing this for Bonnie!* And then I felt warmer; more comfortable.

We hung out with Bonnie in her changeroom after each gig. It was a lot of fun, and this twenty-four-year-old Aussie girl, who never even thought she'd get the chance to see Bonnie perform live, was having the time of her life.

'You two again, ha-haaaah. Fantastic! Come on in. Have a beer,' Bonnie would hoot. Her warm, raspy, signature laugh was a hearty welcoming summons into the behind-the-scenes biosphere of her tour. She knew us by name, and I felt a sense of freedom and exhilaration that has rarely compared.

'I want you to listen to something for me,' she told us over a few beverages one evening. 'It's my new single, released in Germany next week. I'd love to know what you think.'

'Sure!' we said in unison. She encased us in a motherly hug, bidding us farewell with the demo cassette tape in my quivering, gloved mitts. 'She wants to know what we think!' I yelled into the freezing Danish winter air as we ran toward Hans' car. We couldn't believe it.

Hans clumsily stuffed the tape into the cassette deck, and we waited in euphoric anticipation for the sound to come. There was a pretty piano riff. Bonnie's gravelly voice sang softly at first, then built in her signature way. Of course, we LOVED it, convinced it would be massive. With Bonnie's permission, ('Of course you can, darlings!'), we took it to a music shop and 'borrowed' one of their display tape decks to dub the cassette onto a blank tape. Remember when you could speed-dub a cassette? Bonnie sounded like a Smurf, crooning out her new song through the tinny little boom box speakers.

Back to the present, listening to *Total Eclipse of the Heart*, I drove, and wept. More crying – will it ever stop? Maybe it was the hormones in the drugs. Or perhaps I was finding the whole thing just too damned hard. Maybe hearing Bonnie's biggest hit was like a pair of warm, caring arms wrapping around me. So familiar, so many memories, like an old friend assuring me that everything was going to be okay. I was much calmer afterward, my soul soothed.

I fastidiously injected into the right side of my tummy for the next few nights. I also made a point of giving my right ovary pep-talks to ensure it felt loved and encouraged. 'You can do it,' I said. 'Just keep working hard. You've got follicles in you waiting to make an appearance.' I didn't neglect the left either. It was important they both had the nurturing they needed to go forth and produce.

With trepidation, I re-entered the ultrasound room. The same kind nurse greeted me with a 'crossed fingers' gesture to indicate her optimism. Well, my inspirational words must have worked because this time things were looking much more positive. My left ovary kicked butt with at least four follicles, all receiving high scores. Scores I later found out referred to their measurements.

The right side wasn't as good, but I'd expected that. There were a few: three, I think. The nurse smiled reassuringly. 'So much better than last time.' I'd started developing a bit of a rapport with some of the friendlier nurses. I loved those 'knowing' moments where they could tell what I was thinking. We'd share a smile, without needing to say a word.

Sabine-of-the-sperm took my blood (she's clearly multi-talented), and we had a little reminisce about everything that had happened so far which put me nicely at ease as well.

By this point my ovaries were so active, they had become little pressure points bearing down on my bladder, making me want to wee all the time. I thought that only happened in the late stages of pregnancy when the baby was ready to pop. That'll be fun – I'll be needing the loo every ten minutes if this was anything to go by.

I guess my lovely ever-growing follicles were demanding a few extra bunkers down there. But in all honesty, it was a strange feeling. I was acutely aware of the location of both ovaries, something I'd never experienced before. They felt stretched. Tugged.

Meanwhile, I was feeling great. My skin was glowing, my insides drenched in estrogen. I was happy, and in an odd turn of events, not moody. I'd been warned by my work-friend Tonia (pregnant with her first IVF baby – three rounds, two miscarriages, and five embryo transfers, so she really knew what she was talking about), that I would become a right and proper bitch after the injections.

Somehow, I'd managed to skip that part. Tonia studied me when I came into work one day. 'Bags under the eyes. Tired.' She guessed I'd started my meds and gave me a hug. 'Wow! Look at you! You're going to be a mama.'

She was right about the tired thing. I was fucked. Happy, glowing, but extremely knackered. I tried to look on the bright side – feeling a bit weary is better than being moody, right? I'd be back to myself again. Just needed some sleep. Home, inject, dinner, ZZZ.

I had a great visit to the clinic the following morning. My follicle measurements were high, and I was loving the girls at the clinic too. They made it all very easy and fuss-free. Of course, it also helped when the news was good.

Must be the hormones invading my brain because I started developing crushes on everyone. Men? Women? No one in my path was safe.

The first was the compassionate head nurse, Marian, who did most of my ultrasounds. That made perfect sense – she was my carer. It was a mothering, nurturing thing. Will-I-Am was my next victim. He was on the TV show *The Voice* as a mentor and was so kind and lovely to the contestants. The nurturing thing again. Plus, he's a hottie!

Two days later, I was back at le clinique having all the usual procedures, and big news: I'm follicularly spectacular! Marian also found some small but still viable follicles, which was good. I was looking at somewhere between six to ten eggs at the retrieval operation. A decent number. 'Textbook,' Marian told me after the ultrasound. There's that word again. Leaving the clinic, I was jumping for joy.

Because everything was going to plan, I'd be heading out of town the following day for my egg collection. My operation would be early the morning after.

Meanwhile, I had to administer three injections: my usual one, and two others using a pen thing I'd never tried before called a 'trigger' injection, intended to bring on ovulation. This trigger told any eggs hiding out in my follicles it was time to head out and get ready to be collected. The ovulation train was on its way, *toot toot!* I was instructed to do the 'pen' injections at precisely 8pm that evening.

I gave Marian a blank look. 'But I can't. I'm working.'

'It has to be at 8pm,' she replied. 'Can anyone bring them to you?'

No. I don't ask for help. Remember?!!

I gave in, cancelling my last two dance lessons, screeching home in time to prep and administer those mysterious time-adamant meds at 8pm precisely. The pen thing was a challenge, but it was okay. I had to stab it into my stomach and push on a button at the top. I bled and bruised, but it wasn't a drama. Nor did I feel sick, which was a bonus, because you never know.

I tried not to think too much about the operation I was having in thirty-six hours. And more than anything, I tried not to think too far beyond *that*.

10

Just. More. Waiting

Early June 2014, age 40

Waiting, waiting, waiting can go on for so long. Even if in real time it's only a couple of hours, or a day or two, it feels like centuries. We all know this. What I didn't know was how much the egg retrieval operation would knock me around. Rest? My idea of rest was going for a nice long walk. I didn't like to be forced to relax.

The egg pick-up is a quick operation under a light general anaesthetic. The doctor inserts tiny needles through the ovaries into the follicles. Liquid from each follicle is then gently sucked out, hopefully with an egg in it. It took around twenty minutes to half an hour, according to Mum. The concept of time had completely eluded me due to the anaesthetic. I could have been there for two minutes or a week, a million-dollar reward wouldn't have encouraged me to know any different.

The doctor and nurses were all busy, buzzing around checking on me with efficiency and care. I was sad Dr Hopkins couldn't do the op. But the two-hundred kilometre trip was too far, and Dr Mapleton, the local doctor, seemed nice enough. He had silver fox grey hair and deep, dark eyes. His face was harsh but trustworthy, and he seemed proficient. Naturally, I developed an immediate crush on him.

Going into the operating theatre was like walking onto an *E.R.* set, with Dr Mapleton my very own George Clooney. There was a spotlight above the operating table and bright fluorescent lights illuminated the room. Everyone looked ten years older, because overhead lighting does that. Above all, everyone looked competent, as I'd hoped they would. I don't know what I would have done if they were all drooling or wearing clown suits. A very different kind of *E.R.* episode!

The nurses were setting up equipment and lining up scary stainless-steel tools on a nearby table. I was lying on the operating table feeling extremely nervous as the procedure began. No one said anything to reassure me or keep me calm, so I told myself over-and-over in my head, *You will be FINE, Lorena!* That helped.

An anaesthetist tried about six veins on my inner arm, making numerous attempts to find a good one for the cannula. This wasn't encouraging, and the more he tried, the more I flinched. He eventually found one on the outside of my hand. If I hadn't been feeling so apprehensive, I would have laughed at the slapstick comedy element of it all. The backs of both my hands were bruised black. This was the man I was entrusting my life with; to put me into a temporary coma, keep me alive, then bring me safely out of it.

Thankfully, that's all I remember. Next thing I knew I was awake, groggy, recovering in a nearby hallway. All I needed to know was: *How many eggs?*

Dr Mapleton came over when he noticed me stirring. I could see the joy in his soulful eyes as he told me my results. 'We retrieved eight eggs,' he said, with a serious smile. How somebody can smile seriously I don't know, but he did. Eight eggs! I wanted to kiss him. Have babies with him. Oh, hang on…

There was no nausea afterward, either. The nurses gave me tea and toast, which I inhaled. I was a little dopey from the anaesthetic, but so far, no pain. Mum stayed with me the whole time. It must have been a long day for her, but she did her motherly thing without hesitation. I was immeasurably grateful.

We decided to go for a leisurely dinner that night, and it came as quite a shock when my body protested. Mum was driving us to a restaurant when I started to feel weird. 'I'm not sure I can do this,' I heard myself say.

We pulled over and a look of concern washed over Mum's face. 'You look terrible, sweetie.'

I was clammy and lightheaded, either about to throw up or pass out. My eyes went fuzzy, and I could feel the *oh, no* narrative of my injection fainting episode replaying in my head. Mum pulled out one of her trusty complimentary RSL Club wet wipes from the early 90s. She still had a trillion of them, and somehow, they were still damp. She wiped my forehead and opened the car door. The fresh air was heaven. Another moment, I'd have been out cold.

I didn't vomit, thank goodness. But what had I been thinking? I'd been under general anaesthetic just a few hours beforehand, and there I was insisting we go out for dinner? I even had a secret plan to drink a 'spontaneous' glass of wine. I needed to crawl back into my shell and hide for a while, feeling like such a fool.

We headed back to the hotel once I started feeling better. I went straight to bed. On reflection, it's quite amazing the way my body demanded healing time. *You get to bed and sleep 'til I say otherwise*, it had insisted. This was rare for me, and quite confronting. I was so used to being in control, rarely sick.

But.

Control was a thing of the past now IVF had entered the building. And in this instance, it was for the good. I slept, took it easy, and Mum drove us two-hundred kilometres home the following day. None of this had been a picnic for her either as she walked the fine line between worry and encouragement.

It was now time for the next bout of waiting. How many eggs would fertilise? How many would stay fertilised? How many would survive the removal of cells for PGD testing? Out of those, how many would be chromosomally correct? Would any be usable? Would any be transferred back to me? Would I have any extra to freeze? Would I end up pregnant? Would I go to term? Give birth?

My God, this was just the beginning.

The following morning, heading home, I phoned the clinic to find out how many eggs had fertilised. I was shitting bricks, to put it elegantly; nervous and shaky as Mum pulled over so I could concentrate on the phone call.

I poised myself for the worst. Always bracing for disappointment. Because expecting the best could leave me short-changed, so I needed to hedge my bets strategically. 'Five fertilised, Lorena,' an embryologist from the clinic said.

'Oh,' I replied. 'Is that all?' At first, I felt disheartened. Why only five? Why not all eight?

'Survival of the fittest,' Mum suggested afterward. 'You wouldn't want the ones that didn't fertilise – there's a reason they didn't.' I agreed, feeling a little better after hearing it. I love Mum. I love her for being there, and for looking after me. I love her wisdom, and comforting words. I love her for not pushing herself into my space too much, and for knowing just how much support to give. She has been incredible. If I can be half the mum to my little, newly fertilised, six to eight-cell clusters incubating in their petri dishes, I'll be doing just fine.

And though I'd hoped for more embryos, I had to find a way to be happy with five. Statistically speaking, five is in line with the percentage that typically fertilise under similar conditions. Some women get more. Many get less. All I could hope for was that the embryos were balanced and chromosomally sound.

More waiting ahead…

PGD stands for Preimplantation Genetic Diagnosis. PGS stands for Preimplantation Genetic Screening. I'm not sure of the difference. There's also PGT, which is Preimplantation Genetic Testing. But where I was, they called it PGD, which is why I do too.

Of the five embryos I had, only four little fighters survived the weekend. On the following Monday a single cell was removed from each and tested in a separate lab. This was a cutting-edge establishment, world renowned for its excellence in PGD testing. My little guys were in good hands.

Here, scientists analyse the chromosomal content of each cell (and therefore of each embryo). The testing doesn't distinguish between *normal* and *abnormal*, but checks the chromosomes are balanced. A *balanced* chromosome count contains the right amount of information. Not too much (i.e., an extra chromosome as in Down Syndrome), or too little (say, if part of the chromosome breaks off and doesn't re-attach properly, as in Williams Syndrome).

If everything is okay, the embryo would be transferred back to me, and fingers crossed I'd end up pregnant. If there was an imbalance in any of the chromosomes, I would have to decide whether to have the embryo destroyed. That's because if it implanted at all, the result would be either a miscarriage, or a child with a disability. For this reason, PGD is an incredible science, much like a crystal ball looking into the future.

I'd Googled PGD results a million times, specifically trying to work out the odds of a person with a seventh chromosome inversion ending up with an abnormal embryo. The results were uplifting. It seemed unlikely all four embryos would be imbalanced based on that. It may still be inverted – that would be okay – we just didn't want any of it to have broken off. The odds were looking good, so I wasn't worried.

I should have been. (P.S.: I'm never Googling again.)

What I failed to remember was this test was for ALL of the chromosomes in my embryos. Not just the seventh. I was no spring chicken, and the older I became, the more likely chromosomal abnormalities would occur. I simply hadn't considered any of the other twenty-two pairs of chromosomes.

And I should have!

11

The Hardest Part

June 2014, age 40

Genetic testing is a bit like playing with fire, but in the future it will no doubt be used all the time. The sex of an embryo can be determined too, but in Australia we're not allowed to know that unless there's a specific medical reason.

It's possible that genetic testing could one day be used to *create* perfect babies. Perhaps, somewhere in the world, there's an underground laboratory where it's already happening. Eek!

Chromosomally incorrect embryos are usually destroyed. Or given to science for research, depending on the wishes of the family. I wondered whether anyone would go ahead and transfer an embryo if it was atypical. I was fairly sure I wouldn't. Isn't that the point of testing? Still, the power of playing God felt overwhelming. As a solo mum in the making with a couple of genetic anomalies, I wanted to have a healthy baby. Is that so selfish?

I realise that many people label solo mums by choice as selfish because they knowingly bring a child into the world without a father. For me, being the sole parent was even more reason to take extra precaution to ensure my baby was healthy. And as science made that possible, it felt unwise – crazy – not to utilise this technology.

Families are all so different. Some have gay parents; transgender parents; grandparents as parents; solo parents like me. Some have parents who are ill and unable look after their children. Some live in houses filled with extended family. Some parents die. The list goes on.

Then there are circumstances where children are born unwanted, or their birth parents can't take care of them. Some are adopted out (possibly a happy ending). Some are abused, some are orphans, and some have parents who abandoned them. Others have parents who have separated – which isn't necessarily the worst thing, but let's face it, it's rarely easy on the children.

Then there's the *standard* family structure with mum, dad and 2.4 kids, all living together. This was my upbringing (two kids, not 2.4), and I never questioned it. Though this norm is ever decreasing, my theory is that as long as the child is loved and wanted, family structure isn't relevant.

It's nobody else's business, anyway. The human spirit is powerful, and I include the craving for parenthood in that. My specific desire to be a mother was all-encompassing. My desire for a healthy baby, virtually the same.

Driving two-hundred kilometres for my PGD results and possible embryo transfer, my mind was whirling. I was trying not to stress too much about the results I was soon to receive, but it wasn't working. My stomach churned with worry.

Perhaps driving home I'd be a pregnant woman! Why they made me drive all that way without knowing whether I had any transferrable embryos was beyond me. What if the PGD testing revealed disastrous results? But the nurses had insisted on a face-to-face appointment, and if the results were good, I'd have an embryo transfer, so I kept my mind on that.

It was the weirdest thing knowing I had four growing embryos incubating in petri dishes in an embryology lab. All coming to life outside my own body. My handsome donor's sperm, combined with my sensational eggs. Four bundles of potential life. Four potential personalities, faces, bodies, eye colours. Four potential futures!

I was bonding with my baby already, which was dangerous, naïve territory. Everything was in danger of taking a big nasty topple and I wanted, needed, my embryos to be perfect.

Sitting in that waiting room was torture. Mum had offered to come with me. 'I'm there the moment you need me, sweetie.' But I had to do this alone and couldn't fully explain why. I figured I was potentially getting pregnant – a very personal thing, so if an embryo was implanted, I wanted to quietly clasp onto the thought of being pregnant alone for a little while. Ingest it before letting anyone else in.

I mean, whether I had an embryo transferred or not, I was still going to have plenty to think about. Panic came and went. My scrambled thoughts scattered like marbles. *Please let it be good news*, I repeated to myself. Please, please let my embryos be normal – even just one.

The doctor was late, his morning surgery running overtime. He'd be there in half an hour, the nurse said. This didn't help. Why did everything always have to be so drawn out? The waiting room was my torture chamber, and I felt like I'd never escape. The receptionist suggested I pop outside for some fresh air, promising she'd call me when the doctor arrived. I reluctantly followed her instructions and was called back just ten minutes later. Walking back into that clinic was like walking a tightrope. One step at a time.

The news would be good, Lorena. Don't worry.

Dr John Mapleton, whom I had developed a crush on (along with everybody else) had a shaky voice as he delivered the news that none of my embryos were usable for transfer. He tripped over his tongue telling me all four of my cell bundles were genetically incorrect. 'Um, I imagine you had anticipated the news wouldn't be good?' he stuttered. *(Um, no. I hadn't!)*

This man was so proficient as a gynaecologist and fertility expert. Perhaps he wasn't used to breaking devastating news, who knows? I squirmed in my seat as he filled the silence, 'Well, at least we can say that PGD testing worked for you today.'

Suddenly, I didn't have a crush on him anymore. Tears began to well. Again. My 'no more tears' policy was clearly toast. Dr Mapleton kindly went through the full report, showing details of each embryo. I perked up momentarily, quite fascinated by the science and detail.

Embryo one had an extra second chromosome. Embryo two had an extra eighteenth chromosome. Embryo three was missing chromosomes fifteen and twenty-one, and the last embryo was the superstar (unfortunately not in a Liam Hemsworth way), labelled a *complex aneuploidy*, which meant many, many errors. Too many to list. Go embryo four!

So, what the doctor meant when he'd said PGD testing 'worked' for me today, was if I'd had any of those embryos transferred, they would have either ended in miscarriage, not embedded at all, or have gone to term and created a baby with a disability. If I hadn't had PGD testing, those embryos would have all been transferred. Months of hope and sadness had been saved. But that didn't quell my desperate tears in the moment.

All those needles I'd injected. The fainting incident. The money. Driving two-hundred kilometres and back, twice. The money! The emotional ups and downs. THE MONEY!

I was going to have to do it all again. But what if I end up with the same results? Was there something wrong with me? I had questions for the doctor.

'Why didn't my seventh chromosome cause any problems?'

He tipped his head in thought. 'I'm sorry, my knowledge as a gynaecologist doesn't stretch to that,' he said, claiming to know very little about the information on the report. My tears began to stream in little rivulets, dripping onto my jeans.

'Shall I get a nurse?' he asked.

I mumbled something along the lines of, 'Yes, please,' and within seconds, one of the nurses appeared and wrapped her arms around me. After a while, I left the clinic feeling heavy and hollow. Stumbling out to the street, I noticed the sun shining across a freshly mown lawn. How could such a beautiful day not be aware of my bad news? Life kept moving on as always – which never ceases to surprise me when my world had just partially collapsed. I called Dr Hopkins' office, crying my way through a conversation with his receptionist, Gen. Dr Hopkins wasn't in, but she would get him to call me back.

He called within ten minutes, probably from the golf course, because even when he wasn't working, he was still on call. His calm, reassuring, and generally amazing demeanour soothed me.

And he explained a *lot*.

I learned that most of the eggs in a woman's ovaries are chromosomally abnormal. It's to do with the initial creation of the oocyte (a cell in the ovaries destined to become an egg), which requires the forty-six chromosomes of a normal body cell to divide into twenty-three pairs. Sometimes they divide well, and the chromosomes split properly. Other times they divide incorrectly. Some eggs end up with too many chromosomes, some with too few (a fragment of a chromosome, or a missing one). Age, of course, adds to egg deterioration too, as I already knew.

Dr Hopkins assured me my PGD results were, 'Not horrific. You are not chromosomally abnormal, Lorena.' And the sperm. Could I blame the sperm?

Apparently not. Donor sperm is tested for all kinds of things. It's pretty much as good as you can get, quality-wise. The Rolls-Royce of gametes (sex cells). Sperm is made daily so there's also the 'regular regeneration' factor. Yes, folks, back to grade five science class: 'The man's testes produce sperm every day.' (Giggle, giggle.) Plus, there are millions of the little buggers so there's more choice.

But eggs are clever too. In nature, they reject irregular sperm, so they can't get in to fertilise the egg. This is *even* if the egg is chromosomally incorrect. So, a potentially doomed egg can *still* reject dubious sperm. Certainly, one for us gals!

All in all, Dr Hopkins made me feel much better, helping me breathe back to life. He asked me to make another appointment when I was ready to discuss trying again. That felt good.

I started the long drive home down the highway. Suddenly I had the urge to call Mum, so I pulled over.

Speaking to Mum on the phone at times like these always made me cry. This time was no exception. I tried to keep my shit together – was feeling okay, after all. But Mum picked up the phone, I heard her voice and whammo, I was off. I explained everything, particularly my positive conversation with Dr Hopkins. She said all the reassuring things I needed to hear. Once again, I felt better for it.

I headed home and opened a bottle of red wine. That night, I savoured every drop.

I didn't want to leave it too long before my next appointment with Dr Hopkins. I needed to get on with round two.

It was great to see him again, but everything felt lukewarm. Our conversation edged very much back to the drawing board. I'd been expecting more of a 'round two, woohoo, let's DO this' vibe, especially after his positive response to my embryo testing fiasco; so, this was a bit of a smack in the face. He was trying to figure out why my embryos were such a mess. He'd already explained the reasons behind the chromosomal abnormalities, but he was now erring on the side of something being uniquely wrong with me.

Great.

I felt the world heaping onto my shoulders. Not only had I been anticipating an upbeat appointment, I was now facing the idea I was a complete failure. Couldn't even produce decent embryos. Shouldn't that be a given for a woman? I could feel all the emotions welling up but made the effort to push them straight down again. If my doctor didn't question everything, how could I progress? So, I listened with intent.

He thought that perhaps *all* my eggs had a malfunction when formed, possibly due to my chromosome inversion. And age. He suggested I consider the idea of egg donation.

What?

'Not use my own eggs? How is that possible?' I stammered.

It seemed unthinkable.

'It isn't something we need to consider yet, Lorena,' he replied with a lighter tinge to his voice. 'But it's a possible Plan B for later.'

Dr Hopkins had mentioned donor eggs before, but I didn't pay much attention. I always assumed I'd be fine with my own, ending up with a mini-me, a reflection of my own traits. 'Look, she has my eyes; my temperament,' and so on. Isn't that part of the drive of having a baby?

What would it be like if I used donor sperm *and* donor eggs? My child wouldn't be genetically linked to me, or anyone in my family. Would that matter? I didn't have the foresight to imagine. The suggestion was too enormous, and certainly not yet something I could get my head around. I pushed it aside knowing I had to keep trying, trying, *trying* with my own eggs. At this point, I couldn't see any other way.

I woke up the next morning and noticed an unspeakably early missed call from a silent number. It turned out to be Dr Neal Peters' personal assistant wanting to arrange an appointment. Dr Peters was a geneticist who specialised in the PGD testing I'd had done. We had spoken on the phone a few months earlier, an in-depth consultation discussing my inverted seventh chromosome. To have his personal assistant call made my stomach drop. Why did he want to see me now? There must have been something wrong. Why not just another phone call? Obviously, the enormity of what needed to be discussed went beyond another phone discussion.

I booked an appointment for the following week: 8am in the city (Ouch!) at a cost of $480. (Ouch! OUCH!) I prepared a list of questions stemming from our previous phone conversation. The first question on the list was: 'Will I be able to have a baby?'

Until that question was answered, all I could do was try not to fret. Be calm. One step at a time.

Getting to Dr Peters' rooms was a comedy of errors. I mean, I had to get to the city in peak hour – madness at the best of times. And to add to the chaos, for some reason the Harbour Bridge was completely shut down. Why? God only knew, but of *all* days.

I planned to drive to my nearest train station and head in from there. But ended up having to practically park at home and walk to the station, there was so much traffic. No way I was going to be late for my appointment, so I sprinted past the almost stationary cars like a superhero bounding into the city to save the day.

Arriving at the train station, I was a hot clammy mess. Surprisingly, the trains were on time and not too packed. A win! I looked at my phone. Half an hour until my appointment with a lot of walking at the other end. In unyielding *I will not be late* mode, I walked into the building with just three minutes to spare.

I arrived red-faced, hot, and sticky, my hair in an unruly state of mega-frizz. I went to explain myself, but there was no humour behind the reception desk. Sitting and waiting, I immersed myself in a crappy magazine. The building that housed the clinic was an ancient, cold relic with that dank *old museum* odour. Musty, mouldy, but strangely reassuring. There were no pictures or posters: the room felt more like an office than a medical practice.

The 'no worry' thing wasn't working, and my brain attempted to guzzle itself with over-thinking. I put the magazine aside (now sticky from my sweaty palms) and pulled out my list of questions. I tried to memorise them but Dr Peters called me in before I had a chance. He was very serious. Much shorter than I imagined, and quite young, too. Had I been expecting a tall, doddering fossil? He was reasonably good-looking – not in a Hemsworth way – more like Elijah Wood, slightly nerdy but striking.

Overall, he was a pleasant, knowledgeable man. He didn't throw too many curve balls. In fact, I left wondering why I'd needed to battle my way in for a face-to-face appointment at all. There was very little in our consultation I hadn't heard before. The biggest revelation was that he seriously doubted my inverted seventh chromosome was enough reason to do PGD. I was so confused.

But wait… What was that other part I heard? 'Do PGD?' I could go *again*?

'Yes, there's no reason you can't do IVF again,' Dr Peters said. And that's all I needed to hear. I'm goin' again, y'all. Woohoo!!! The whole appointment was worth it just for that.

I paid my $480 and left feeling happier and relieved. A small part of me felt it was such a lot of money for very little new information. But reassurance was what I ended up with, and that was definitely worth something. There was a small Medicare rebate too, which helped.

I was now well and truly back on the onwards and upwards trajectory – just needed a couple of months to save up, and I'd be good to go.

IVF round two: This fighter's back in the ring. *Ding, ding, ding!*

12

The Alternative, AKA Possible Plan B

August 2014, age 41

I'm one of those people who likes to have a Plan B on the back-burner. I find when there's a Plan B in place, it often isn't needed. A *Murphy's Law* thing. For my IVF mission, I had a Plan B – and C too.

Plan C was a bit lame, but still potentially viable. If all else failed, I planned to get a dog and become a fur-mum. I mean, that was going to happen eventually anyway – I really wanted a dog. Not exactly a substitute for having a baby, but I needed to broaden my focus, and this helped.

I've mentioned Plan B already: donor eggs. I began educating myself about egg donation. Google-overload, again.

I could choose an egg donor with comparable traits to mine. Someone with a similar temperament; colouring; build. But then again, with time to think after the initial shock of the suggestion, and Dr Hopkins talking about egg donation quite a bit during subsequent consultations, I started to wonder, how much of that really mattered?

Egg donation in Australia can be a trying process. As things stood, it was likely I'd need to find my own donor. Some people ask a friend or a sister. Some advertise. Egg donors go through the whole rigorous IVF injection and egg pick-up process, a huge ask! I don't have a sister and would find it weird asking a friend. How confronting to look into my child's eyes and see my friend's traits instead of my own. I knew I'd struggle with that.

Perhaps I needed to keep a closer check of my ego? I'm not normally overly egotistical, but was I closing off options just because my offspring may not look like me? A known egg donor could be like an 'aunty' to my child. But I knew I'd feel forever indebted in a way I wouldn't with a sperm donor – which is strange in itself. Well, I knew I needed help in the sperm department. I was clearly unable to produce it myself. But an egg? That would represent a particularly cruel sort of failure. Could there be jealousy or awkwardness from either side of the egg donation? What if I felt paranoid, as though being watched and monitored by the donor? An 'Is she bringing this child up right?' kind of thing.

What a rabbit hole. The notion of advertising for a donor seemed like a labyrinth too. People put ads in newspaper classifieds and online. Plus, Australian donors are not paid, other than for medical expenses, so it can take a really long time to find someone suitable.

Another way to find donor eggs is to source them from overseas. America, South Africa, Greece, and many other countries have viable donor programs. The laws in these countries differ from ours, which makes it possible to pay donors for their eggs (and sperm too). For a princely sum, you can help a Harvard college student pay their tuition by buying her eggs. To be honest, this didn't sit well with me at all. If I ever needed to buy donor eggs, or sperm, it would be from somebody doing it for the good of humanity, to help others. *Not* for the money.

In many of these countries it's legal for donors to remain

permanently anonymous. I wasn't sure how I felt about that either. How would it sit with my consequent child? I was beginning to enter a headspace that was too colossal for my tiny IVF-riddled brain. So, I decided to save it for later if, heaven help me, my IVF rounds continued to fail.

One person who blew me away with her acceptance of the donor egg notion was Mum. I couldn't believe the conversation we had about it.

I'm sure you've gathered by now that I have a very high opinion of my parents. Mum has been incredible throughout my IVF shenanigans, and this helped increase Dad's acceptance as well. He was on board but needed a bit of an extra nudge to fully get there. I think the fact that Mum was always so supportive helped. They're a team after all and come as a package: the true parental unit.

When I mentioned Dr Hopkins' suggestion of perhaps using donor eggs in the future, Mum's answer was to the point and remarkable: 'I wouldn't have a problem with that at all, sweetie,' she said without hesitation.

I was momentarily surprised. Then floored. Then relieved. That was just the way Mum saw it – very plainly. She certainly opened my eyes.

Our conversation continued. 'A genetic connection doesn't make a mother.' Dad was sitting right behind her, nodding in agreement. Neither of them so much as flinching at the thought.

'So, you wouldn't mind if your grandchild wasn't genetically linked to you?'

'Of course not!' Mum said, smiling. Dad was once again nodding in resolute agreement.

I wallowed in the thought for a moment. A double-donor

child created from a donor egg and donor sperm was a truly amazing concept. If someone used donor eggs but had a partner's sperm, they would still have some sort of familial connection. But a double-donor conceived child with no genetic connection at all? Should I be panicking about that? Could I really do it? My parents' response helped, because I knew that if the important people weren't worried about it, then I would surely have less cause for concern.

There's a whole nature versus nurture debate that goes with double donation. And the concept of epigenetics too; something I find exciting and utterly fascinating. Epigenetics is the science of how a birth mother's pregnant body can modify the ways genes are expressed in a growing foetus. I'll go into this more later on.

I also considered adoption as part of my Plan B. Giving birth to a baby using donor eggs and sperm wouldn't be entirely unlike adopting where in both cases, there's an absence of a genetic link. I hoped that wouldn't lessen the emotional connection, but I didn't really know. You often hear adopted kids talk about the parents who raised them as their 'real' mum and dad. Their true family. After some research I learned that in Australia as a single person in my early forties, I didn't qualify to adopt. So, for me, it was off the table.

Meanwhile, not everyone had been so open-minded when I broached the subject of egg donation, even among the special few I trusted. One friend surprised me with her response. 'It… could be a bit weird,' she said. Sometimes it's those short sharp sentences that strike the hardest. 'The child wouldn't really be yours. Would it?'

All my fears were realised in that moment. My mind went

numb. What the hell was I doing even thinking about donor eggs? Thinking I could play God? Creating happy families like some sort of fairytale?

Well, it was good for me to hear her honest opinion, I guess. To be fair, I've used the words 'potentially weird' when referring to egg donation in the past as well. Still, the sense of my friend's judgement felt real, even if had been unintentional.

I realised that in the future I needed to be careful who I spoke to and what I revealed. Best to keep my guard up, because there would be opinions – and lots of them. In fact, the ones that potentially hurt the most are often from people you love the most. I redirected my thoughts back to the positivity I'd received from my parents.

My brother and his family came over a couple of weeks later. Their reaction was the same as Mum and Dad's.

'Why wouldn't you?' they said.

I was relieved. They hadn't even faltered. I was particularly happy because they are a 'say-it-as-it-is' family and would have spoken up if they hadn't approved. I took a breath, reminding myself how lucky I was to have landed such a phenomenal family. The abundance of love in my life felt incredible. To be understood, and to have their support and love was just amazing! All this reminded me of my great-uncle who had passed away the previous year. Uncle Doug was ninety-five when he died. He and our Aunty May had been married for over sixty years. They used to hold hands walking down the street – right up until the end.

Our family was devastated to lose Uncle Doug, and the love in the room was more than evident at his funeral. Aunty May barely made it through the day, propped up by loving relatives desperate to ease her pain. She lived solely for him, and at ninety-three herself, she was already frail, now heartbroken.

We were *all* heartbroken. Uncle Doug was one to pull your leg, and we never quite knew whether the yarns he told us were true or not. But here's the thing: he wasn't genetically related to any of us. His birth family had long disappeared and he never had kids of his own.

He ended up raising Aunty May's daughter, even though he wasn't her biological father. Nothing about genetics mattered. What a revelation during my ongoing internal debate on donor eggs. It stubbed out any remainder of doubt – and made my Plan B entirely viable and solid. I trusted my instinct, leaving uncertainty by the wayside.

Thank you, Uncle Doug, for providing that extra special final piece of reassurance.

13

Here We Go Round Again

September 2014, age 41

I'd saved up some money and had a bit of a rest from all things IVF. Well, as much of one as I could when all I really wanted to do was get on with it.

I headed back for another consultation with Dr Hopkins, feeling like I'd been away forever, although it was just a few months. I arrived full of enthusiasm, raring to start again. He kicked off with, 'Oh, Lorena, what are we going to do with you?' which was not reassuring. Especially after our previous appointment that had a similar tepid tone. What was I expecting, a big brass band? I knew I was being uncharacteristically pedantic.

The doctor got to work, planning my next round. 'You had eight eggs last time, so the medications did their job. I want to repeat the protocol for this cycle.' He was typing instructions and prescription orders into his computer as he spoke.

His receptionist, Gen, was particularly lovely, telling me she had 'a good feeling this time', wishing me all the best.

I remembered to rub the magic Dali egg on the way out. No surprises what I wished for.

Holy Shit – I Know You!

What happens when you're sitting in the waiting room of an IVF clinic and right opposite you is someone from your childhood ballet class?

Panic! That was me, anyway. Admittedly, I can be a reticent soul. A normal person may have struck up a conversation about old times or even shared a knowing smile. But for me, this was an *Anonymity Unveiled* moment. The sheer horror in my eyes! If the pot plant in the corner was bigger, I would have dived directly into it.

There I was, waiting to get blood tests done. Been there a million times. Strangely, I have often wondered what I'd do if I recognised anyone. Who might it be? And how would I react?

Well, wonder no more. There she was: Belinda Stanley from my *City Ballet Academy* days. I remember her as a freckly kid with a massive ballet bag in the shape of a pointe shoe. Now, she was a businesswoman with an oddly small briefcase. My brain couldn't figure out the transition, and I'm surprised I recognised her at all.

We shared so much history, stemming from ancient times in our young years under the tutelage of Barbara Bunyan. It was strange to be in such close proximity to someone who was both a stranger and a childhood acquaintance. I glanced at her from the corner of my eye. Her gaze was stoic, straight ahead, giving nothing away. I doubted she was thinking about Barbara Bunyan.

Mrs Bunyan. My dad used to nickname her *The Dragon Lady*, and I'm sure she would have taken that as a compliment. She did everything short of breathe fire, let me tell you – a very scary woman. We were all terrified of her. She yelled; she screamed. Heaven forbid you should make a mistake, because you'd be done for, even at the tender age of five. The quintessential old-school ballet teacher, she was small, loud, with shitloads of make-up. I actually think she might have *invented* false eyelashes.

We knew she was a good teacher, though. She demanded so much, and as teenagers we quivered in our pointe shoes, too scared to say we were in pain, because we knew her response would be, 'Until I see blood dripping through your shoes, I don't want to hear about it!' Pointe shoes are made of resin, so for blood to seep through, you would pretty much have to have a toe falling off.

She instilled something in me that created a lifelong love of ballet. To this day, I can't explain it. She gave me discipline, a strong work ethic, morals, and motivation. I still thank her for all of it.

As these memories burned through my head, I knew if I just murmured those two magic words, 'Barbara Bunyan', into the clinic waiting room, Belinda Stanley would jump to attention. The exact same images would flash into her head. It would've been a great experiment, but I resisted. I could more easily satisfy my curiosity by talking to her. 'Still dancing?' 'Why this clinic?' 'Any baby success yet?'

Instead, I rummaged through my bag, yanked out my phone, and did the only thing I could think of: I developed a sudden and profound obsession with Bubble Mania. I was shooting bubbles like there was no tomorrow. *Up. Across. Pew-Pew!* I beat the level I'd been stuck on for weeks in a single go. Pure adrenalin overload. I think my hands were even shaking a little from the sheer rush of it all.

I could sense Belinda's every move in my periphery. She was casually swiping her phone. Perhaps she'd seen me too and was also in avoidance mode. Or maybe she hadn't seen me at all? Why was I even bothered?

Of course, my name was called out first, but Belinda didn't notice. You've never seen anyone move into that corridor as fast as I did that day. Olympians would have been impressed. Whether she saw me or not, the truth is, we were two people in the same boat at the clinic for the same reason. In the end none of the other stuff mattered.

Still, I couldn't explain why I hated the thought of sharing MY clinic with someone else I knew. Barely knew at that! This was the place where *I* came to for treatment. *Me!* How selfish of me, and in hindsight I can't believe I gave such a vast amount of energy to such a ludicrous notion. Other patients who were strangers didn't bother me. But to share this experience with someone I knew? I loathed the idea. Don't ask me why; it was just a thing I had. A CRAZY thing. The IVF process had already become so much a part of my identity, I was engulfed. Somehow, it also made me a more 'interesting' person. (Whatever that means.) Innovative too. And brave. And all the things my friends told me I was. My grand IVF journey would seem dull and pedestrian if there were other people I knew doing it too.

I was also snorting hormones at the time which was bound to have an effect. I mean, how dare Belinda be trying to have a baby! And she'd better not have one before me, either. I couldn't face the news if she became pregnant, which would inevitably be shared on social media. There I was worrying about something that may never happen. Yet. Again. Will I ever learn?

But I had another question. Why was I so reluctant to bond with other women doing IVF? What was wrong with me? These were people I could theoretically look to for support and camaraderie, because we were all going through much the same thing. There was a direct support network available to me. What was I going to do, shun them all?

I logged onto a solo mum by choice website for about five minutes before catapulting straight back off. (There's that Olympic speed again!) I'm sure those forums are great for some, but they weren't for me at that time. Too much information, and too many failures. So many miscarriages. I couldn't take it. So heartbreaking and confronting for the still-hopeful newbie that I was.

But you never know where your next support network is going to spring from, so I tried to stay a little bit open. It wasn't until much later in my treatment marathon that I came to know a bunch of outstanding solo mums, mostly through various solo mum by choice Facebook pages. There's a wonderful community of strong women out there who are super supportive. A subject for later.

And as for Belinda Stanley…?

Well, I never did find out whether she became a mother. I hope she did. Despite myself, I would genuinely love to call her and chat about the old days. Wouldn't it be nice for our babies to meet?

My, how I have changed.

14

IVF Round Two: Ding Ding, Back in the Ring (Again)

October 2014, age 41

The head ultrasound nurse, Marian, always gasped when I told her my date of birth. Confirming my name and age was part of the clinic's identification process. Marian *never* remembered me. It didn't matter how many times I'd been in, she always gave me the same blank look. I had to introduce myself 'for the first time' every time, which became absurd. Honestly, it started to feel like *Groundhog Day*. Here's how it went:

Marian: 'What's your name, love?'

My answer: 'Regina Porridge. Heh, just kidding. Lorena Otes.'

She looks at me from over her reading glasses, uncertain how to proceed. 'Yes, er okay. Your date of birth?'

I decide not to give her the run-around on this one: 'Fourth of the eighth, seventy-three.'

She pauses, removing her glasses, giving me a look of utter disbelief. 'REALLY? You don't look a day over 30!'

I would always respond with, 'Well, it's a pity my reproductive system isn't aware of that.' And we'd both have a laugh.

Happened. Every. Time.

I was officially early-forties by now (ouch!), so my age wasn't a joke at all. I was teetering on middle age, though reluctant to admit it. To me, the term 'middle age' meant fifty-plus, conjuring images of elasticated trousers and spongy 'sensible' shoes with therapeutic soles.

As far as greater society is concerned, women are seemingly encouraged to start withdrawing into their caves at forty – around the time grey hairs begin their invasion. If I were a newsreader, I'd be out of a job by now. Sandra Sully is one of the last ones standing, and good on her. She must be a hundred percent grey by now, but who would really know? Many other middle-aged female newsreaders have crawled under their rocks. Not the men, though. They can be as grey and *distinguished* as they like. Or bald as an eagle.

Around 2016, Madonna threw it all back at the critics regarding ageism during her *Billboard Awards* speech when she said:

'And finally, do not age. Because to age is a sin. You will be criticised; you will be vilified... People say I'm controversial. But I think the most controversial thing I have ever done is to stick around.'

Her refusal to disappear just because she was past her mid-fifties has led the way for future generations. Perhaps someday society will even accept women having babies at a later age. Because I'm not the only one doing it: there are thousands. And millions more in the future. We need women like Sandra and Madonna to pave the way and increase the visibility of women over forty. We live in hope.

But none of that was solving my current problem.

If only someone could find a way to update a person's

ovaries by letting them know that forty is the new thirty. I was still very active – especially as a dance teacher. I definitely *felt* young enough to have a baby. Plus, I only owned two pairs of sensible shoes: Ugg Boots (strictly indoors only), and sneakers.

Every time I did a new round of IVF, there were a million papers to sign: agreements, contracts, medication orders, surgery forms – it felt endless. The cogs were turning again though, which was both exciting and terrifying. I made the big decision to repeat the PGD testing for this round. Despite Dr Peter's advice, it felt like the right thing to do, purely because of my age.

I was doing everything I could to prepare to go again. I needed to be in top form. For starters, I hadn't had any alcohol in three whole months! A miracle for me. This wasn't intentional, it just ended up much easier than I had anticipated. I'd begun to look forward to my after-work glass of wine a little too much. Like I couldn't cope without it. But it turns out, even with the additional IVF stress, the opposite was true, and I thrived. I suspected that stopping for a while wouldn't hurt. That it wouldn't (and I can testify, didn't) kill me.

It had been easier and quicker to receive my medication from the nurses this round too. Probably because I knew what I was doing, they just handed over what I needed sending me on my way – no instructions or demos required.

I wasn't too enthralled with the idea of starting the injections again, but there were no problems this time. I was more relaxed, more in tune, making things much easier.

Before long, it was time for the first ultrasound. Marian forgot who I was again. Perhaps it was becoming our little game. It certainly lightened the mood! We went through the same routine of checking my name, date of birth, and just like every other time, she was *astonished* by how young I looked for my age. I wasn't complaining though. I could never hear enough of that.

My stomach prickled with nerves. Were there going to be any decent follicles? Were the drugs working? I'd been injecting for a week. When I compared this round to my first, I'd had at least two ultrasounds by this stage. Round two seemed faster, cleaner, like clockwork. Maybe this was a good sign? Maybe I shouldn't be looking for 'signs' at all!

Well, my left ovary appeared to be going for it with at least six follicles measuring well. My right was lagging with only two smaller follicles. Come on, righty!

Once Marian had left the examination room, her assistant came over to help me along. I mentioned how great I thought Marian was. The nurse replied, 'Ah yes, she's been doing this a *very* long time. So efficient. In and out, and she's done.' Then she caught herself, realising what she'd said. With a pause and a giggle she hurriedly added, 'Well, so to speak.' She was quite embarrassed once she realised, obviously not meaning for it to come out that way. Regardless, it was nice to have a giggle.

We had warmed to each other a bit, and once this lovely lady found out I was on my second IVF round, she smiled and added, 'Well then, let's get you a baby for next Christmas.'

I left wondering what 'next' Christmas meant? Shouldn't she have said 'this' Christmas? It was October already, after all. Could I be over-thinking it? (Who, me?) But yes, let's get me pregnant. By this coming Christmas. Pleeeease!

I have already mentioned some of my incredible friends. Let me give you a brief history, because I don't have a million of them; just a few, and they are the real deal. Some I've known forever – my early childhood 'buddy-bug', Cass. Others are schoolmates, London friends from my ten-year stint over there, and work friends from various jobs over the years.

I'm talking about friends at this point because it was around this time I realised I would need my tribe to rally around me. Going through all this scientific baby-making with uncertain outcomes and tumultuous mental strain had created a bit of a psychosis in me. I knew it wouldn't sit well with just anyone, so I carefully chose who I invited into the hysteria.

I'd had a phone conversation with an ex-colleague, Olivia, chatting about my second IVF round. 'I don't know how you do it,' she said. She'd been asking me what it was like doing the injections, and I was giving her an uneventful answer because, in truth, that's what the injections had become. She was intrigued, also quizzing me about what it's like to choose a sperm donor.

I guess most people wouldn't know any of that stuff, because they've never needed to do it. I'd already told Liv a bit about my donor when I first chose him, but those things sometimes take time to sink in. The questions came later.

I was becoming more open. I'd already gone through one IVF round, so my friends were much more comfortable to ask about it. They probably hadn't wanted to cross the line before, and, let's face it, I was so busy just getting on with it and freaking out, I wasn't really up for the cross examinations.

In the distant past, a few of my friends, especially some of the married ones, had shied away from me a bit. I noticed it particularly after I first returned from the UK. I copped a bit of attitude at times, particularly about the fact that I was single and without kids. In those days, most of my friends and acquaintances were either trying for kids, had babies, or were wrangling vivacious little toddlers.

It really pains me to think of it now, but sometimes I'd get passing comments like: 'Coping with lack of sleep is the hardest part of being a mum, Lorena. You don't understand yet. But some day you might.'

Still makes me cringe. I also copped sentiments like: 'No one can love a living creature the way they love their own child. If you ever have kids Lorena, you'll understand.'

'Yes. I guess so,' was the usual response I dithered out.

Those comments defined me for a time. I was in my late twenties and didn't have a clue where my life was going. I'd just left my favourite city in the world, London, after ten years there, to come home to a country I hadn't yet come to know as an adult. I didn't have a partner, and wasn't even sure I wanted one. I definitely hadn't thought about whether I wanted kids – I was only just getting by. I just needed space. To be cut some slack. Released from the hefty shackles of judgement.

In the meantime, I relished hanging out with everyone else's kids. I became the 'cool aunty' to friends and family alike; not least my own nephew, an incredible human who I love to bits. I exhibited this *amazing* example of a child-aware, super child-friendly, fun, childless adult. To show that I 'got it'.

I didn't think of it at the time, but this was also the beginning of something else. A little portal into the future of intensely craving a kid of my own. People often assumed I was leading the super exciting, fast-paced life of a ferociously happy single person. I wasn't. That was my London life. Back in Sydney I was home in front of the television most nights. Not unhappy, but certainly not living it up. Possibly (definitely) drinking too much wine.

Sometimes I felt inferior because I didn't have children. Like I wasn't 'good enough'. Not in the club. So, hearing Liv ask questions about my IVF journey was refreshing. It created a balance between the idea of a married family woman and a single woman, who both wanted the same thing: to be a mum. We have no idea what others are going through. Sometimes a childless person has tried for kids and it just hasn't happened for them. Or they could be having fertility treatment. Maybe they just don't want children. And that's okay too, isn't it?

It probably took a while for some of my mates to realise there was no threat or need for judgement. I wasn't trying to impose my ideas or lifestyle onto anybody else. I certainly wasn't 'weird' because I was single. Or a loser. Nor was I hoping to snap up a friend's husband – not in a trillion years.

I returned from London at twenty-eight years old. It wasn't until I was thirty-eight that I realised I had such an all-consuming need to become a mum. That's a lot of self-analysis and growth time in between. And as I've said, I'm bloody lucky to have a tribe of loved ones who stuck by me through all that uncertainty.

Even if originally, some of them weren't so sure.

15

The Solo Parent Life for Me?

Late October 2014, age 41

Marian was happy with me. And I was happy with her too. For starters, she had begun to recognise me when I came in for tests, so that was a plus. She always called me 'Hon', or 'Darling', which could have been irritating, but somehow, she pulled it off.

My ultrasound scans were starting to bring some fantastic results. I had a 10.5mm endometrium, which is apparently good. My left ovary was the star performer with eight nice juicy follicles. The one on the right was kicking into gear too with a little more gusto than before.

Marian was confident about my numbers and was pleased to see my right ovary doing better.

'I gave it a little pep-talk,' I told her.

'Good on you,' she laughed. 'I'm sure that'll work.'

It looked like I'd be ready for my scheduled egg pick-up in a few days. Relieved to hear it, I immediately organised accommodation and time off work for the trek. Everything seemed on track.

A few days before my appointment, I landed myself in a bit of a pickle. Driving onto Sydney Harbour Bridge, I felt my steering wheel suddenly tug to the right. It felt like a flat tyre. With nowhere to pull over, and the only option to keep moving forward, I slowed to thirty kilometres an hour – a snail's pace, trying to figure out what was going on. This was the WORST place to break down, and I could feel sweat beading on my brow. Don't they fine you thousands for breaking down on 'The Bridge'?

The drivers behind me were getting irritated. Tailgating me, because everyone in Sydney does that. If only I could have projected a sign across my rear window explaining my predicament. With a completely flat tyre, my car bumpety-bump-bumped its way to the nearest exit ramp. The NRMA did a quick patchwork job, but my regular mechanic saved the day, squeezing my car in for a tyre replacement just hours later.

It was a great excuse for coffee and a chat with Dad; the mechanic was around the corner from my parents' place. We had a good old chinwag about this and that – something to do with our favourite tracks on Bonnie Tyler's latest album, and whether Mum was going to have a win at bingo that afternoon – the important stuff.

The reason I am Bonnie Tyler's biggest fan is because of Dad. He used to play her cassettes in the car on road trips when I was a kid. I wanted *Lost in France* over and over again on repeat, which involved rewinding the tape a trillion times. I've loved her ever since.

The conversation flowed on to my as-yet-unborn munchkin. This wasn't a subject we'd broached often, if at all, unless Mum was around. I was intrigued to see where it would go. Dad always listened carefully when I talked about my IVF life and future plans, but he never said a lot. Today, after updating him on my latest positive scan results, he asked, somewhat out of the blue, 'What will it be like for you when your kid is a teenager, and you are in your sixties?'

The compulsive realist and over-thinking side of Dad's brain was always present. And he was right. I'd thought about it, and it was going to be tricky – but it wasn't enough to stop me from becoming a mum.

'It is what it is, Dad,' I replied, in a matter-of-fact tone. What more could I say? I just had to hope I was going to be an energetic sixty-year-old.

One of my concerns, try as I might to fend it off, was still the absence of a father. I'd tried to imagine what life would be like without my own dad, but couldn't. In particular, I didn't want to dwell on the parallel universe of life without him in it. I just couldn't imagine being brought up without him on the scene.

Now I was planning on bringing up my own offspring alone. No dad. Who knew what would happen further down the track, but as it stood, I'd be flying solo with a fatherless child.

Would I cope? How would *we* cope? Would my child hate me for my decision? We would adapt; that's for sure. There's a theory that you can't miss what you never had, and I believe that's part of the solution. I mean, I can't imagine life without Dad, or Mum, or my brother; and conversely, it's hard for me to imagine life with a sister, because I never had one. Nor did I have a grandfather. And if my dad hadn't been around, would I have missed him? In all honesty, I wouldn't have known any different. I would have survived.

It was a tough conversation, but in the end, Dad agreed. He knows how much I love him. If he had been absent or unloving, maybe I wouldn't have felt so torn. The question remained: could I knowingly go into parenthood alone? How could I deprive my future children of that father-child bond, especially when it meant so much to me? Should I even be doing this?

Well, probably a little bit of 'yes' to all those questions. You can't always have the choices you wish for. Sometimes you have to just put it out there – what your heart really desires, like a fairytale with three wishes. And hope the fairy godmother comes to the party.

The conversation with Dad continued.

'Seeing you do this alone worries me too,' he said. 'Mum and I have often wondered how you ended up with such dickhead boyfriends.'

I couldn't help but agree. There had been a lot of dickheads. A couple of real arseholes too. And a certain Shithead. But, as I said to Dad, you can't choose who you fall for. They all had some nice qualities, and not everything had been awful. I always seemed to fall for men who ended up being no good for me. Like a titanic mega-magnet, I seemed to attract a lack of desire for commitment.

That good ol' *c-word*: commitment. Turns a grown man into an Olympic sprinter. Sometimes I wondered if I was just using 'their' lack of commitment as a shield to hide my own. Several self-help books later (yes, I read *He's Just Not That into You*), having wobbled my way off the dating scene, I realised that perhaps I was also terrified that if I took the risk and met a guy I really liked, I would have to commit my life to him. Did I really want that? I was never sure. The stars collide when some folks meet their 'person', and perhaps then the fear fades away. But I was far from reaching that stage, far more than content to plod on with my solo parenting plan.

The other massive worry for me was risking my child's safety by bringing a man I barely knew into our home. This honestly kept me up at night, and is the sad truth of how I felt: wary, fearful, and fully on guard. This has ignited anxiety in me where I just know I could never, *ever*, risk leaving my child alone with anyone except for my parents and close family. Never a future partner, no matter who he was. I felt somewhat crippled by the dark places my imagination took me. In the end, it was best to just remove all potential likelihoods of this ever happening and stop thinking about it.

Back to my *D&M* chat with Dad. He told me he wanted to be involved when the baby was born – particularly when I had to go back to work. 'It's not just Mum stepping up,' he said. 'I'm up for helping too. I've changed nappies before. I'm here all day. The baby can be upstairs, and I can be right here to help.' I was blinking back tears.

I'd be chuffed to have Dad do all those things. Part of my dream was to have both of my parents closely involved in my future bub's life. See? How the hell could I have a baby without a dad around? It felt contradictory, but strangely, also something I would happily live with. I figured Dad's *Grandpa* powers would bring plenty of male energy, as well my brother, who would also be in the mix. Friends too. There would be ample blokes in our lives.

And regarding the 'lack of father' stuff, there will be questions like: 'Why don't I have a dad?' I'll be prepared and honest when the time comes. My child will know their conception story – I'll make sure of that.

Furthermore, I'll strive to provide a safe, happy, loving, and fun environment for my little one, doing my utmost to find the right balance to include 'dad' things in my child's life: *Soccer?* Sure, let's enrol. *Cricket?* Yep (cringe), I'll take you to a test match.

Rough'n'tumble play? Well, that's what mums are for, right? Just don't whack me on the boob!

I collected my freshly-tyred car with a smile on my face, feeling more ready than ever to get on with this round.

16

Super-Pre-Ovulation Mode

Late October 2014, age 41

I could actually feel my ovaries. I knew their exact location in my abdomen because they felt swollen, as if struggling to fit within their allocated space. Their obvious presence was a reminder of my mission. There were no other symptoms of the drugs I was once again injecting. I didn't feel that different, and tried not to symptom-spot.

That's a bit of a lie: I'd been having the occasional impure thought. Mostly about George Clooney. Must've been the whole medical procedure *E.R.* thing from my previous egg pick-up, and the hormone surges. Well, ovulation happens when the body is ready to release an egg, which is traditionally *game-on* for having sex to get pregnant if you're going to do it that way. Being on the drugs I was taking meant an increase in the ovulation effect, so it goes without saying those feelings of sexual desire were probably on overload along with everything else.

I had follicles all over the place, according to the ultrasound nurse. Marian was away, which was disappointing. How dare she have a rostered day off at my time of need! I mean, the woman is supposed to be Superwoman, right? Today's nurse nearly ripped me in half, delving around trying to locate my right ovary. Perhaps she was a trainee, her technique clumsy and torturous.

The sense of invasion eroded once I heard my results: about thirteen follicles that all seemed to be progressing well. When I called for the official rundown later that afternoon, the nurse told me that Dr Hopkins wanted to lower my injection dose to make sure I didn't 'overstimulate'.

Ovarian Hyperstimulation Syndrome (OHSS) is the terrifying circus act of the unsuspecting IVF patient. Too much medication can tip you off the tightrope into the abyss of long-term damage, even death. Not enough, and the trapeze artist will not grab your hands properly, catapulting you into the net, forcing you to start all over again. Thankfully, OHSS is a relatively rare condition, and usually mild.

I was buzzing with hormones, my ovaries having a wild teenage party. I felt relieved to be responding to the drugs so well. The nurse booked me for my egg pick-up on Halloween. Ooh, I was hoping for some good omens. The name of the doctor performing the operation was Dr Angela Jolie. Huh? How could that be? And how fabulous, at the same time.

I looked her up on the internet – she was young, blonde and very fabulous indeed. Not unlike her Hollywood *almost* namesake, in fact. I looked forward to meeting her on that hallowed eve of spirits and ghosts. Hopefully, she wouldn't cut me up and put me into meat pies. No wait, that's Helena Bonham Carter.

Before I knew it, I was heading back to the far off PGD clinic with my superstar mum. Once again, we nervously packed ourselves into the car, not saying much about the reason for our little getaway. Blasting Mum's favourite *INXS* CD out of the tinny old car speakers, we hit the road. We were there in less than three hours.

Three weird things happened upon our arrival.

One: We'd just checked into our hotel. I was getting out of the car when my upper body had a peculiar arm spasm, somehow shooting my beloved hand-made purple topaz cameo earing out of my left ear. It completely disappeared from sight. Down on my hands and knees, I searched everywhere for the thing. I couldn't lose it. For the sake of superstition alone, I needed it back in my ear. I crawled unsuccessfully in all directions, including underneath my car, desperately searching for my nugget of unsubstantiated good luck.

No findies. *Shit!*

Meanwhile, Mum was watching from the hotel lobby, wondering what the hell was wrong with me. I tried not to see my failed search as a bad omen but was flirting with complete insanity. The immensity of the reason for our trip was consuming me. I had to breathe. It was just an earring.

We headed upstairs to our tiny twin room and did a quick job of unpacking. Hunger drove us back outside pretty quickly. I couldn't help but resume my search. Miraculously, I saw a shimmer in the sunlight. Was it? Nope. Just a piece of gum wrapper. Then. Amazing! Almost directly under the front left tyre of the 4WD parked next to us, there it was. My earring!

Of course, that was a sign everything was going to be alright, and I was going to be pregnant with triplets by the end of the week.

Two: We were driving slowly through traffic toward the 'CBD' of this town. I mean no offense people, but for a CBD, don't you need a city? Where were the high-rises? Anyway, I'm usually good with directions but do you think I could get into the centre of this place? Every road seemed to lead to suburbia. Unexpectedly, a police car filled my rear vision mirror, lights flashing, telling me to pull over. Damn it. What now? I had all the usual thoughts you have when the cops are after you, including the big one: *'Faaaark!'*

I pulled over, frantically trying to work out which law I had broken, manually winding down my window. I know: my car is from the Jurassic era.

The police officer squinted through his sunnies, channelling Tom Cruise from a scene in *Top Gun*. 'Can I see your driver's licence, please?' I did the handbag shuffle, fumbling around to fulfil his request.

He studied my licence, taking forever, but staying by my car. 'Do you know why you have been pulled over today?' he asked, not looking directly at me. Aloof with power.

'Not quite sure,' I answered, looking squarely through his sunnies. There was a pause.

He broke the silence. 'Why did you stop in front of the white line at the traffic lights back there?'

I didn't know what to say. How can you answer that without being a smart-arse? I decided to keep it pleasant. Being on a tight budget meant I wanted to get out of this potential traffic violation situation without a fine.

I mumbled something along the lines of, 'Umm, well, we're from Sydney and don't really know our way around here. Mum's got a map…' Right on cue, Mum waved the enormous *NRMA NSW Roads Map* I kept in the glove box. 'I was just trying to get a better look at the name on a street sign, I think.'

I held my breath.

Why would a policeman pull me over for something so

trivial? I mean, yes, I broke the law, but didn't he have criminals to catch? Perhaps it was a simple case of being over-blessed with spare time. He leaned in and cast the hairy eyeball over Mum, who was clearly my accomplice, egging me on to commit the atrocity in question. He really gave her the once-over. It took me all I had to stop myself from making a cutting remark like: 'Yeah, that's my mum. She put me up to it. My partner in crime.' But I resisted.

I ended up with a warning, and no fine. Phew! While very grateful for that, I was still quite shocked to be pulled over for such a small thing. My maroon 2001 *Toyota Corolla* hoon-mobile must have made me look suspicious. And the hard-core *INXS* fan in the passenger seat probably tipped the officer over the edge.

He followed us around for a bit, which was annoying. I drove with white knuckles, trying not to give him another reason to pull me over. But eventually he turned off, no doubt to chase another illicit wrong doer. Perhaps someone, somewhere in town, was jaywalking or something. He'd find 'em!

Finally, food time. We eventually found the fabled, elusive city centre and sat down to lunch. Then, weird thing number three happened: I got elbowed in the head by the waiter. And not just a little nudge. It was a corker. She whacked me so hard I saw stars. She was quite embarrassed, but didn't even apologise. I was left seeing double, wondering what my name was.

Knowing that weird things usually happen in threes, I could now relax. I certainly didn't want something in tomorrow's operation to be 'weird'. I trusted my quota was full – for this trip, anyway. But then…

We returned to our hotel, settled down to sleep, when the

bang-banging of the guests next door started firing up. And I do mean BANG-BANGING. Clearly having a bout of after-dinner, er… delight. Not the ideal scenario when you're in the room next door with your mother.

Thank God it was a *wham-bam-thank-you-ma'am* effort because by the time Mum was aware of it, it was over. That poor girl next door made a lot of noise for what was an extremely fast event. *He's got a few things to learn*, I thought to myself as I turned over and went to sleep.

Mum was already snoring.

17

The Marvellous Dr Angela Jolie

October 31st 2014, age 41

Dr Jolie. What a woman!

She turned up late for the surgery. I was first in for 8am, but she didn't rock in until way past 8:20am. Actually, it would be fair to say she *wafted* in, just like a movie star. Blonde, young looking, fabulous. A little dishevelled after possibly getting home late from cocktails the night before. I could hear her high heels clicking on the sterile surgery floor.

With her near-superstar name, I imagined she had actually turned up in costume. Well, it *was* Halloween! 'The evil Dr Jolie, at your Surgical Service,' she would hiss, before turning to the nurse and whispering, 'Scalpel, please.' Well, as long as she knew what she was doing, I was content to lie back and think of *La-La Land*.

'Who do we have here?' she asked the nurse.

I introduced myself, and she smiled. 'Well, let's get you some beautiful eggs this morning, lovely.' I was dazzled.

As she scrubbed up for the procedure, she mentioned that she lived near me in Sydney. I immediately added *psychic* to her list of outstanding credentials before realising she'd just read my patient info that listed my home address. Then the anaesthetist stepped in, and – next thing I knew, I was waking up in a corridor. It was all that quick.

I got NINE EGGS! Couldn't believe it. That was beyond what I'd been hoping for, and I was tingling with joy. Everything was worth it when the results were good, giving me the feeling I'd worked hard and achieved something. Plus, I felt surprisingly well after the surgery – nowhere near as groggy as the first time, with no nausea at all. There was a bit of soreness in my abdomen, and I was about as tired as I'd ever been, but things were looking up.

Mum was also thrilled and relieved. She'd been living this whole thing right by my side, and I knew it was never easy for her watching her daughter go through so much. But she was there, steadfast and ready to cheer for joy, or to catch me when I fell; whichever came first.

After a bit of a nanna nap at the hotel, we ventured downstairs to the restaurant for dinner. Dinner! Last time I couldn't stand up without nearly passing out. This time I was in a restaurant having a steak.

Hail thee, Angela Jolie, and her marvellous sidekick, the anaesthetist. Somehow, they worked a bit of Halloween magic that day, and it seemed I was in really good hands. These guys were my new heroes, and I couldn't have been more grateful.

Sadly though, it was always going to be a treadmill of results and waiting, waiting, and waiting some more.

While shopping with Mum the following morning before driving home, it was time to call the fertility clinic to see how many of my nine little potential bundles of life had fertilised. They had all been injected with a single sperm cell some time the day before. Once again, I was so nervous about the results I was shaking.

I hoped all nine would fertilise. I knew it was unlikely but had to aim for the stars. Realistically, at a push, I would have been happy with five or more. Last time it was four – a fifty percent success rate, so I was banking on those odds. I should never have done that.

I dialled the clinic number and waited anxiously to get through. These phone calls always, *always* made me sick. The line was constantly engaged, because no doubt a bunch of women were phoning in at the same time for the same reason. Finally, a nurse picked up, but I was put on hold while they transferred me to the science lab. By the time an embryologist took my call I was pacing up and down the fruit and veg section of Coles, light-headed and dizzy. I just needed to know.

'Three eggs have fertilised for you today, Lorena.'

Just three?

'Oh. That doesn't seem like many.' I could feel the world dropping around me. How could it be only three? My light, woozy head seemed to levitate. Why so few? WHY SO FEW? Massive waves of disappointment heaved over me. I had to squint to comprehend the words that kept coming at me through the phone. The pragmatic scientist combed through some finer details, telling me that only five of my nine eggs were mature enough to be injected with sperm, and that only three of those took. My heart sank to the depths of my aching ovaries. Everything hurt; my heart thumped.

Why did it have to be so hard? The odds were stacking up higher against me. The next thing to start reeling through my head was, *What if none of them survive the weekend? I'll end up with none.*

A swarm of worries battered me.

I couldn't function. Telling Mum made me even more numb. Thankfully, she jumped into mum-mode, bounding around the shops with a level of enthusiasm only she can muster. 'Let's look at the summer dresses over here,' she said.

I tagged along pretending to be okay, but my mind was on only one thing: three embryos wasn't enough. It wasn't going to work. Ratios and percentages. Nine eggs, three embryos. 3:1 Those odds were awful. If only two survived the weekend, that would be bad enough. What if *none* survived? How was I going to handle that?

The IVF failure rate for women over 40 is reported by the former Victorian Assisted Reproductive Treatment Authority (VARTA) to be as low as 90%. By these statistics, I was facing almost certain failure.

I had to perk up – for Mum's sake if nothing else. We looked around the shops for a while, got petrol, and commenced the long, quiet drive home. I really didn't have much to say. We talked about the results, but even Mum's unyielding optimism couldn't pull my mind from its anguish.

I had pretty much talked myself out of this IVF cycle by the time I unlocked my front door.

The next day was a bit better; Sunday, a well-earned day of rest. Trying to stay calm by not thinking about things too much was impossible. I managed to find a sliver of hope, though: perhaps there'd be at least one fighter in those petri dishes. One little embryo that wouldn't take 'no' for an answer.

Distractions. I needed distractions, so that night, I sat down and had a glass of wine. It helped to calm me, making me feel happier and more relaxed. Given it was my first touch of alcohol in three months, I felt a little tiddly, which was nice.

I still had three precious embryos incubating and growing. I could be pregnant by the end of the week and had to be careful I didn't let one glass of wine turn into more, or even slip into a daily thing. Staying healthy was just as important; eating well, and somehow, magically being stress-free. Was there an ointment for that? I'd buy it!

The good thing to come out of all this was Mum's optimism. She kept assuring me the cycle would work. Whether she was right or not didn't matter. She evoked a strong positive energy, something I was really struggling to find. Mum had the pompoms out, cheering for my little team of cell clusters to go forth and become my baby. 'Never write this off, sweetie,' she said. 'One of those little embryos is going to make it. I just know.'

Could a mother's instinct be right? I'd take all I could by this point. Thanks Mum! I went to bed feeling good. Still shitting bricks slightly, because the next morning I would find out how many of my embryos survived the weekend. But I was oddly calm all the same, falling asleep with all fingers and toes crossed.

I woke up late, exhausted. I shook my head to boggle my brain awake and grabbed my phone. Four missed calls and voicemails from the fertility clinic. *Shit!*

Shit, shit, shit! This couldn't be good. Why hadn't I set an alarm? They'd been calling since 6am. It was now nearly 10am. How could I have been so stupid? I fumbled a call back, finally getting on to embryologist Kathy, a lovely lady who sounded genuinely distraught.

'Only one embryo has survived the weekend,' she told me.

'The other two fragmented, meaning they were no longer any good.' Probably chromosomally incorrect, I figured.

I was surprisingly stoic. Maybe subconsciously planning to save my tears for later? Or maybe the grief had already peaked on Saturday when I'd found out so few of my eggs had fertilised. I mean, I couldn't have been more disappointed. Perhaps I'd talked myself into this result? Perhaps I should have been more positive like Mum! As it was, I'd managed to buck the very lowest end of the odds for this round with nine eggs and only one embryo.

'What should I do?' I asked Kathy.

'Well, the remaining embryo is only just hanging in there, Lorena. It barely fertilised.'

'Oh.' I was lost for words.

'We've taken a cell to prepare for genetic testing. Do you still want to go ahead with PGD?' That's where the early morning phone calls came in.

It was a tough call. It was going to cost me a fortune if I went ahead. (One to four embryos cost the same at the time of writing.) And let's face it, after Kathy said my remaining embryo was mediocre at best, I was left confused. I never thought I'd be faced with a decision like this. Not in my wildest list of imaginary IVF/PGD preparations. It was totally fucked.

I tried to organise my still sleepy head. If I *did* the genetic testing, the cost would be extortionate, especially for just a single embryo. But if I *didn't?* I'd risk having a child with a disability. Oh God, oh God. Should I really be thinking about money? You can't put a dollar value on a healthy baby. It was just SO MUCH money. Thousands! My whole next IVF round, an entire additional go at this. The ethics and dilemmas put me in a daze.

Then clarity emerged. Very simply, I had to make the practical choice. To save my money and use it for the next round. After the initial shock, my decision became a no-brainer. I'd write this round off, and go full steam ahead into the next one. Kathy agreed, though she'd been careful not to sway my decision.

And even though they'd already recovered the cell from my embryo ($5,000 of the total cost), they didn't charge me. A huge relief! Very compassionate too, and I was tremendously grateful. What a potential balls-up. Just because I'd slept late, missing Kathy's calls, the testing could have gone ahead and cost me eight-thousand dollars! Eek!

I'd been an idiot. A hugely appreciative, humble idiot, and I'd learned my lesson.

I was absolutely shattered by Monday morning, drained emotionally and physically. With my body still hurting from the egg pick-up operation, and my head reeling from that horrible decision, I now needed rest, recovery, and restoration.

Yet there were still more prickly decisions to make. What was I going to do with my remaining embryo? Should I let it go? Have it transferred back and take the risks? Should I freeze it? Was it even going to survive another night?

According to Kathy, it was weak and shaky, but could be a fighter. Possibly that one-in-a-million little trooper. The strongest in the litter, therefore the survivor. If I froze it, I could save it for future genetic testing with my next batch. Or even get it tested in a couple of years when the technology would become better, more accessible, and more affordable.

I needed to speak to my doctor before deciding. I knew the risks. I'd been through them already, a thousand times. It was going to come down to Dr Hopkins' advice. And what a bit of advice he gave. He returned my call almost immediately, and we talked through the results together.

'Have a punt. It's Melbourne Cup Day,' he said.

Had he been drinking?

'That's my medical advice,' he continued. *Wow!* He chuckled a little as he finished his sentence and rationalised his apparent callousness, 'It's a numbers game, Lorena. You're aware of the risks. We'll manage them if and when they come up.'

It made sense, and I immediately felt better. He'd always assured me that the advice he gave was what he'd give his own daughter. I knew he'd be there for me if things got ugly, so I decided to take his advice and go for it. The entire IVF cohort lived by the mantra: 'It only takes one embryo to make a baby', so I counted that as well.

There were still plenty of immediate worries. Yep, that's me – still looking for things to worry about. The embryo had to keep dividing and surviving. That was the next hurdle. I needed to be ready for a 7am phone call the following morning with embryologist Kathy to see if my little creature was ready for transfer.

If so, I'd be doing the three-hour drive immediately.

18

The Reluctant Embryo

November 2014, age 41

After a restless night of worry, I was drowsily devastated when the arranged 7am phone call contained another torrent of bad news.

'Your embryo isn't ready to be transferred yet, Lorena,' Kathy told me, her voice laced with concern. By now, it was supposed to have reached what they call 'blastocyst' stage, but mine hadn't, and may not. Another blow to the head. But what could I do? I just had to keep a lid on my distress, remembering that if this didn't work, I could attempt it all again.

Kathy was genuinely concerned, hearing the wobbly anguish in my voice as I asked her whether she thought my embryo was okay.

'I haven't seen it, Lorena. I'm just looking at the report from the other embryologist.' I could tell she wished she had better news. I was advised to ring again the next day to see if things had improved. Maybe they could transfer it then? Meanwhile, I had to get up and get on with my day – somehow. Even though I knew I'd be thinking of nothing else. Aah, come on, beautiful embryo! It's time to blast into a blastocyst so you can come and meet your mama.

That afternoon I received the best voicemail message I think

I've ever had. It went like this: 'Hi Lorena, it's Kathy from the lab.' I could already hear the happiness in her voice. I'm sure everyone who's been through IVF is an expert in reading the undertone of a nurse's voice in the first moments of a results phone call. By now, I could tell if the news was going to be good, bad, or neutral. She continued, 'We've just checked, and your embryo has reached blastocyst stage.'

WHAT?! 'That's amazing!' I screeched, my heart dancing a jig.

'It's looking lovely and will be ready for transfer tomorrow.' Now her voice was a full moon of smiles.

I jumped up and down: happy, relieved, and excited. I was going to have my first ever embryo transfer! And I felt sure all signs pointed to pregnancy. The universe had flung plenty of hurdles my way. I'd certainly been tested. Now it was the smooth-sailing part of the success stories I'd heard. I breathed a massive sigh of relief, not even trying to quell my excitement.

The following day, I skedaddled to the clinic without hesitation, having already planned the day off work in hopeful anticipation. I was thankful that for once I hadn't been let down.

I selected some of my best mixtapes for the drive. And by mixtapes, I mean actual cassette tapes. My car only played tapes and CDs. As for Bluetooth – well, that was still a long way off for me. My ritual was to listen to the tapes I'd lovingly made in the 80s and 90s. It made the drive fun, taking my mind off things.

The trip took almost three hours, as expected. The closer I came, the more nervous I was. Once again, I'd chosen to do this part of the journey alone. Although Mum wanted to come ('Only if you want me to, sweetie'), I felt it would be better to do the transfer solo. I wanted to indulge in this part, in my own headspace where I could dream of parenthood while also keeping fears of another failed round at bay.

I felt sick with anticipation, knowing it could all go kaput at any time. I walked into the clinic reception area at 11.45am and spoke to the receptionist. 'Won't be too long,' she said, directing me to sit and wait. By half-past twelve, there were a few other hopefuls in the waiting room. I assumed they were probably having transfers too. They all had partners with them.

It's a Miracle by Culture Club was playing in the background, appropriate for so many reasons, including the title itself: having a baby is a miracle – cheesy, but true. Also, I'd wanted to have Boy George's baby when I was a teenager. I know – weird, given that he was dressed as a woman most of the time, and was clearly into men. But I thought he was gorgeous and charismatic. There was just something about him.

I was called in first, fashionably late once again, by Dr Jolie. I walked into the room where the *magic* happened, peering at Dr Jolie in the lab next door, looking fab. So it hadn't been an illusion under the anaesthetic at the egg pick-up – she could indeed star as herself in a Hollywood movie, giving her near namesake a run for her money. What a stunner!

Suddenly, a funny look came over her when she saw me. The lab door slammed shut. I sensed doom. The nurse apologised, telling me, 'We're still working with the embryos,' hurriedly ushering me back to the waiting room.

Something was wrong! I sat for over twenty minutes waiting, feeling like throwing up as one by one all the other patients were escorted in, then back out. My head was hot, then suddenly frozen with chills. I could feel my dreams slipping through my fingers, like trying to cup water in your hands but watching it trickle out. I looked over at the receptionist for clues, but her eyes were firmly directed at her computer. Something must have been amiss with my embryo. Why else would they have rushed me out like that?

What's Love Got to Do With It started playing on the stereo. 'EVERYTHING,' my heart roared back in desperation. If I were looking for signs, this wasn't a good one.

The fact that all the other women were having their embryo transfers before me played heavily on my mind. Dr Jolie must have been saving me for last because she had to break bad news. I was so convinced of this, by the time I was ushered back into the little room, I was a shaking sweaty mess. My body so strung out I was at risk of being unable to incubate my embryo even if they did still plan on transferring it.

Everyone in the room was smiling as I walked in. *What the hell?* 'Is everything okay?' I stammered nervously.

Dr Jolie swung her head around in what seemed like movie-set slow-motion. Her blonde hair had that wind-machine look. As she smiled, I think I recall a tooth-twinkle. She replied, 'Yes.'

She had a deep, husky voice that didn't quite match her slight stature. I think I was developing a bit of a girl crush on her. Well, she was about to make me pregnant, so why not? It turns out my embryo was 'beautiful', and I had nothing to worry about. They could have told me that earlier! Apparently, the holdup was because another patient's embryo had begun to hatch, so they had to transfer it immediately. I wasn't sure exactly what a hatching embryo meant, but it was evidently cause for urgency.

I mentioned to Dr Jolie how worried I'd been out in the waiting room. I didn't want to over-exaggerate or carry on – but there was a limit. She showed concern, and the nurses apologised. They hadn't intended to cause distress. Lovely of them because they really didn't have a clue who I was. Technically, I wasn't their patient.

As for Dr Jolie – she was both funny and caring. While setting everything up, as we were chatting, she spilled some liquid from a petri dish. 'Oops,' she said, and looked over at the nurse. I was staring at her trying to restrain impending horror. I gasped. 'That wasn't my—?'

'Nooo,' she laughed. 'That's just the liquid I'm going to use to clean your cervix.'

Phew! I was so geared up for bad news that an embryo spill onto the floor wouldn't have surprised me at all. Dr Jolie hoisted me into the ungainly embryo-insertion position, not dissimilar to the ultrasound probe one, or that of the all too familiar pap smear.

She chatted away as she lugged me around. I'm a reasonably small person, but so is she. Small but mighty, I tell you, she is *strong!* She knew where she wanted to shift my legs and pelvis – and that's where they were going. All the while, she chatted about how she was off to Paris the following week for a work conference.

'I've just got to make sure I don't spend all of my money on shoes,' she laughed, throwing her hair over her shoulder (of course). It felt like an episode of *Sex and the City* as she cleaned my cervix, popping her head up every now and then from between my knees to better emphasise a point. Like the style of shoes she was *not* going to buy in Paris. She would definitely not be buying a pair of ballerina slippers from the new *Monsieur del Sezane* range.

'Now, let's return this embryo,' she announced.

I love that phrase. The idea of 'returning' the embryo. What a beautiful way to describe the procedure. Because that's exactly what it is. An egg is removed, fertilised, incubated, and now returned. From where it began, to where it belongs. I started welling up. Was I about to become pregnant? Please, Dr Jolie – make me a mum.

They had another look at my embryo under the microscope. 'Yep, it's a good one,' scientist Kathy said, filling me with hope. It was lovely to meet her in person.

Somehow, they sucked my embryo up into a curved catheter-looking thing. I think they draw up all the liquid from the petri dish, because the embryos are too small to pick up on their own. They then released it all into my uterus. I wasn't sure if there was any particular aim required, or whether they just try to get it near the endometrium wall where it would eventually implant. All I knew was it was a painless and easy procedure.

I thanked Dr Jolie wholeheartedly. 'Call me Angie,' she said, 'And good luck. Take it easy today. Do you have the day off work?' I reminded her I was from Sydney, and had a long drive home. She started recommending places to stop enroute for shopping and lunch. I shouldn't have expected any different.

The journey home was quiet. I wasn't sure how mellow I was supposed to be after an embryo transfer. I stopped off at the recommended place, visiting boutiques and a cute cafe. I was careful to stroll – no fast walking. I had a baby on board! I knew I needed to take it easy for a few days.

My legendary car cassette player died on the drive home. Was that a sign? *No, Lorena.* I had to stop thinking every minor thing was a sign. I'd tried to eject a tape while it was rewinding.

You NEVER do that.

Clearly a convincing case of baby brain.

19

Painful Endurance

November 2014, age 41

I didn't slow down as planned. Instead, I worked. The next day my alarm shocked me awake at 7am. With drowsy reluctance I rolled out of bed, pulled on a pair of trackies and a loose t-shirt, psyching myself up for a long day of teaching.

First to arrive at the studio, I let my student in so she could warm up for her lesson. I was doing my best to concentrate but I knew it was going to be hard. My mind was in silent panic, absolutely sure I was pregnant one minute, scrambling with doubt the next.

I started the lesson, demonstrating the choreography I'd prepared the previous day, but realised I was struggling with the floorwork. Staggering around the studio, I found myself drawn to the piano stool, the need to sit down overwhelming. I still had nine private lessons to get through, and then three contemporary classes in a row without a break.

By rights, I should have been at home on the couch watching crap daytime TV, but I had to work to pay for my treatment. As a casual dance teacher, I didn't get sick leave, despite my regular weekly hours. I was in survival mode telling myself, *As long as you don't end up in a heap on the ground, you'll be okay.*

Between each lesson, I'd race to the loo to check if there was blood on my undies. Bleeding would be a sign the transfer had failed. The sense of relief each time there wasn't blood gave me confidence that I was definitely pregnant. The longer the day went, the better I felt. The distraction of teaching temporarily veiling my worries.

I raced to the loo after private lesson number six. Locked the cubical, checked for blood and saw exactly what I had been dreading: a small red stain. With sickening, shaky trepidation, I rang the nurse then and there.

'Don't worry – it's not a bad sign,' she assured me. 'It could be irritation from the egg-pick-up. Or even implantation bleeding.'

'What's that?' I asked.

'When an embryo implants, there can be a little spot of bleeding,' she explained.

This was great news, and exactly what I needed to hear. *I MUST be pregnant*, I assured myself. With a warm glow, I floated back into the studio and spent the rest of the day energised and optimistic. Implantation bleeding. Who would have known?

I had five more days to wait until the pregnancy test. I fretted each time I went to the toilet and continued to check for blood every hour, on the hour, without fail. I'd Googled 'implantation bleeding' by this stage, and it was usually a one-off, with only a few drops of blood. Exactly what I had experienced. As long as there was no more blood, I remained convinced I was pregnant.

Checking for blood became a task. A labour of love. A primal need, like checking on a sleeping newborn. Blood would mean no baby. I couldn't survive without this regular assurance confirming that my dreams were still on track, and my baby was safe, settled, and growing in my uterus.

I remained dizzy with anxiety, looking for pregnancy symptoms. Metallic mouth taste? Surely, I could taste metal. What kind of metal though. Rusty nail? Aluminium can? I was sure I could taste both.

Nausea! I felt sick. Could it be morning sickness? I knew I'd worried myself sick, but no, no, this had to be more than that. It had to be because I was pregnant. I was *absolutely* pregnant, without a doubt, because I also felt bloated. Surely that couldn't still be from the egg pick-up. That was over a week ago. It must be a pregnancy symptom. Women are always bloated when they're pregnant. *Er, yeah – at around sixteen weeks, you crazy lunatic.*

I had been prescribed progesterone pessaries, to be administered vaginally every morning and night. These are little waxy progesterone pills, a hormone that helps maintain the early stages of pregnancy. The gross waxy stuff dissolves, ending up all through your undies, often mistaken for the gluggy feeling of blood. In a nasty twist of fate, progesterone also mimics pregnancy symptoms. All of them. So, my overly zealous symptom-spotting frenzy hadn't been unwarranted.

I decided I really needed to slow down while teaching. Normally I demonstrate movements, but for a few days, I taught as though I was injured and unable to dance.

'Roll on your backs, class,' I instructed on the Sunday before my pregnancy test. 'No, not a backward roll, a sideways roll. Eh, does anyone understand?' I occasionally raised my voice, and then began to fret that the added stress would prevent my embryo from implanting.

On the way home from teaching, I pulled into my local shopping centre car park. Before I knew it, I was standing in front of the bottle shop, staring inside. All resilience burned out, I walked inside and bought a bottle of shiraz. I needed a hiding place from the never-ending symptom-spotting. I was wrung out. A few sips of wine would take the edge off at dinnertime.

I had two glasses. The warmth in my head provided the respite I needed. I sat back and relaxed for the first time in a fortnight, allowing myself a night of freedom from worry. Totally crazy in my reasoning that most people don't even know they're pregnant until four or five weeks in and they drink wine, so why couldn't I?

The following morning, I jolted awake, remembering it was pregnancy test day. I felt guilty and weak from the night before. Ashamed. What if the nurses detected alcohol in my blood test? What would they think of me? No two ways about it, I was a mess. I was sure I'd worried myself into a big fat negative result. I wasn't exactly creating a relaxed, easy environment for my little embryo. *'Get out now while you can. Your mum's a nutcase.'*

I was instructed to wait until 2pm to call the clinic for my pregnancy test results. Argh! I'd then have to go straight into teaching from 3pm onwards, so I needed to be prepared for all scenarios. There was no way I could have a breakdown in front of my students.

With my heart beating in overdrive, I was immersed by fear that I wasn't pregnant. All I could do was wait.

Waiting, waiting, waiting can go on for so long. Waiting in queues that never seem to move. Waiting in the WRONG queue that isn't moving when all the others are. Waiting for your 'big break'. Waiting for the waiter (to whom you have become invisible).

So. Much. Waiting.

The *worst* kind of waiting is for clinical results. I didn't know what to do with myself, unable to stop pacing. I thought that going to the shops might take my mind off things. Nope. Just walked around like a zombie for an hour, buying nothing, looking at less. Time didn't go any faster, so I headed home.

I was only able to think of one thing: what if I wasn't pregnant? How would I cope? I'd been happily convinced after the 'implantation bleeding' phone call, but doubt was rising. I needed to get back to that former mindset. Of course the test would be positive. It *had* to be.

Housework. I tried to clean up a bit. I looked up a recipe for Christmas pudding. Well, it *was* November, after all. Managed to track down some new pine shelves online for the bathroom. Didn't stop all day. Then 2pm came. I was in the car, just driving around, because I had exhausted all other options. I pulled over and rang. But they'd mixed up the times. It was Monday. I was supposed to call between 2:30 and 3:30pm on Mondays because that was their busy day.

I looked at my watch. It read 2:01pm. I got back in my car and started to drive around a bit more, not knowing what else to do. Five minutes later, it was somehow still 2:01pm. I drove in a trance, no idea where I went.

At 2:25pm, I found myself pacing the back alley behind my workplace. It must have been garbage collection day because the narrow road was flanked by a rainbow of coloured wheelie-bins. The stench of them, a whack in the face. I stared at a patch of graffiti that could almost pass as a mural. The area was 'trying' to be artsy but hadn't quite got there.

2:30pm eventually slumped along. My sweaty finger pressed the touchscreen of my phone, dialling the number of the clinic.

I tried hard to breathe.

But my results hadn't arrived yet.

'You'll need to call back after 3,' the nurse advised.

After 3? How was this happening? I hastily cancelled my 3pm lesson so I had a bit more time to absorb the news when it finally came. My poor heart was pounding in my chest like a wild, frantic baboon.

I slumped into the gutter like a vagrant, not knowing where else to go. My hands trembled as my third call to the clinic was transferred to a nurse. She wanted my identification details, which only added to the wait time. I closed my eyes, and in my imagination ran though the words I was sure I would hear: *'You're pregnant, Lorena. It's the strongest positive we've ever seen. You are so pregnant, we think you may have broken the world record for how pregnant a person can be! Congratulations.'*

I jumped at the sound of the nurse's voice back on the line, poised for the inevitable.

Whenever I hear a sentence beginning with the words 'I'm sorry,' I know I'm in for a rough ride. This time was no exception. 'I'm sorry, Lorena, not this time, unfortunately,' she said.

I was unresponsive. Frozen.

'Are you okay?' the nurse asked.

'I'll be fine,' I lied, as my world crashed in around me, everything in a wild maelstrom all at once.

All my life's failures, no matter how unrelated or insignificant, landed squarely on my shoulders in that moment. My failure to find a father for my child; failure to succeed as a professional dancer after a career-ending injury; failure to own a home, even my failure to achieve a high first in my degree. Where did THAT come from. I never knew I cared! And then the biggest one: the ultimate failure of my body to become pregnant and make a baby. Everything came back to that.

What a useless clump of failures I'd become, sitting in the gutter like a big, hopeless piece of nothing. And there was nothing growing in my uterus either. Nothing, nothing, nothing!

There was an awkward silence on the phone as I caught my breath, my eyes staring out into the suburban setting but seeing only black. The realisation hit me again, and again. There would be no baby.

No baby.

The words pounded in my head. I was not going to be a mum. I was *never* going to be a mum. It wasn't going to happen for me.

My breathing hiccupped as I attempted to hold back tears, trying to find the words to end this phone call. There weren't any. So instead, I babbled something to the nurse about how these calls must be the difficult part of their job when it's bad news. I assured her I'd be fine, hung up, and sank into the gutter, letting torrents of tears escape.

I called Mum immediately. She and Dad had been waiting nervously all day to hear my news. 'Mum, it's a negative,' I sobbed. 'It didn't work.'

'Oh, sweetie. Where are you? I'm coming over.'

'No, Mum, I'm about to go into work. I've let you down. I've let everyone down.'

'No, no! Not at all. Now, are you sure you should be working? I can come and help!' Mum has never done a contemporary dance class in her life, but there she was, willing to do anything and everything to help me survive this, including helping me teach. Things were always so crushingly real once I'd told her. She had been optimistic about this embryo from day one, so I genuinely felt I'd let her down. Robbed her of a grandchild.

Eventually, I calmed down. Speaking to Mum helped me get on with the rest of the day. And with all the stress I'd put myself through in those last few hours, my mourning had largely been done. There was very little left in the tank.

Now it was time to switch to overdrive and let work take my mind off things. Surprisingly, it did. But the other thing about grief is that even though you can temporarily cover it up, once the veil slips off, you relive it in excruciating detail, as if for the first time.

That was my drive home, in tears once again, the traffic lights blurring in colourful circles as all remains of hope washed down my face.

PART TWO

20

Total Eclipse of my Dreams

Summer 2014/15, age 41

The unbearable pregnancy test day burned in my mind for weeks. But the grief began to lessen with time, and I noticed a few funny little things happening in the aftermath. It was as though the universe was saying, 'Okay, this girl's been through some shit, let's give her a break.'

And boy, did I need one.

Things got better and in small ways. Wandering around my local suburb one day, a woman stopped me to say, 'Excuse me, those colours look fabulous on you.' I thanked her. It's so rare to get a random compliment from a stranger, I was quite taken aback as she smiled, disappearing into the crowd like an angel sent to help restore me.

I met up with Monica, a friend who I hadn't seen in ages. I finally felt able to tell her about my IVF stuff. It was a tough topic for me still, and I hadn't been ready to broach it with her before. Monica is one of the most selfless, caring people I know. Out to save the world, and I have no doubt her small, but countless, gestures will one day make a big difference. Her calm demeanour and eyes radiate an empathy that has always made me feel nurtured in her company.

Funnily enough, we met years ago after both falling off our

motorbikes in a comedy of errors at a learner riding course. I was attempting a tight left turn and fell right into a ditch; Monica had an epic fail, dropping her bike halfway through a U-turn. Our egos hurt as much as our minor injuries, both of us sitting in the gutter holding broken clutch handles, teary from shock and embarrassment. A great friendship forged there and then.

It felt good to divulge everything to her. Then she absolutely blew me away. 'I'll give you my eggs if you need them,' she said. 'I don't want to have kids, but I'd be a great aunty. Only if you wanted me to though. I wouldn't want to get in the way.'

That's the way Monica speaks. She offers you the world in a sweet, almost apologetic way.

I was dumbfounded. I could technically use her eggs. I think the cut-off is around her age, thirty-five. I'd previously researched this possibility but had written it off, at least for now. I just didn't think my ego could handle looking into my child's eyes and seeing the resemblance of the friend who'd donated. I knew, if it came to egg donation, I could only go anonymous.

But Monica's gargantuan gesture was truly astounding and she wouldn't take 'no' for an answer, instructing me to go home and think about it. I knew, though. The answer had to be no. But her offer filled me with confidence. It was Monica's way of saying, 'I see you, I care about you, and I'll help in any way I can.' And, truly, that's all I really needed. I texted, 'No, but thank you,' to her a few days later, and she was genuinely disappointed replying with, 'Tell me if there's anything else I can do.'

When I say I wasn't alone in this process, I really mean it. Having a partner is great, and possibly the ideal we think we want, but having rock-solid friendships and a caring, supportive family: give me those any day. Made me realise I was by no means going it alone. Far, far from it.

My girlie crush on Dr Angela Jolie had begun to resurface. I didn't know where it had come from, or how it happened, but I must have had a void that needed filling, and she was it. I even tried stalking her online, but she was well hidden. Only a few professional bits of information. No visible Facebook, clever girl.

A few months later, I found out that a friend of mine, Mabel, from college, had moved to Sydney. We were never the closest of friends, but we'd loosely kept in touch over the years. One of our rare catchups was for a mutual friend's birthday celebration at a bar in the city. It was a breezy, warm, summer evening as we reminisced about our college days in London in the 90s.

Then the conversation moved to what was going on in our current lives. I mentioned my plan to become a solo mum by choice. Mabel's eyes bulged. 'Wow! I could never do that.' Her priority was to head back to Western Australia to her family for a while, to recharge her batteries and attend to her declining mental health. 'I do want a baby,' she said. 'But no way on my own.' She was still on the dating carousel and wanted to meet someone first.

She said she thought I was very 'brave' for going it alone – a not uncommon sentiment I had heard before. I shrugged it off.

Brave?

Brave is fighting terminal illness. *Brave* is walking into a lion's den to save a child. *Brave* is so many things, but having the luxury of choice, money, and time to achieve a dream is not what I call brave. I wasn't sure why my friends sometimes put that label on me, but I smiled and thanked Mabel all the same.

A few weeks later, Mabel messaged me on Facebook to tell

me she was trying IVF. I sent her the obligatory, 'Good luck with it all,' response and thought very little of it. I didn't want anything to do with her IVF, really. After all, I still had that weird aversion to bonding with anyone else going through it. I certainly didn't want to discuss needles and failed cycles.

If I'm brutally honest, I was also a little miffed that she'd stolen 'my' idea. Where did her 'braveness' suddenly come from? I was being entirely unreasonable. I knew nothing about Mabel, and here I was claiming her IVF plans as my own.

You probably know what's coming next.

Six months later, I received an admittedly lovely direct message from Mabel: 'I just wanted to let you know, I'm thirteen weeks pregnant. Yay!'

Ouch.

She wanted to let me know before she spilled the news across social media. I acknowledge that it was truly noble of her to consider my feelings like that. But HOW DARE SHE!!? How the fuck dare she be pregnant when it was all *my* idea in the first place. How! Dare! She!

I ran to the toilet and threw up. To this day, I have no idea why my reaction was so carnal. I must have been that gut-wrenchingly upset. Angry. Sick to the stomach. I felt cheated, she'd run away with my idea, having it work while I was struggling and failing to even get close to pregnancy.

I still feel a twinge when I think about it. It was the same physical response I'd had when I found out Richie was cheating on me. Somehow, I managed to type out a friendly congratulatory response to her, but deep down I was bitter and resentful.

By this stage, I'd only just finished my second IVF cycle. I was so raw. Mabel had no idea where I was in my own journey. She never asked, probably fearing the answer. I felt suddenly very alone. If there was one aspect that was tough about doing IVF solo, it was having no one to come home and talk to. It's that primal need in all humans to be comforted and heard when the going gets tough.

Regrettably, this feeling of resentment stayed with me for weeks. I figured that the only way to dispel it was to try and talk to Mabel and offer an olive branch. She must have known I was bitter. Would she really care? She had her baby to think about. The last thing she was thinking about was shitty old me.

Fast forward half a year, and she had a six-month-old. I never got in contact.

Not long after, a clinic nurse suggested I chat to a counsellor after I opened up about my reaction to Mabel's pregnancy. This 'counsellor', as she called herself, told me I had every right to feel bitter and twisted about a friend stealing my baby idea. Wrong answer! She *should* have suggested I toughen up and look at the reality of the situation. That the longer I held onto resentments, the more they'd eat me up and make me unhappy.

I was in a deep, dark place. I could barely recognise myself, watching my senses of kindness and empathy all but dissipate. No one called me out on my behaviour, and I guess I had to go through it to come out the other side. It took the time it took, but I needed to toughen up to face the next round of the fight.

I scraped myself off the floor, breathed, reassessed, and continued to move forward, leaving all thoughts of Mabel, and any other pregnant friends, by the wayside.

21

It's a Heartache

March 2015, age 41

My saga continued apace, and IVF round three happened very quickly. After that, round four came and went. Both failed miserably. Apart from a few changes in medication, it ended up as another two rounds down the gurgler.

Dr Hopkins had advised me not to continue with the PGD genetic testing. We'd weighed up the cost and results of the first rounds and decided to just wait and test at the foetal stage. The worst-case scenario was that the foetus would be chromosomally atypical, and decisions would arise on whether to abort.

While all this was happening, I seemed to be on some sort of gradual overall demise.

I fell up an escalator. Yes, *up*. I had thongs on and was wrangling an armful of toilet paper (of all things), so my hands were full. I went BANG, tripping and ripping half my big toe nail off. I staggered around in disbelief for a while, about to pass out from the pain, when a kind security guard escorted me to the doctor. A few needles later and some dressings, I was okay.

What a klutz, though. I was in 'good riddance to 2014' mode at the time. It had been a trying one and I was more than ready for the fresh New Year to kick in. Another tough gig was at our family Christmas dinner when my exceedingly enthusiastic,

156

unintentionally thoughtless, sister-in-law asked us all, 'So, everyone, what were your highlights of 2014?'

Ugh. Do we *have* to?

Those questions are easy when life's good, but it had been a shithouse year for me and I was feeling low, unable to find an answer. Couldn't for the life of me think of one damn thing. Everyone else was going around saying amazing things.

My brother proclaimed, 'The birth of my nephew!'

Mum said, 'Getting the hearing back in my left ear.' *Big* stuff.

I was left thinking, well, I have nothing.

I got away with being a bit of a party-pooper (I still had my party hat on) that night. But I was unhappy. It was an enormous magnifying glass shining over my life, proving I was a complete dud. Of course, it was family, so they didn't think that at all.

Getting the violins out? Yes. In fact, the violin solo was rapidly turning into a sonata. I had to pull myself out of it. New year, new start and all that.

So, what did I do? IVF round five, of course.

People, even close friends and family, never really knew how to ask, 'How's the… er, baby thing going?'

So awkward.

It had become quite funny, really. I was now able to say 'sperm donor' without giggling, and could have a serious conversation about ovulation without thinking twice. I could locate my ovaries, and remember that uterus and womb are the same thing. I was progressing.

So, when people fumbled the uncomfortable pauses between the word 'how's…', eventually reaching the words 'baby-making', I just smiled and watched them squirm. I mean, the awkwardness was appropriate. If someone was trying for a baby naturally, you wouldn't ask that question. You'd say, 'Are you still trying?' or 'Is a baby still on the cards for you guys?' or something like that. It's rare to ask a single woman how her baby plans are going.

Marian called to see how I was doing. 'It's been a while and I've been thinking of you,' she said. 'How have you been?' We chatted for a while. She suggested I think about changing my sperm donor, that perhaps my current one and I were somehow incompatible.

Noooooooooooo!

My stupendous sperm donor was the one positive facet in all of this. But deep down, I knew she was right. I was willing to take her advice and try anything, so I booked an appointment with Sabine-of-the-sperm to discuss options.

Looking at sperm donors again felt like a step backward. I'd been so full of hope the first time, but now just felt jaded. I knew I had to perk up and get on with it. There would be someone just as amazing as my original donor hidden in the realms of Sabine's folders.

In no time at all, I found a good one. An Aussie architect (brainy!) with three kids (his swimmers could swim!). He had a warm personality and was in his late thirties. Sabine loved him, enthusiastically telling me that whenever he came to the clinic he was well dressed, softly spoken, polite, and kind.

'Is he good looking?' I casually mused.

'He's er… nice,' Sabine answered with a smile.

Nice? What's that?

'He's pleasant looking,' she added, noting my hesitancy.

'Oh, okay, so not as good looking as my original donor?'

'Not quite,' she said. Well, at least she was honest. 'But he really is lovely.'

Okay, I could live with lovely. When did I become so superficial?

Sabine went on to explain that sometimes they had left-over vials of sperm if women didn't complete their rounds. You had to buy five at a time, so if someone became pregnant after one try, there would be four left over. No refunds. Sabine was going to swap two of my previous donor's vials for two of the new ones at no charge. I left the clinic happy and relieved I hadn't needed to pay extra.

This round was going to be slightly different. No nasal spray. I would do what's known as an *Antagonist Protocol* where injections (called *Antagonists*) shut down the pituitary gland to prevent ovulation. It's a much faster approach than the nasal spray. I didn't know whether I liked that idea, but I was willing to try something new. Perhaps it might work better?

My first ultrasound was soon after, and bloody Marian forgot who I was again. Admittedly, I was now blonde, and she'd previously only seen me with black hair, but really? After all we'd been through?

She squinted at me. 'Nope.' Total lack of recognition in her eyes.

'I've changed my hair a bit.'

She tipped her head, moving closer, peering over her reading glasses. I had to hand it to her; she was giving it a red-hot go.

'Hmm, well, maybe I'll recognise your ovaries.'

Very funny. I confirmed my age and yet again she was aghast. 'You look so much younger,' she gasped.

She didn't seem to recognise my ovaries on the ultrasound

screen either. There were only a few follicles. 'About average size,' Marian assured me. I went home feeling worried. A few days later when the following scan wasn't much better, my hopes began to plummet.

This had all happened during school holidays, and my now seven-year-old nephew was staying with me for a few days. It felt weird doing the injections while he was there. He never knew, but it reminded me how hard it must be for women with children – especially if there was no one else to look after them.

Dad looked after my nephew when Mum drove me to the egg retrieval surgery. We'd taken him to the Easter Show the day before where we'd ridden the Rocky Monster Truck ride. I was worried I'd jiggled my ovaries too much. Maybe I'd jiggled the eggs out of them? Or squashed them. I can't believe the things I found to worry about.

Walking into the operating theatre, I immediately felt comforted to see Dr Hopkins. Next thing I knew, I was waking up after surgery. Sore. More tender than previous times. I must have been poked and prodded a lot. Perhaps something had happened?

Just two eggs were retrieved; neither had matured, so they couldn't be fertilised. Somehow, I wasn't massively disappointed. In my gut, I already knew this hadn't been a good round since the first ultrasound.

Dr Hopkins came in and sighed. His caring eyes held a concerned look as he said, 'My mystery lady.' Goodness gracious, no one wants to hear their doctor refer to them as *that!* 'What are we going to do with you?' He sat next to me. 'Something must be going wrong, because none of your eggs were mature.' He paused for thought, drawing in a deep breath. 'We'll do the next round on Medicare,' he said. 'You'll still have to pay for meds and surgery, but not the round itself.'

Perhaps he felt he'd failed me? 'I want to leave no stone unturned,' he added.

'I trust you. I'm prepared to do what it takes,' I replied, still groggy from the anaesthetic.

He nodded and left. I got dressed and staggered with Mum back to the carpark where I threw up a couple of times – thankfully into a spew-bag – the nausea lingering through the night.

I had to work the next day from 11am to 6pm, which was gruelling. I could barely sit and was still bleeding. Christ, they must have been really digging around in there for those eggs. *Any* egg. Anything in there? Anyone? Cue eerie echoes and a haunting tumbleweed.

Marian called later that day to see how I was doing. I always knew when there was bad news or sad times, because Marian made those tough calls. I told her I was okay. 'While there's hope, I'm fine,' I said. And I truly believed it. Hope was keeping me going, and without it I would surely have folded.

22

Putting on the Brakes

July 2015, age 41

I went to see Dr Hopkins a few days later. This visit felt relatively positive and, more than anything, proactive. Sitting around waiting for things to happen was not an option for me. I wanted, needed, to keep moving forward.

In the back of my mind was the lingering thought of my approaching birthday. I'd be turning forty-two in August, just a month away. I thought I'd be up the duff or at least up all night feeding a baby by then. I'd pegged forty-two as some sort of landmark of infertility, and needed to keep the ball rolling.

Dr Hopkins remembered our chat about doing my next round on full Medicare rebate which was a relief. 'This time we'll monitor you and stop treatment if there aren't enough strong follicles developing,' he assured me. That made sense.

'Should we wait a bit before the next round?' I asked. 'Do people become immune to IVF medication?'

'There's a small chance of that,' he replied. 'But very unlikely. You can go onto your next round as soon as you feel ready. Wait one period; then you're good to go.'

I had to visit the clinic for some baseline blood tests. In theory, this was supposed to kick-start the meds for IVF round six. Yet something in me was pleading to slow down. Rest a bit before the next round. If only I wasn't so fucking old, this would have been a no-brainer. Then again, if I were younger, I wouldn't be in this predicament in the first place. I decided I needed to chat with Marian. She always told me to grab her if I had any concerns.

'I know you're busy, but do you have time for a quick chat?' I sheepishly asked as she bustled past me in the corridor. I always felt a bit nervous speaking to her. She's a very strong, intimidating woman, always busy, like I was interrupting her. Especially during ultrasound time, her peak-hour rush. But there was only one person in the waiting room today.

Marian glanced at me. 'Not really,' she replied in a neutral tone.

'Oh, okay,' I whimpered as another nurse ushered me to one of the blood test rooms.

After a minute, Marian popped her head in. 'Talk to me,' she gently commanded.

'I'm just not sure I'm ready for this IVF round,' I began. 'My body still doesn't feel healed from the last one, and I don't know if I'm being silly or not. Dr Hopkins gave me the go-ahead, so I should be alright, but I feel tired, and…'

'You're getting teary,' Marian said, tilting her head. Aah, the good old caring nurse head tilt. She was softening.

I nodded. 'The last two rounds have been awful. My eggs didn't mature, because *I'm* too mature. And I don't feel ready to go through it all again just yet.' She sat down beside me as tears streaked my cheeks.

'Your body is the incubator,' Marian explained. 'If you don't feel ready, well, you won't be able to provide the warm healthy environment your embryos need to grow.'

The other nurse came in. 'We won't do Lorena's bloods today,' Marian told her.

'But I'm letting Dr Hopkins down,' I protested.

'We're working for *you*,' Marian reminded me. 'You won't be letting anyone down. Go home, have some quality 'you' time, and come back when you're ready. We're not going anywhere.'

'Will you please let Dr Hopkins know?' I asked.

She reassured me, 'Yes.'

I sat there and cried for a minute, both nurses remaining by my side. They spoke kind words and gave me space for my moment. I wept my way out to the lift and pressed the button when Marian came running after me. 'If finances are part of your worry, Lorena, I've just looked at your file, and Dr Hopkins has marked your next round as full Medicare.'

'Thank you,' I smiled through the tears. She kissed me on my forehead and sent me away with good wishes.

I continued to blubber the whole way home and then some. It was a weird combination of relief, because I had been given a 'pardon' to sort myself out; and a sense of immense panic because time was ticking away.

Usually, by going straight into the next round, I was kept busy. There was an addictive component to the 'round after round' of IVF treatment. I felt isolated and wobbly, but I knew I needed this time to get my body match-fit for the next round.

In the meantime, I had to get my shit together to teach class in an hour. I showered and fixed myself up.

I decided to visit a Chinese herbalist who ran his treatment clinic from inside a broom closet at the rear of a fruit shop. Alarm signal? Should have been, but not for this little duck. A work colleague who had done IVF recommended him, so I thought, *why not?* From the minute I arrived I had a weird feeling, walking out just five minutes later, clutching bags brimming with $380 worth of tiny pills. ('A bargain price, no charge for my time, just for the pills. Cash only. No, no, NO receipt!') He'd instructed me to take some before meals, after, before bed — over ninety infinitesimal pills a day. Some to cleanse my liver, others to aid digestion or make me 'healthy', whatever that meant.

I pictured myself on *A Current Affair. 'Dodgy Herbal Practitioner preys upon crazy middle-aged woman desperate for a baby'.*

He was dodgy, alright. Still, I couldn't get my hands on those pills fast enough. They didn't last long — in less than a month I found myself back again. This time my predicament was apparently 'way worse'. I needed even *more* pills. Over $450 worth. Having taken some of the pills but seeing no positive change, my pill-popping urgency miraculously petered out.

Yet still, I didn't feel comfortable sitting around doing nothing. So again, rather spontaneously, I made an appointment with an acupuncturist. I'd been carrying her number around for months, given to me by a friend. I'd always meant to use it but never did, keeping it up my sleeve as a future insurance plan.

The acupuncturist's name was Mai, and she was lovely. Her thick Chinese accent made her tricky to understand at times, but that wasn't a problem. A Chinese acupuncturist felt right, given that acupuncture was an ancient Chinese therapy. Mai came to my home for treatment and spent ages with me twice a week over a couple of months.

I'm not exactly sure what I was hoping to achieve out of it. A baby, I guess. Mai went hell-for-leather with her ideas and plans. Small in stature, her commanding voice would stop a plant from growing if she'd ordered it to. She always wore black, and was never without a massive bottle of water that almost certainly outweighed her. On arrival, she'd walk through my door as if in a rush, trudging through my loungeroom to set up on the coffee table, ready to get down to the business of my treatment. She began by listing things I could and couldn't eat.

Here we go.

'Nothing cold. Cold foods shock the system. Reduce caffeine. Eat plenty of warm vegetables. And NO alcohol.' Hmmm, well, I could see that one coming.

We finally came to the acupuncture itself. I was a bit nervous about the needles. An odd thing to say, as I'd jabbed myself many times for IVF. But it was different when someone else was doing it. Acupuncture needles are incredibly thin and didn't feel anything like an injection. But they *did* sometimes hurt. At times, they ached.

Then there were the herbs which tasted like horse manure. Not that I've tried horse manure, but the smell! Some were for pre-ovulation to strengthen my blood and mature my eggs; others for post-ovulation, to ensure a good period.

Yes, folks, my life now officially revolved around ovulation.

Just before she left, Mai told me I needed to be in bed each night by 11pm, because 'That's when hormones are made' following the rules of circadian rhythms. Bed by 11? Unheard of. But I was going to have to try. What else could I do? Anything for my as yet unborn firstborn!

23

Sixth Time 'Round

March 2016, age 42

It was a rainy autumn day when I found myself at my friend Tonia's place holding her six-week-old baby. Having been conceived through IVF after multiple miscarriages, he was a special one. Staring at his wrinkled little nose, I listened to the tiny baby noises he quietly gargled in those peaceful moments before hunger screams were sure to surge.

Blinking my eyes, I tried to suppress tears. It didn't work. I watched a salty drop fall, settling on the baby's chin. I quickly wiped it away, embarrassed. Looking at this perfect bub was like being hit in the face with everything that had gone wrong for me over the past eighteen months.

I tried not to cry. I mean how would that look to Tonia? So selfish, creating an awkward situation. But she didn't feel that way at all. Nor did she think I was being self-centred, although I'd well and truly convinced myself otherwise.

'This will be you soon,' she assured me. 'Your time is coming.'

'God, I hope so,' I replied, letting the tears flow. 'I really do.'

Afterward, driving home, I tried to work out why I'd been so overcome with emotion. It was okay to feel sad. I mean, I'd been through a lot, and was hoping I'd be cuddling my own baby by this time. But standing there holding a friend's newborn, unable to stop bawling because of my own failure to conceive? I probably needed to look at where my life was headed.

Meanwhile, I was still stressing about my age. Forty-two! And nearing forty-three! Time was certainly marching on. Middle age was all over me. Menopause was still a long way off (at least I hoped), but my windows were closing. Metaphors, middle age, and menopause. Yet the only 'm' I was really after was motherhood.

When round six finally arrived, I was more ready than ever. This was for several reasons, most of them obvious: I'd waited a while, giving my body a chance to properly recoup. The acupuncture had helped to relax me and prepare mentally as well.

Only problem was, this time the spray turned me into what I can only describe as a moody shit for three weeks. I'd used it before but hadn't noticed anything. When I mentioned the mood swings to a nurse during my blood test, she replied, 'Oh yes, that spray puts you in a perpetual state of pre-menstrual tension.'

Er, what?

'Yep – it should ease up when you start the hormone injections, but you've basically had PMT for the last three weeks.'

That explained a lot! I had been getting pissed off with myself for little things. I'd also been dropping stuff. Toothbrushes, my hairbrush. All hurling floorward through my klutzy fingers with words like 'Bloody gravity' habitually flying from my lips.

The nurse said that once I started on the *Menopur* hormone injections, life would become less erratic. And it did. I calmed down, stopped dropping everything, and world peace seemingly resumed.

My egg pick-up was same-old, same-old. Woke up in recovery with a nurse staring down at me. 'Seven eggs,' she said. 'Congratulations.' She phoned me the day after to tell me only three had fertilised. I'd prepared for that. But I was curious: 'So the embryologist defrosts the sperm, then choose an individual swimmer to inject into the egg?' I mean that's a huge responsibility, akin to playing God, ultimately choosing the child I was perhaps going to have.

'Yes. They take it all in their stride,' she replied casually. 'It's exciting though, when we all meet the baby nine months after and think, "Yep, we had a hand in that".' I thanked her and hung up the phone, pondering this concept for days after.

From that point I found ways to measure my optimism and happiness in careful increments for my own mental health and survival. All three of my eggs had fertilised this time, but I didn't get too excited, because they might not divide and grow. Then again, I didn't want to be pessimistic either, because that might attract bad luck.

How many would still be going the following day? I needed to prepare for the worst, just in case there were *no* embryos that made it.

What a total mind-fuck!

I was *due* to start worrying two days after the fertilisation results. Until then, I'd allowed myself to relax a bit. Off the hook until the big phone call telling me how many embryos made it to day three for a transfer. When the phone rang, I felt sick. *You've been here before*, I told myself, but it never got any easier.

'Are you on your way yet?' the nurse asked. I was not expecting that.

'On my way? Do I have an embryo?'

'I'm sorry, I think there's been some confusion, hang on—' She paused.

Confusion? But this was my future child, how could there be confusion?

'Can I please have your ID? Name? Date of birth?'

I complied. *Come ON, get on with it!*

'Okay, so your embryo transfer is today at 2:30pm,' she told me.

'But I didn't know I had embryos. No one phoned me.'

'You have two beautiful embryos ready for transfer, Lorena. Can you come now?'

I knew I couldn't. For starters, I was about to walk into class. And besides, Mai would want to acupuncture the bejesus out of me before I had my transfer. It would need to be tomorrow. The nurse understood, so 2pm tomorrow it was.

In all that confusion, I had forgotten to react. Happiness was on the cards this time: two embryos were going to be transferred. Huge and exciting news! I called Mum to let her know and she was beside herself, as always, yelling to Dad, 'Matey, two embryos! The transfer's tomorrow.' I could hear his excitement in the background.

'You have two stunning embryos, Lorena.' I'd just run from my acupuncture session and was ready for my transfer. 'One is eight cells,' Dr Hopkins continued, 'and the other is six.'

The sacred moment when the embryo was placed in my uterus remained the most emotional for me during my IVF cycles. Where hope was at its highest. Where optimism both lifted and held me. I lay there during the procedure, breathing slowly, praying to the gods of fertility or whoever was watching from above, hoping with every ounce of my heart that this was it.

Walking out to Mum afterward was a significant moment too. She looked at me, beaming, with that *there's my pregnant daughter* face. There's never been a time she wasn't one-hundred percent sure I was pregnant when I emerged from a transfer. Beautiful memories, and the best parts of IVF that I cherished.

That's the thing about IVF: everyone dwells on how hard it is. And yes, getting failure after failure *is* bloody hard. But amid those failed rounds, there were moments of beauty and love, unspoken between a mother and a daughter. Moments where friends stepped up, offering love, tears, and support that I never ever expected. Moments among the failed attempts that made me realise, through it all, that I was loved, and that my absolute need to do everything in my power to become a mum was heard, validated, and respected. My little group of people were utterly on my side. Without that, for me, doing IVF would have been impossible.

For round number six they also gave vital support when, after the *two-week wait*, my period arrived, and I realised the embryos didn't take, and I had to tell my beloved tribe of ever-loyal loved ones.

That was *always* the hardest part. And that's how round six ended for me.

24

Do I Want This Enough?

Winter 2016, age 42

Truth is, sometimes when I was really in the mood for over-thinking and torturing myself, I'd sit with my excruciating thoughts and wonder if my embryos weren't implanting because maybe I didn't want motherhood enough. Was it all a test?

Was I allowing myself snippets of complacency? Underlying, barely detectable *feeling-ettes* of relief when IVF didn't work? Had I dodged the parent trap? I was putting in all this effort to become a mum. Did all the failure silently absolve me?

Perhaps the IVF treadmill was becoming a mere habit. Perhaps I'd become addicted. Perhaps I needed to be a better person. Kinder to others, more charitable. Was I somehow too proud of my grand total of 'Six Failed IVF Rounds', wearing them like a badge of honour? 'See how determined I am? Six failed rounds and still up for more.' What a martyr.

I re-programmed and wiped as many of these thoughts from my mind as I could. I wasn't about to let them dissolve my mental health to shards. I'd come too far for that.

The next two rounds blurred together. Nothing marvellous came of them and I certainly didn't end up with my baby.

I met up with Nicole for a coffee one afternoon. 'I'm pregnant,' she announced out of the blue, her eyes glassy with tears of joy.

'Oh my God, Nic. That's amazing!' I replied, leaning across the table for a hug. I could feel an unexpected wave of vertigo shiver across my skull. *What's happening?* A private panic party was setting itself up in the deep darkness of my brain. I was happy for Nicole. Of course, I was. But I'm disgusted to admit that my first response was otherwise.

I heard myself say, 'Wow! How far along are you?'

'Just over fourteen weeks,' Nicole replied. 'I know this must be hard for you.'

She knows!

'No, no,' I said, as convincingly as I could. 'I'm happy for you. This is your moment!'

Nicole looked at me, and we sat in silence for a few seconds. 'Thank you,' she gently said. I could see in her eyes that she understood.

I held it together and continued to make all the right noises. But in truth, I was gutted, jealous. Barely holding on, feeling that same horrible nausea that I'd felt when Mabel announced she was pregnant.

Nicole's only a couple of years younger than me, so I figured it'd take her ages to fall pregnant, but it happened quickly. She and her husband had been seeing a naturopath, who she'd named her 'miracle worker', and he really must have helped. Nicole gave me his number. I put it in my back pocket as my next insurance policy. I'd stopped seeing Mai by now, so perhaps I'd give him a call.

A few other things happened over this period too. I moved

house. After living in a small one-bedroom unit for eleven years, I suddenly decided, 'Why not? I'm moving!'

I liked the first place I inspected and moved in a fortnight later. It was perfect: bushland as far as the eye could see and a huge deck. For the first time in my adult life, I was going to be able to have people over for a barbie! I couldn't wait.

The place was a small granny flat built under a redbrick house. It was open plan, with enormous windows on every wall. It felt so big and fresh. I overlooked the slightly Dickensian kitchen, torn curtains, and roughly finished touches. This was going to be my new haven, representing the next chapter of my life as a future mother. I was feeling blissfully positive and content for the first time in ages.

'What's the catch?' Dad asked, looking around as he carried a box of my stuff across the threshold.

'No catch. I'm just lucky!' I replied, a sunny tone to my demeanour.

I remember that conversation vividly, because a month after I moved in, my lovely, quiet, considerate upstairs neighbours announced that they were moving out. And then, everything changed.

The following day began my year of hell. I could hear a woman yelling. 'JUST PUT IT OVER THERE!' *Put what over there?* 'YOU IDIOTS, CAN'T YOU JUST LISTEN TO ME FOR ONCE? PUT THE FUCKING COUCH OVER THERE!'

A mother moved into the flat above with her two teenage boys and a man who came and went. Something about them felt dangerous. Threatening. Their angry energy seeping through the ceiling. My hopes for a peaceful, idyllic dream home all but dissipated.

One night, the teenage boys had a party where their mates threw glass bottles, cigarettes, and spliff butts off their balcony into my garden. The music pounded with increasing volume, the alcohol intake of these underage drinkers seemingly infinite. Frozen and scared, I waited for the revelry to end, not wanting to 'overreact' by calling the police. Nor did I feel safe to go up and ask them to stop. Eventually, just after 1:00am, the music stopped. I sat there, teary with relief.

The estate agents didn't care. Their attitude was, 'Move out if you're unhappy'. I nearly did.

But just as I'd made my final decision to move out, presto, the harridan upstairs went too far, smashing a window in a fit of rage. They were immediately given their notice. It had taken fourteen months to finally get to that. But still, my life instantly turned around when the nicest couple in the world moved in and peace resumed.

Then I did something way out of character: I got a cat.

Ordinarily this wouldn't be strange, but I'd never liked cats much, so I even surprised myself with this move. I craved a pet! A dog was my first preference, but they can be clingy. Given that I lived alone and was out of the house a lot, it didn't seem fair to have an anxious dog fretting at home, all alone, probably barking.

At one point I decided to get a rabbit. They're cute, right? I could keep the hutch in my back garden where there was plenty of grass to eat. Then I'd bring it in at night for TV snuggles on my lap.

'Rabbits don't snuggle,' rabbit-owner Nicole told me.

'You sure?' I asked, hoping she was confusing rabbits with some other creature.

'I mean, ours will sometimes, but only for a few minutes, and usually when he wants a carrot.'

'Oh.' I was disappointed. Next thing I knew I was casually perusing pet rescue websites looking at cats. And that's how I ended up with Fonzi. I loved him instantly. He had such a cute little face, and a heart-shaped patch on the back of his neck.

'He's the runt of the litter,' the rescue cat lady told me. 'But don't let that confuse you – he's by far the most curious of all his brothers. Into everything.'

I could perhaps have taken that as a warning sign, but I didn't. I liked that he had some get-up-and-go. 'How did he end up here?' I asked, hoping he wasn't found in a bag at the bottom of a dumpster.

'His mum was a one-year-old stray. We couldn't keep her in foster care, but look: they have an adopted *dad*, see?' Pointing to a larger cat, curled up on a squishy couch, she added, 'The kittens think he's their mother.'

I loved it. The story fitted perfectly with the solo parent family I was creating. I left that afternoon with Fonzi in a carrier. He was a little weepy, whimpering quietly as I drove the ninety-minute trip home. I felt awful pulling him away from the familiarity of his siblings but knew he was going to have a wonderful life with me.

It didn't start off that way, though. We got home, and though Fonzi was a little purring machine, I had to abandon him and go to work for a few hours. That meant leaving him at home. Alone. I couldn't relax at work, racing home the minute I clocked off, wondering what I'd find. Relief, *relief* when Fonzi came bounding out of his new room, purring away contently in my arms. It was official: he was mine, and I was his.

Over the coming days, I became quite overwhelmed by the love I had for this little guy. On one occasion, lying on the couch, he crawled up to my chest and lay there, purring. Tears filled my eyes as my heart opened as wide as it's ever been. He had me hook, line, and sinker.

Meanwhile, my IVF rounds were becoming a continuous haze of failure. Seven and eight whizzed by like an ungainly out of control truck. There was no stopping my determination; my levels of hope and optimism were still high, but as had become the pattern, they weren't amounting to a baby.

Whenever I received bad news during IVF, I went numb. Perhaps it was a mechanism that lessened the pain. Because bad news clearly hurt. The numbness eventually began to seep away. Manifesting itself into liquid form, escaping my eyes in the tears I cried. And boy, those tears could flow. Usually in secret.

Hope was the solution. Once I lost hope, the tears would really become infinite, and I'd be on a tragic downhill slide. It kept me going even when my goal of being a mum seemed impossible.

By the same token, hope was also my nemesis. What if it was false hope I was clinging to? What if it kept me going for all the wrong reasons? Hope could be truly empowering *and* debilitating at the same time.

I wondered what it would take for me to make the decision to stop. By this stage, I'd had so many failed attempts, how many more could I endure? *Perhaps my next round will be a success*, I'd tell myself, time and time again. Or the round after that?

I was frustrated as all hell, but that was certainly not going to damn-well stop me.

25

A Newer Approach

October 2016, age 43

It was a blustery spring day when I hot-footed it to the clinic to get started with round nine. In the waiting room, my eyes caught a new sign by the door. It showed all the medical staff in the building alongside professional headshots. My eyes scanned the poster until they stopped at – what?

'Dr Jolie's HERE?' I said out loud.

'Oh, ah, yeah. She's been with us for nearly six months.' I didn't realise nurse *Trunchbull* was at the reception desk, listening.

I turned to her and smiled. 'I know her. I LOVE her – she did one of my egg pick-ups. She's amazing.' I was excited. I mean, you've got to be kidding me. If that woman was here, I'd be making an appointment with her for SURE! Not that Dr Hopkins wasn't great, but eight rounds, all with pretty much the same protocol and without success?

I asked *Trunchbull* if it would be possible to transfer to Dr Jolie. She nodded and organised an appointment. I couldn't believe it. That easy!

While on a roll, I decided to call the naturopath Nicole had used to help her get pregnant. No better way to recover from the disappointment of previous rounds than to saddle up and get straight back on the horse with a new set of tactics.

As always, I needed to keep busy. Focus on my mission. Keep the ol' addiction fed, and the hope flame burning.

I was surprisingly nervous before my first Dr Jolie appointment, but she was exceptional. I've never had such a down-to-earth 'human' doctor before. She swore like a trooper, had an outrageous sense of humour, and had me immediately at ease. Plus, because we already knew each other, it was straight to chit-chat, and business. That seems like a paradox, but Dr Jolie had a way of not crossing into over-familiar territory, yet still talking like a friend I'd have coffee with.

I was convinced if anyone was going to get me pregnant, it was her: a strange statement in itself, really. I was able to open up to her a bit too. 'It's been difficult at times,' I sheepishly offered, not wanting to overdramatise things. Typical me.

Her response was what I now know as 'typical Ange':

'Difficult? Well, let's see – you women have to shut down part of your hormonal system, inject drugs into your body, undergo minor surgery that may or may not be successful. And you're in pain for weeks afterward.' She paused for breath. 'And that's just the retrieval of the eggs. What do men do to retrieve their sex cells? Have a wank!'

'Oh my God!' I gasped.

'Not that I'm waging a battle of the sexes, but yes, Lorena – you have been through a lot, and I imagine it's been more than difficult. Now, let's come up with an innovative strategy and get you pregnant.' Her plan was something new. 'Have you ever done a flare cycle before?' she asked.

'Nope. But I've worn a few pairs of flares in my time, heh-heh.'

Dr Jolie ignored my ill-attempted humour – which surprised

me. She had her head down, concentrating, working out the medications I would need. Turns out the flare cycle is a fast one, where the meds are administered in such a way that there is a sudden flurry of action (the 'flare' response) that should *jolt* my ovaries into producing more follicles. That's how I understood it, anyway.

With acupuncture over, it was naturopathy's turn. Arthur, the naturopath, had his consulting room in Campbelltown, a real pain in the arse to get to from my place. I figured it would be worth it if he was good, so didn't begrudge the trip. His office was in a peculiar little corridor of shops beside a health-food store. The earthy, muddy, biscuity 'smell' all health-food outlets seem to have wafted through, which I found strangely comforting.

The door opened, and there stood Arthur McCoy: an older man with a sour face and a physique that suggested a vigorous penchant for sugary snacks. The consultation was brief. He looked me over, snorted when I dropped the words 'donor-sperm', and handed me a leaflet on how I could improve my fertility through diet. I walked out thirty minutes later with a large cardboard box bursting at the seams with potions, pills, and powders – over four-hundred dollars' worth, my mind flashing back to the dodgy Chinese herb dealer fiasco from a few rounds ago.

I sensed that Arthur didn't like me much. His brusque, impersonal tone made our monthly appointments more of a potion dispensary than anything. Yet once again, I persisted for four months in the name of preparing for my next round. Spending my child's future inheritance on consultations and medicines, all in the desperate hope this would be the therapy that would work.

I was now up to IVF round nine. Talk about a marathon. Never in my wildest dreams had I anticipated so many rounds. But I now had a new doctor, Angela Jolie, who I loved. Who would make a difference.

Dr Jolie's 'flare' cycle was hectic. Pretty much the same doses of the same medicines but in half the time. A fast, aggressive protocol. And the upshot? My body didn't like it. I wasn't surprised. By the time I was due for the egg pick-up there were five semi-decent follicles that all resulted in eggs. But none of them were mature – like so many times before – and poor Dr Jolie had to make the phone call to tell me.

'Darling, I'm so sorry. I thought with five eggs we'd be all right, but they just weren't good quality.'

I was gutted. 'Maybe it was too quick – the flare method?'

'Maybe. We'll go again, Lorena. I'll have a think, and we'll do something different. We're going to do this.' Her reassuring tone calmed me, giving me the next dose of hope I so greedily craved. 'You're a trooper Lorena, that's for sure,' she told me as she hung up the phone.

The next few months were a killer, money-wise. It was as though my bank account had an invisible but unrelenting leak in it somewhere. It was late November, just before the summer holidays. My work slows down over the Christmas holidays, which I'm normally prepared for, but all my savings had gone on my previous IVF rounds. Not to mention alternative therapies. I was deep in the shit.

I somehow managed to get through it with Fonzi lovingly

by my side. We were never in danger of starvation or destitution. Just as my money ran out, some work would come in – holiday classes or private lessons for solos, keeping me afloat. The bummer was that because I was so skint, I wasn't able to save. And until I was able to save, there would be no IVF.

There was something else in sight, too: Bonnie Tyler.

For the first time in nearly twenty years, Bonnie was touring Australia. I was beside myself, attending every single show, centre front, sobbing, singing, and savouring every moment. Bonnie saved me, inspired me, and gave me new hope.

In Canberra, I waited by the stage door after the show for her to come out. Eventually she emerged, all smiles with an autograph pen at the ready. I was so nervous, wondering what would come out of my mouth when it was my turn to speak to her. Hopefully something coherent and not just fanatic babble. The guy before me was taking ages. But Bonnie was generous with her time, and when it was finally my turn, she took the record I'd brought for her to sign, scribbling, *Love Bonnie Tyler* across the cover.

'Did you enjoy the show?' she asked.

'Yes!' I replied. 'It's not the first time I've met you.' I gave her a brief rundown of our previous meetings in Denmark and London. She didn't remember me. Why did I think she might? I became overwhelmed with emotion, nonetheless.

'Your music has been the soundtrack of my life,' I told her, a river of tears running down my face.

'Oh, that's lovely,' she replied. I suppose she'd heard a million fans say similar things. Her very patient, kind husband, Robert (who I'd also previously met, but he didn't remember either. Damn!) said, 'Don't cry. It's a happy time.'

'I know,' I blubbered, fixing my face as best I could for a photo with my idol.

I watched them get into their car and drive off. They waved through the window at the congregation of fans, like farewelling long-lost friends. What a beautiful lady.

Bonnie's shows helped heal me after all those IVF failures. My CD player was blaring her tunes for months as I re-re-rediscovered her back catalogue for the trillionth time.

Driving to work a few days later, belting out a rendition of *Holding Out for a Hero*, carpool karaoke style, I was rudely interrupted when my phone rang. It was a sunny day, and I was happily psyching myself up for hours of teaching. Spinning, kicking, and choreographing in my head, preparing exercises and planning, as I always did before my workday began.

It was a nurse called Lana from the new IVF clinic. She spoke with a soft but confident voice.

'Is that Lorena?'

'Yes, hi.' I wondered why she was calling. I hadn't booked anything with them yet, still saving up.

'I just wanted to check you were still planning to do your IVF treatment at our clinic?'

'I am. I'm so sorry, I've been meaning to call you, but somehow, it's July already.'

'We were discussing you in our meeting this morning. Would it be easier for you if we made this round more financially achievable? We can organise a gap payment, so you wouldn't need to pay the whole amount up-front?'

I was so surprised! 'Oh my God, yes please. Thank you – that would be amazing.'

'That's okay,' she said with a smile in her voice. 'We figured this'd help you get back faster. You don't have time to lose.' She was right on point there. I certainly wasn't getting any younger.

Round ten started a few days later. My medication delivered, I started injecting, back on that old familiar horse. At trigger time I needed to do all the injections at 3pm precisely. But that was in the middle of a lesson. I couldn't just walk out and leave my young students alone. Why was everything always so bloody complicated? Doing the injections in front of a room of students wasn't an option. But the toilet there was so rancid, I couldn't imagine injecting in there either. I had to work out a way.

Wednesday came, and I was nervous. After sweating on it all night, changing my mind a million times, I decided the best plan was to inject in the loo. Telling my boss wasn't an option, because then I'd have to confess my whole IVF secret identity. Besides, she was on a day off and wasn't going to be there anyway.

What could possibly go wrong in the middle of a fourteen-and-under Eisteddfod group rehearsal? I imagined the kids running riot the minute I closed the cubicle door, even though I knew they wouldn't. I was only going to be a door away, able to hear everything. Still very much in charge.

I decided to keep my students busy by setting them a fifteen-minute choreography task. I often gave them a bit of space with tasks like this so they could work in peace without a teacher breathing down their necks. So, my disappearance wouldn't seem out of the ordinary.

Once that was done, I snatched my meds bag and legged it to the loo shouting, 'I'll just be a minute. Keep working!' So engulfed in the task, they barely noticed me leave.

The dank cubicle was tiny and grubby with the tell-tale pungent urine stench synonymous with public washrooms. I placed a towel onto the toilet lid and began organising my meds.

The mixing of the medications was tricky – an exercise in haste and precision. My hands were shaking. I couldn't afford to make a mistake, because I didn't have the time to redo anything. And anyway, I didn't have spare medication with me.

Squatting by the toilet, much like a junkie in a nightclub, I lay the three syringes out. Number one was going to be quick, just a jab, ready to go. Number two was a complex task of drawing up liquid through a massive horse needle, depositing it into the powder vial, mixing it, drawing it back into the syringe and then with a different needle, administering the injection. I got all that done, laying that needle carefully next to number one, like soldiers ready for battle. Number three was the trigger. For this, I needed to wind the bottom part to a certain number, put a needle on top and inject.

Standing by the toilet, I searched for unbruised patches of tummy to insert each needle into. It wasn't easy, because my stomach was a patchwork of track marks.

I listened for my students. They were enthusiastically getting on with their task next door. Good, all was well.

My gaze shifted to a line of white paint peeling from the bottom of the cubicle door. Why would anyone choose white paint for a public toilet? There were dirty stains in shades of beige at all the points of human contact – especially around the lock. And germs everywhere, I could tell. As I stared, with all these pointless thoughts going through my head, I picked up the first soldier in line, then slid the needle into my stomach. I pushed the button at the top and felt the familiar sting of liquid passing from needle tip to flesh, sighing with the familiarity of it. The other two needles followed with similar precision.

Then like a flash of lightning, I scooped up all evidence of my 'illicit' activity, piling it back into the small bag I'd brought with me.

Racing out the door I looked at the clock. 3:08pm. *Eight minutes*. That had to be a world record. It scared me that I'd become so accustomed to administering those needles. Walking back into the rehearsal I was relieved to see the kids were still working, deep in concentration. I took a breath, held my chin up, and let them continue. I was proud. Proud of them for working so well, and proud of myself for managing the impossible. Just another notch on the post of unusual things I'd done in the name of making my baby.

The on-call anaesthetist for my egg-pickup was Dr Veronica McNamara. She was a youngish petite woman with a tan. Not pretty, but well-maintained, with long dangly earrings that seemed out of place in a medical environment. She must have forgotten to remove them.

Dr McNamara was filling out my pre-op questionnaire, but I could tell she wasn't concentrating, her eyes scooting past me. And the notes she was scribbling were much briefer than the information I was giving. My head bobbed sideways to keep in track with her eyeline. My stress levels were elevating as I desperately repeated, 'I have been sick after having anaesthetic before.'

'Well, that's the hormones,' she replied with a sniff, her gaze shifting to a bird that had just landed outside on the windowsill. 'IVF medication affects your hormones.'

'It's just that I seem to become extremely nauseous after some of my egg retrievals,' I added, remembering the vomiting into a bag in the carpark incident, trying desperately to catch her eye.

'You'll be fine,' she replied, snapping her notebook shut. Then her face ignited. 'Oh, hi, I'm back!' She was looking straight through me at a nurse.

'Oh, my GOD, how WAS it, Roni?' the nurse asked.

'Exactly how you'd expect, ha-ha. Unbelievable!' 'Roni' was looking straight at me again. 'I just got back from Bali,' she said.

'That's nice,' I replied, unable to fully engage.

'Well, I can't guarantee you won't be sick again,' she added. 'But I'll do my best.'

Most of the other anaesthetists I'd had were extremely thorough, but 'Roni' was already pushing her chair back to leave, without asking if I had any other questions. I felt rushed. Unprepared.

She pointed to a door behind me. 'You can get undressed in that room.' I knew. I'd been in 'that' room six times before. I could hear her telling someone else about her Bali trip as I fumbled out of my clothes. I had butterflies in my tummy as I always did at that point in the proceedings. But things got worse.

Dr Jolie must have been away because I had someone else doing my pick-up: Dr Lauren Cruikshank. As I walked in, Dr McNamara was regaling a story about a drunken night she'd had in Bali at some place called Potato Head. I crawled up onto the bed and pretended I wasn't in the room.

'Oh, this is Lorena. She's Dr Jolie's patient,' McNamara told Cruikshank.

Cruikshank looked me in the eye for the first time since I'd walked into the room. 'Oh, I'm not as good as her,' she said, and threw her head back with a *nya-nya* giggle.

I flinched at her off-putting humour attempt. Where was *my* doctor? I guess even Superwoman needed a day off. I muttered something along the lines of, 'Oh, I'm sure you're great.' But I think that only annoyed Cruikshank more. Don't upset the doctor, Lorena. But it was too late.

Next thing I knew I was under. It happened so suddenly. Much faster than normal. Usually, I felt the slumber trickle over me for around twenty seconds but this time I was out like a light. The whole thing felt like a scene from *Frankenstein*.

I woke up feeling awful. Barely able to register the result of three retrieved eggs. Light-headed, with an intense nausea pulsating through my abdomen. I couldn't sit up without feeling like I was going to vomit. The nurse tried to feed me a biscuit, but the thought of eating made me heave. My blood pressure was low. Too low. I ended up in the recovery room for six hours. Unheard of.

They eventually had to send me home because the clinic was closing. The longest car ride I've ever had. Poor Mum, who had been by my side the whole time, was trying to drive so gently, but every curve in the road made me dry heave, every bump causing my ovaries to scream.

The craziest part was that I had somewhat optimistically planned for Mum and me to see The Australian Ballet's latest triple bill at the Opera House that evening. The light at the end of the tunnel after my medical procedure. Dad ended up going in my place. He could have done without it but went willingly. So, I lay in bed, while my parents skedaddled off to the ballet. They really enjoyed it even though it was quite modern and peculiar in places. Dad gave me a detailed description of all the pieces, and even though I knew he'd rather have not gone, he still made the most of the night which made me smile.

The next day I decided to do some investigating. Rustling through my old IVF payments folder, I searched for the anaesthetist who was on call the day I'd vomited in the carpark. I had a pretty good idea whom it was, and yes, sure enough, there was the name: good old Dr Veronica 'Roni' McNamara (not her real name). That woman! She'd robbed me of two days' work, and a night at the ballet because of her indifference and ineptitude.

Regardless, somehow, two of my three eggs fertilised. One survived the night. They were going to transfer it, but my phone rang just as we were pulling into the carpark.

'We can go ahead with the transfer, but the embryo is only twelve cells, so there's really not much point. It's not progressing.'

Mum and I turned the car around and went home. Another round down the toilet.

'Sweetie, is it time to start thinking about Plan B?' Mum asked a few days later. I could feel the tears starting. I'd been thinking the same thing. I mean, how many times was I going to *do* this? I looked down and didn't answer. How could I tell Mum that I was ready to go again if Dr Jolie would let me?

I couldn't face Plan B yet. Though I knew it was looming closer, I wanted to give my body one more try. Always 'just one more try'. The only thing that scared me was the anaesthetist. I needed to talk to Dr Jolie about her. There was no way I was going to let that woman near me again!

26

Last Rounds Before I Turn Forty-four

June 2017, age 43

Dr Jolie was, as always, a comfort and a superstar when I broached the subject of 'some problems I'd had' during the last egg pick-up.

'Okay, well, there is an option to do the egg collection at our sister clinic without going under a general anaesthetic. We use a local instead, and you'd stay awake the whole time. It can be more painful during the procedure, but the recovery's usually much faster'.

'Sold,' I said. I loved the idea. It piqued my curiosity as well. I'd always wondered what went on during those egg collections. Now I was going to find out.

It was 8am on egg pick-up day, and although Dr Jolie was in, she wasn't doing my surgery. 'I'm here as a nurse today because we're short-staffed,' she told me.

'You're amazing,' I gushed.

'Well, what else would I be doing at home?' she said, swishing out of the room in her little blue theatre booties. Strange things, those. Like shower caps for feet.

Dr Harry Reeves was doing my retrieval. One of those older 'dad-joke' doctors who would normally make me cringe. Today, they felt oddly comforting. He paraded into the pre-op room.

'We're back from the pub now, so we're ready for your surgery.' His light-heartedness brightened my mood.

I was wheeled into the operating theatre: the usual brightly lit, sterile ambience, filled with silver medical instruments. Dr Reeves got on with it with a stream of pleasant banter, explaining everything as he went. This was by far my most 'enjoyable' pick-up. I say enjoyable because it was really interesting to witness.

A big screen showed the procedure as the needle pricked my ovary and drew out liquid that hopefully contained an egg. Slightly high on happy gas ('Champagne, anyone?'), I watched the follicle getting smaller and smaller with the liquid being sucked out. Then the fluid was raced over to the scientist who put it under a microscope to reveal if there was an egg in there.

'Yippee, there's your first one,' the scientist celebrated.

I smiled. I felt so content under the influence of the gas, the sound of success was heaven. Dr Reeves delved in again. 'Another egg. Oh, my goodness, two? Now I'm just showing off.' He then drained the others.

He retrieved five eggs in total. At my age I was lucky to get any, so five was a bonus. It was satisfying to be awake and part of the procedure, and the pain wasn't too bad. It was uncomfortable, for sure, but way better than the lasting effects of a general anaesthetic. The recovery time was next to zero. I felt a bit dizzy afterward, but it didn't last. I was home within the hour.

That afternoon I was sweating on the results phone call, hoping the numbers hadn't diminished too much. Turned out four eggs were mature and two fertilised. Not too bad. One embryo was suitable for transfer. 'It's perfect,' the nurse told me on transfer day with a tilt of her head and a broad smile. 'There's no reason it wouldn't implant.' They always said that.

It did give me hope, though. Always hope, hope, hope. The driver of this machine. I hoped I'd be pregnant that round. I was, once again, absolutely sure of it. POSITIVE! I'd been bleeding during the days before my pregnancy test, but not much. I assumed it was implantation bleeding. It wasn't. The result was, once again, negative.

Was I really going to say 'back to the drawing board' again? *Oh yes.*

But really, *was* it time to quit? The argument was getting old.

27

And One Last Time
(Unless I Decide to Try Again)

April 2018, age 44

My Medicare rebate came through quickly, helping me contact Dr Jolie sooner. We had a phone consultation as there was really no need to go in. She was noticeably casual during our chat. Maybe she was becoming bored with me?

'Oh, I assumed you had decided on egg donation,' she said.

'Not yet, Dr Jolie,' I replied, as sunnily as I could. 'I can keep trying until I'm forty-six, can't I?' She *had* mentioned that.

'Yes, okay then, off we go. Maybe adjust the medication again.'

'Well, I'm up for whatever you recommend,' I replied.

What a marvellous patient I am, I thought to myself. *So easy going and grateful.*

We were off the phone a little too quickly, I thought.

I was always on the lookout for more information. Kinesiology, for instance. I Googled it. The big question was: bullshit or not? I was ready to enlist some additional hocus-pocus for what could possibly be my last time in the IVF ring.

I found an acupuncturist, who also specialised in

kinesiology. I must admit, I wasn't entirely sold, but *fuck it*, I decided. *It's worth a try*. I'm a sucker, because how many times had I uttered that exact sentence, often resulting in hideous expense and little result?

Anyway.

Jenny, the acupuncturist, was lovely. A motherly Italian woman who was a 'people person' through and through. She was surprisingly tall with Italian features – prominent nose, dark regrowth, and a strong melodic accent. She was touchy-feely, always up for a hug. I took to her instantly. During our appointments, I felt I was being nurtured and didn't have to make any decisions on my own. That's how it started, anyway.

Jenny's clinic was in a converted federation house. Charming ceiling roses, cold corridors, ancient oak floors, and dusty pink walls adorned with framed prints of peaceful scenery. It felt quaint with a homey vibe. She had a heater in her consultation room that made it toasty enough to melt my qualms away. Or so I'd hoped.

Turns out, kinesiology is not my thing. It involves an unusual way of reading the body. First, Jenny 'asked' my body for permission to be treated. Squeezing her eyes shut, she'd place her hands above my solar plexus, posing the question, 'Do we have permission to ask some questions today?'

I suppressed a giggle but held my composure, resisting the urge to squeak out a ventriloquist's, 'Yes'. She continued to mumble questions to my body that I couldn't hear or understand. Then she asked me to think a happy thought, (Fonzi, my cat). Then an unhappy one, (my IVF failures).

'I want you to open up to receiving,' she told me, managing to hit all my buttons in one sentence. I welled up. She was referring to my job as a teacher. When I thought about it, my job was all about giving. And when did I receive? Not often. Didn't even have someone at home to make me a cup of tea. She got the violins out for me, and I assembled the orchestra.

At the time it felt insightful, but in hindsight I started thinking, *Hang on, how much information did I actually give you to run with? Are you just rebounding off that or are you really reading my body?* I was trying to be open, but my bullshit detector was buzzing. I wondered if Miss Kinesiology detected *that* from my body.

Regardless, there was something about Jenny I liked, so I persisted. She made some interesting suggestions, and I put my trust in her and went with it.

One such suggestion was setting up the baby room. Until then, I'd been way too superstitious for that. 'You will be sending a strong message out to the universe this way,' Jenny insisted. 'You'll be saying *I am having a baby, and this is where it will sleep.*'

I was reluctant, only daring to put a couple of pictures on the wall, sorting through some of the baby clothes people had given me over the years, which had been carefully stashed out of sight. I'd kept hold of a baby bath given to me five years earlier. I dreamed of bathing my future baby in it, a symbol of hope as much as anything. It was a monumental dust ball by the time I dragged it out from under my bed. I spent time cleaning it up – carefully wiping off the dust and washing the cream-coloured plastic surfaces. This was going to be where I'd clean my baby. I put the bath on a stand in the corner of the baby's room.

Notice I didn't say 'future baby's room'? Another one of Jenny's guidelines.

'Don't use *meh* words, Lorena,' she told me one day – words like 'try' and 'can't', and 'if' and 'sorry'. Apparently, those words are non-descript and don't help anything progress. I needed to be assertive and positive. I tried. Even though 'tried' was another banned word. It wasn't easy, and I found myself apologising a lot for getting it wrong.

Setting up the baby room was a tangible example of positive thinking. It said, 'Yes, I'm going to have a baby.' And in the strangest way imaginable, that felt scary. There I was, on my humungous twelfth round trying for a baby but scared about the idea of that dream coming true. Absolute insanity.

Jenny was good for me in that way, though. Always reminding me to focus on the prize, not just the process. I certainly needed that. But our appointments became problematic for me when she began to forget details of what we'd gone through previously, pretending to remember after I'd prompted her.

The reality was, I'd done so much alternative therapy, I'd inevitably become cynical. When she 'fluffed up' my aura, I had to suppress laughter, because it sounded so ridiculous. Past lives? I just couldn't go there.

I took the advice that suited me, quietly rejecting the rest. In the end, my cynicism took over. I ended up letting her go just after my embryo transfer.

I'd like to say this twelfth round was my IVF success, but it wasn't. It was another drawn out, needle-fuelled bunch of nothingness. A few follicles here and there and an unsuccessful embryo transfer.

Plus, it all climaxed at the worst possible time: during the middle of the Sydney Eisteddfod on contemporary groups day. I'd directed my group through a warmup, preparing them to go on stage, quickly blowing air-kisses to them before heading into the theatre auditorium to watch them perform.

I was just about to go in when I decided to duck into the loo to check for blood: standard procedure for me by now. The assumption was there would be no blood. I'd then murmur the word 'Phew!' and get on with the next thirty minutes of the day before checking again. But this time – there was blood. Lots of it. Why hadn't I factored that in? As usual, I'd been so sure I was pregnant, I'd rendered myself unprepared.

Bad move. Dumb move.

I returned to my seat with the other teachers to watch the group, pretending nothing was wrong. Worse still, afterward, talking to the kids and their parents, having to console them because they didn't win a place. In between all that, I'd duck back to the loo, rechecking for blood while holding in cries and screams of grief. It was now gushing like a full period. I walked to the car at a blistering pace because the tears had begun to overflow and I couldn't let anyone see.

Why? Why again? I'd been so sure this time. I always was, wasn't I! WHY was I always so bloody sure?

I could feel the IVF premise slipping through my fingers, this time with a thunderous timpani-fuelled finale; the end slamming down on the floor in front of me. Swerving around it, and in a frenzy of 'what now, what now?' I could once again, somehow, feel an emerging new hope already beginning to surge. I was like Muhammad Ali, always rising up to continue the fight with a new tactic to ensure I could get back into the ever-illusive ring.

Somehow, I was still in the game.

28

The Last Part – At Last!

Winter 2018, age 44

There had been a total of:

- 12 failed IVF rounds
- 85 follicles
- 57 eggs retrieved
- 30 eggs mature enough for insemination
- 24 eggs fertilised
- 18 embryos
- 8 embryos transferred with 6 embryo transfers (twice they transferred two at a time)
- 6 times I swore I was pregnant
- 6 negative pregnancy tests
- 0 miscarriages (forever grateful for that!)
- 6 long years of IVF
- **Not one pregnancy!**

Extremely sobering statistics that I will always find impossible to fathom. When I look at them like this, it seems so very, very clinical. Obviously, it hadn't been, but in pure numbers? Devastating.

It was interesting to note that the best rounds I'd had, (apart from round one, which was statistically *the* best) were the ones involving acupuncture or seeing the naturopath. It wasn't until I'd analysed each round, comparing their successes and failures, that I realised the positive effect alternative medicine actually had.

Of course, I believe that ultimately, no matter how good the egg 'quality' is, there was nothing that could be done to change its chromosomal shortcomings. My eggs were aged and that's irreversible. If acupuncture could fix that, I'd have had four babies by now.

In some ways, after everything I'd been through in the six years since my first appointment with Dr Hopkins, I wondered whether I would have been better off skipping all the IVF rounds and just going with an egg donor. The answer to that had to be 'no'. Everything must happen for a reason. No regrets.

But. *All* that money I'd spent. I could never add it up. My house deposit, gone. Trips to see my friends in the UK, gone. Savings and future superannuation, gone, gone. Never in my wildest dreams did I imagine I'd use up so much cash. Mind you, without Medicare, I wouldn't have been able to do half of what I did so that's a consolation of sorts. I was very lucky to have the support of my doctors there. Nevertheless, it had been an achingly immense amount of money spent willingly, unconditionally, hopefully. But without success.

My body really, truly failed me. I was always terrified it would. That was one constant throughout all of this, and in the end, it did. I had never been so comprehensibly locked out of the control console. As a dancer and teacher, I'm used to being in control. I know my physical limits, and I work within them, pushing right up to the edge.

But IVF hadn't been like that. It was a daunting chasm of unfamiliarity, so far out of my comfort zone it may as well have been on Mars. Twelve rounds. Twelve completely different results. Same outcome, though. Each time I entered the ring, I'd been knocked out. I say my body failed me, but IVF failed me too. I was gutted I couldn't get there, propelled once again into a state of sombre mourning. It was going to take some time before I could move on.

Maybe I was finally at the end of the road after all.

29

The Next Step

January 2019, age 45

In a trance of deep silent thought on the plane, a crew member announced our descent, jolting me back to reality. I disembarked, my stomach in a thousand nauseating tangles; my motherhood craving still so tormenting I could barely breathe. I didn't know at the time, but I was heading into my last ever round of IVF.

Months before, I'd had my final, desperate appointment with Dr Jolie. She had kindly made time for me at very short notice for a fifteen-minute *between appointments* consultation. Not sure how that worked, to just conjure up fifteen minutes like that, but she didn't charge me, so I was extra grateful.

'Lorena, you're now forty-five,' she said, her worry lines working overtime. 'And I've only ever treated one woman your age who made it to a live birth. Your egg-quality has deteriorated, and I'm not sure it's going to happen for you.'

The words I'd been dreading for so long were finally unleashed. My shoulders sank. 'Not going to happen?' A massive wallop in the guts. Before I allowed the familiar sting of tears to lace my eyes, I took a deep breath and fought to concentrate. I knew my doctor would have a solution. This was Superstar Jolie. She always had a well-thought-out, shiny new strategy.

'I know a fantastic doctor who can help you,' she began. 'But

"

you would have to fly out of the country. And you would need to be open to egg donation.'

'Overseas?' I couldn't believe it. What was the point of doing an egg pick-up halfway round the world? Then, it hit me: egg donation. Plan B! I was going to find an overseas egg donor and travel for my transfer.

By this stage, I was more than ready to seriously consider Plan B. I'd pondered it regularly, and comprehensively. The hardest part to get my head around was mourning the loss of my own genetics. I sat with that for a long, long time, contemplating all possible ramifications. What if I didn't feel like my baby's *proper* mother? What if we looked different? And, most of all, what if my child grew up with an identity crisis because there's no one they can connect to in that genetic way?

Well, there are ways around all of it. And I relentlessly went through each and every one of them in detail. I had to be sure. I didn't know anyone who had used donor eggs. Nor did I hunt anybody down on social media. I needed to make this decision for myself, going on my own instincts.

Then it hit me one day: *Let go of the worries.* It all came down to one thing. Love. And I had love in abundance for my future child. I could feel it like particles in the air all around me, just waiting to come together and be activated. This wasn't an ego thing. Or a selfish thing. It was a feeling so deep, there was nothing that could stop it.

By the time I boarded the plane, Plan B was no longer even a thing. I refused to think of it that way anymore, feeling very sure this was all a steadfast continuum of Plan A. The division between the two all but vanished. Plus, I had my family's support. They'd given me the thumbs-up for donor eggs from the moment I'd first mentioned it.

An old, familiar excitement began to trickle over me. It tingled across my skin and pounded in my chest. I was going to have a double-donor baby. To my surprise, I found myself just as excited as I'd been way back when I first made the decision to do IVF. The jaded, experienced, tired veteran had miraculously evaporated. In its place was a naïve, thrilled newbie. Like the one I once was, so sure I'd only need a single round to become a mum.

Ascending the stairs of what would be my third and last IVF clinic, I gathered my wits, wiping an emotional tear from my eye. I couldn't believe my baby-making quest had landed me here on the other side of the globe. Mum was with me of course, and I had a feeling – a HUGE feeling – that this was going to be it. My lucky round thirteen.

Sitting in an overseas IVF waiting room felt no different to the ones I'd frequented back home. There were nerves, uncertainty, along with the usual anxious anticipation. We happened to sit next to a young girl who turned to me and asked, 'How's your day going?'

I wasn't really in the mood for small talk or hearing another person's life story, so I reluctantly turned to her and said, 'Good thanks. Transfer day.' Then looked away. Not exactly forthcoming. But there was something about her. She was young, wearing baggy, ripped jeans, and had bright pink streaks in her hair. Her eyes were alive.

I turned back to her. I had to know. 'What brings you here?'

'Egg dona—' she began.

I'd blurted my response before she had even finished, 'You

guys are amazing. I have an egg donor, and what you go through for us is above and beyond.'

'—tion'

She didn't add anything else, but there was a glint of a smile in her eyes.

'Thank you for what you're doing,' I added, expecting the conversation to draw to an end. She wasn't *my* egg donor, but all the same, this felt like a destiny-driven opportunity to annunciate the words 'thank you' to someone who clearly should be hearing it.

There was a pause.

'Hey, it's nothing,' she replied. 'It's one minuscule thing I can do to help someone else. Why wouldn't I do it?'

'Minuscule?' I asked. This was so interesting to me, finding out how it felt to be on the other side of the fence. I like to help people too when I can. But injecting hormones? Having ultrasounds up the clacker? Going through a procedure that requires anaesthetic all for someone you don't even know? That's pretty major stuff.

'It's just a few weeks of appointments that will hopefully help make someone's dream come true. It's an opportunity for me.' We held eye contact for a few seconds, and then she stared straight ahead. The nurse called out her name.

'That's me,' she said, getting up from her chair, 'Off to my egg collection. They're predicting ten to fifteen eggs, so fingers crossed.'

'Yeah, fingers crossed,' I replied, wishing now that our conversation hadn't been so short. She walked toward the nurse, but turned back to me before she got there. She had a big smile on her face, and her eyes were on fire. 'Best of luck with your transfer.'

'Thanks,' I said in a slightly wobbly voice to her back as she walked around the corner.

'Who was that?' Mum asked.

'Someone who has just made everything clearer,' I replied, and then explained everything that had happened. By the time I was called in for my transfer, my body was so filled with love, gratitude, happiness, and readiness to have *my* particular dream come true, I was about to burst.

'Two embryos,' the doctor announced as I walked into the transfer room. I looked up and saw them on the monitor. Their incubator had just been opened, and the nurses were preparing them for their journey to my uterus. I imagined the nurses giving them pep-talks along the lines of, 'Yep, it's your turn now guys. Now you've both gotta get in there and burrow in tight – this lady is going to be your mother, and she's really lovely.'

'Okay, we're ready,' the doctor said, waking me from my thought bubble. 'These two little beauties are the best I've seen today.' I could feel that old familiar wonder called 'hope' hovering over me again.

'One is hatching,' the doctor continued. I lay there with a stupid grin on my face. Hatching often meant success, from what I'd heard.

With that, and hope taking me by the hand, I knew I was in good care.

PART THREE

30

Stick, Little One, Stick!

February 2019, age 45

My hopes were as high as the return flight I was on, imagining I was heading home with a stowaway on board. I got back and tried to get on with life, somehow managing to wait the obligatory week or so before succumbing to a home pregnancy test.

Fonzi was the first to know. 'It's two lines, Fonz!!! I'm friggin' pregnant!' I collapsed at the top of the stairs, clutching the test in disbelief. This was the first time I'd ever seen a positive. Fonzi nuzzled at my forehead as if he knew, sensing my elation. After all this time, those two coveted lines I'd dreamed of were right there. Holy fucking shit, I'd done it.

I phoned my parents, tentatively letting them know. Not wanting to get too excited before the official blood test. Good old superstition was never far away, always on the prowl to steal my joy. Regardless, Mum, Dad and I had a cheerful moment on the phone as we savoured the news.

There was a lot to organise. Firstly, I had people to tell. But who? I didn't want to jinx myself by telling everyone. But at the same time, I'd climbed an enormous mountain and was desperate to shout from the summit to the whole frigging world, 'I'm PREGNANT!'

The official call from my family GP a few days later was magic. Something I'd been dreaming of for over eight years. The blood test had been in the morning, and I was quietly confident the result would be positive. Well, I'd peed on three pregnancy tests by then and the second line was getting stronger. Unless the universe was about to chew me up and puke me out again, I was fairly sure I had a *BFP* (*Big Fat Positive* in the IVF world) on my hands.

The phone rang at 2pm. A little earlier than expected. I could hear the smile in my GP's voice as he asked me, 'What kind of magic is this?'

I started jumping. 'It's positive?'

'It's positive. Congratulations.'

'I did it!'

'You did it! Remember. It's still early days, Lorena. No hot baths, keep taking the progesterone. And above all, take care of yourself — you have a kiddo on board to consider, now.'

A stowaway.

I hung up and samba danced around the house singing, '*A Stowaway-a-ya-ya,*' over and over. Fonzi thought I was nuts, giving me that cat look of, 'I don't know this woman'.

I called Mum and Dad, who were as ecstatic as I'd predicted. Mum jumped around their place cheering, 'Oh, sweetie. You did it!!!' Then I texted my brother, Nicole, Alice, and all my key people. What a rush to deliver those glorious words. Having been so rigorously focused on the technical and medical processes of getting pregnant, I was overcome by the avalanche of emotion of the reality of my baby. I'd imagined these moments so many times. They were even better in real life.

I sat on the couch afterward, giving myself some time to

breathe. To process. It had taken me forever to get to this very first and only *BFP*. But somehow at the same time, it all seemed sudden. A strange trick of the brain.

Cuddling Fonzi and imagining life in this very house with a baby, I decided it was time to get organised. Make lists. Buy stuff. Previous superstitions had prevented me from going there, so with implicit confidence, I grabbed a pen and started scribbling. Once the seven-week ultrasound scans were done, I'd start ticking off the list. I just needed to reach that milestone.

This was, of course, a brand-new worry. The milestones would continue to pile up, preventing me from fully relaxing until I had a healthy baby in my arms. I knew there were countless worries hurtling toward me. Something I'd need to come to terms with.

The next fortnight dragged on. I wasn't sure how 'easily' I was supposed to take things. Depending on what Google landed on, I should either 'go on with life as normal', 'rest, and avoid shellfish', or 'have lots of sex because intimacy lowers stress levels'. Well, the last one wasn't really on the horizon, but I could certainly find a balance between the first two.

Typically, I decided to go to the first scan alone. It was a new ultrasound venue unaffiliated with any of my previous fertility clinics. Still, it could have been any of them, harbouring the same beige carpet with those squeaky black faux-leather 'office' seats arranged in a U-shape around the border. Medical posters and still-life prints were plastered across blush-pink chipped walls, and the usual clinical smells abounded, along with the crisp air of efficiency behind the reception desk.

This scan would hopefully find my baby's heartbeat. In a

painful process of being ready for all outcomes but hoping for the best, I'd prepared myself for the fact that they might not find anything. If there's no heartbeat, there's no life. I couldn't fully prepare for that level of devastation, but I had to remain vigilant.

They were running late. Impatience clawing at my sanity, I made my way to a nearby seat, immersing myself in a spontaneous game of Bubble Mania – still my waiting room favourite.

Hours (twelve minutes) later, I was called in. 'Just strip off from the waist down.'

Huh? Just when I thought I'd never have to contend with the good old internal ultrasound probe again! I lay down, my own heartbeat soaring as if trying to convince my little one to put on a great performance.

In went the probe. I was past the point of flinching. My bulging eyes were square to the screen, which the sonographer swung around for easy viewing. Familiar black and grey swirls appeared. I'd been here so many times, but in search of follicles, not heartbeats. Perhaps I was dreaming. Perhaps this was just another follicle count and I'd be packed off home with another number to obsess over.

Maybe being here to find a heartbeat was expecting too much. That I somehow hadn't done enough to prove to the universe how much I really wanted this baby.

'There it is.'

'Huh?'

'I'll turn the volume up so you can hear it. Hang on.'

The sonographer leaned across me to adjust a knob on the monitor, after which a symphony of audible pulses filled the room.

'One-hundred-and-fifty beats per minute. That's strong!'

'Is that my baby on the screen?' I was looking at a little fluttering black dot, trying to make out any human likeness.

'That's it. A perfect heartbeat. Well done, Mama.'

I lay there, stunned, staring at the monitor.

The sonographer shuffled some papers. 'Um, I'm just checking if there are any others. Your report says you had two embryos transferred.'

'Yes, I did.' I waited, unsure how I'd feel either way about another heartbeat.

'Just one, this time.'

I sighed. Part of me had hoped for twins. But most of me was relieved, overwhelmed, and grateful to have one.

'Would you like some pictures?'

I couldn't say yes fast enough as waves of laughter took over me. 'My baby,' I kept saying, both out loud, and in my head. 'I'm a mum!'

A few days later, I was teaching some of my very talented and dedicated full-time dance students. We were preparing for their mid-year assessment. Something they took very seriously, because an external panel of esteemed examiners were invited and, well, in the dance world, that kind of thing could lead to future employment.

This was clearly *not* the optimum time for morning sickness to kick in.

I was scooting across the floor, demonstrating a move called 'around the world', where you lie on your back with your bum skyward as your feet circle your head. Nausea-inducing at the best of times.

Suddenly, the urge to vomit overtook. I stood up suddenly, which made it worse, and ran. I couldn't tell the class where I was going, so they sat in a haze of confusion as I worked to avoid retching spew across the floor.

Making it by milliseconds, I heaved into the bathroom basin, then collapsed onto a closed toilet seat hoping nobody would come after me.

What was that?

I'd been hoping for a bit of morning sickness. I'd read in Kaz Cooke's book *Up the Duff* that it's a sign of a good, solid, here-to-stay pregnancy. What I hadn't banked on is how it pulverised me like a tsunami, so suddenly out of nowhere.

I didn't have long to gather my wits. I needed to get back out there. Well, at least to show my face, which I did briefly, before rushing back to disinfect the basin. The potent smell of antiseptic was almost enough to press repeat on my expulsion.

A week later, I was sitting across from my GP as he prescribed the mildest available nausea tablets to help keep me up and running through the morning sickness phase of my pregnancy. Images of thalidomide babies filled my brain as I cursed myself for not coping. I'm used to getting carsick, and morning sickness was akin to that but constant.

I saved the tablets for the most severe bouts. They didn't help much, only taking the edge off slightly. I really hated taking them. After all I'd been through to get pregnant, struggling to handle a bit of nausea seemed insane.

Feeling ill constantly was truly wearing. I carried one of those plastic vomit bags with me everywhere, regularly ducking out to the back alleyway for a quick spew while teaching a class. No one knew. I'd become the master of disguise hiding seven years of IVF, so this was child's play.

My fourteen-week, (*Nuchal Translucency*) scan crept up, and I was not comfortable to go public with my pregnancy news until those results were in. My parents were away at the time, so even though Mum wanted to be there, she was busy traipsing across the hills of Lapland, dangling off the edge of a reindeer-driven sleigh. No doubt she and Dad were thinking of me still, as always.

Calling a friend to come along didn't cross my mind. Even though I'd had a line-up of offers – Nicole, Alice, and many others insisting they were 'only a phone call away', and to *please* call if I needed anything. I rarely did. Asking for help still wasn't in my vernacular. And I can honestly say that at this point, I felt more than able to get on with things alone.

Meanwhile, paranoia and superstition still hovered as veils over my pregnancy, and I couldn't get rid of them. If I had a day of not feeling sick, I worried I was going to lose the baby. If I had a day where I was a bit crampy, or my boobs weren't hurting as much as normal, it'd take all my energy and courage to convince myself that this wasn't the end. I couldn't rest and enjoy the idea I was pregnant. Not at least until the next milestone had been ticked off.

Today's scan would check bub was still there with a strong heartbeat. And identify any potential atypical foetal characteristics such as Down Syndrome (Trisomy 21). Sitting in the waiting area, pondering the miracle of being here for a second pregnancy scan, my thoughts took me back to that very first HyCoSy ultrasound I'd done seven years ago. SEVEN! If I could go back and speak to that version of myself, I'd say, 'Keep positive. It'll be a rough ride, but you're going to do this!'

Except in truth, I still didn't have a final outcome. And as my mind clicked back to the present, I became increasingly aware that today's scan, like the previous one, could reveal devastating results. An all-familiar sense of panic washed over me, this time with just a tingle of hope in the mix as well.

Finally, the sonographer called me in. I lay on the table as the sonographer fired up the equipment. 'I'm measuring the nuchal fold,' she said.

'Sorry, what's that?' I'd never heard of it.

'It's an area at the back of the baby's neck. It helps detect Trisomy 21.'

I'd already seen and heard my baby's heartbeat, a cascading river of joyous tears streaming down my temples. And the sonographer was pleased with the developmental stuff, telling me my baby was 'on schedule' for size.

'Do you want to know the sex?'

My stomach fluttered. Yes, I did want to know! I'd had enough surprises already, and needed time to prepare for, well, this is going to sound terrible, but as much as I didn't want to hope for one sex more than another, I couldn't help hoping, just a little bit, that I might be having a girl. I suppose it was easier to picture myself mothering a daughter, especially as a solo parent.

As I'm talking about this, I need to mention; there are many, many solo mums by choice (and other parents too) who say that even though they were desperate for a girl, having a boy ended up being the best thing. A healthy baby is all you can ask for, right? But back at the time of my scan, I was crossing my fingers and toes in the hope my baby would be a girl.

The sonographer ran the scanner across my stomach. Thank goodness it was external this time. Bubs was in there having a party. Moving about like a breakdancer from the 90s. *That's my kid*, I thought to myself with a smile.

'Um, I'm having trouble getting a clear picture.' The sonographer pulled away and tilted her head in that nurse sympathy way, as I braced for impact. 'We're going to have to fire up the internal probe to get a closer look.' *Gawd!*

It didn't make a skerrick of difference. Bubs was doing windmills, head spins, the robot man. You name it, this kid was popping and locking to the *S-Club-Beat*. There was no way the sonographer was getting anywhere close to photographing anything in detail.

'Maybe go for a walk and come back in an hour. Sometimes the baby rests when you're moving. Kind of like being rocked to sleep.'

I was so happy, skipping out of the clinic, knowing I had a healthy baby growing in my uterus. But now curiosity was burning a hole through my brain. I needed to know whether I was having a boy or a girl, and I needed to know now!

I paced the backstreets across the road from the clinic. Scenarios of taking my boy to AFL matches flooded my head. It wouldn't be THAT bad. On the other hand, I imagined taking my girl to AFL matches – because just my luck, my future daughter would somehow end up a massive football fan. The craziness of it only made me smile.

Reassuming my position on the clinic bed, the sonographer gambled on an external ultrasound to start off with, assuming bubs was now worn out and sleeping.

'Well, there's still a lot of movement going on.'

'I can't feel the baby moving. Is that okay?'

'That's normal at this stage. People feel their babies move at different times, but not usually until seventeen to twenty weeks. You'll know.' She paused. 'Oh wait. Here we go. Aah, well done, little one. Are you ready?'

I was ready.

'It's a girl. You're having a little girl, congratulations.'

My heart fluttered. I was absolutely, unequivocally, overwhelmingly floating on a cloud.

31

Some Reality Checks

May 2019, 15 weeks pregnant, age 45

The official scan results came back a few days later confirming I had a healthy little female breakdancer on board. Given my age, the sonographer was surprised I hadn't opted for the extra blood tests designed to detect DNA anomalies of the foetus.

'I used a donor egg, and the donor was only 23,' I said, for the first time out loud to someone other than a close friend or family member. The words caught in my throat. Should I be telling people this? I had no intention of keeping my daughter's conception story a secret – but suddenly saying the words out loud, with no forethought, felt like I was revealing something I shouldn't. Perhaps I needed to start rehearsing what to say to people. In this case, the clinic staff had seen it all before, so I had nothing to worry about.

Meanwhile, in the back of my mind, I pictured all other thirty-five plus pregnant women trotting off for their tests, as I sat back and did nothing for the first time in my entire fertility quest.

It felt wrong: like I was cheating my age. But strangely lovely as well: like an unexpected advantage of using a donor egg.

Morning sickness continued apace. Perhaps I could have taken a few days off here and there, but as always, if I didn't work, I didn't get paid. And as I was the sole income provider with an incoming dependent, I needed to earn!

My daughter's welfare was now at the forefront of my mind. The more I worked now, the more time I could take off after she was born. I'd suck it up, continuing my coping ritual of ducking out to the alleyway, fire escape, or nearest toilet for a quick spew throughout the workday.

I lived on a diet of lemonade and peanut butter sandwiches. For a while that's all I could handle. The nausea wasn't extreme. Just a pest stopping me from revelling in my pregnancy the way I'd hoped to. It wasn't until I was home at night, tucked up on the couch with Fonzi purring softly on my lap that the seasickness would ease.

One such night, after a particularly difficult and long day, I flopped onto the couch and started shivering. Winter was setting in, and I was getting a cold, feeling a bit miserable. The logical left side of my brain suddenly pulled out a previously hidden fencing sword and started challenging the right, creative side.

'Okay, missy. So, you've created this baby. Well done. Many years of hard work and blah, blah, blah. But tell me. What are you planning on doing now?'

The right side of my brain froze. 'What do you mean? We did it! There's a baby on board.'

'Um, you did it. Yup. So, now what? You think that because you've outsmarted your biological clock and beaten the system, you'll automatically become Supermum?'

'I… um… er.'

Holy shit! My left brain was right. While I'd been doing all this creating and reviving; mourning and picking myself up to repeat the cycle time and time again, I'd lost track of the reality of what was coming. What if I turned out to be a crap mother?

What if, after all this effort, I ended up with post-natal depression, or that 'mum rage' I'd heard about? What if I don't love my baby? Using an egg donor means we don't share DNA – what if that becomes a problem? What if I don't even bond with my baby and want to hand her back?

I bolted upright. Blinking away my panic, trying to shut down the thoughts invading my head.

Sometimes those dark moments would clutch me for a while as I imagined the tough times motherhood might bring. It was one thing to revel in the glory of it all, and on the outside, I was a happy solo mum-to-be, proudly announcing to the world that I was pregnant after such a long battle. Was I kidding myself?

Mostly, I knew these demons were just out to play. The occasional fencing bout that every first-time parent endures from time to time. I put it down to that, staying vigilant in case those little voices became loud and constant. They didn't return very often. Usually in unexpected moments like when I was tired or overwhelmed by nausea.

At the other end of the scale, announcing my pregnancy to the world was a solid mixture of pleasure and, well, weirdness. I received every reaction you can imagine ranging from, 'I didn't know you were seeing someone', through to the anticipated 'congratulations', and 'I'm so happy for you'.

There were actual tears when I stood across from Nicole in a Westfield health food shop, nervously revealing to her that, 'It looks like my embryo might have become a foetus.' She nearly knocked over a display of gift-boxed herbal sleepy-time tea in her beeline to grab me into a hug, tears rolling.

On one occasion, I was parking my car in the notorious 'spew' alley at the back of work when a student's mum approached. 'I hear you've got good news,' she said.

I nodded, clumsily unpacking equipment for the lessons I was about to teach.

She continued, 'So, one of the mums said to me, "You'll never guess who's pregnant. Only the last person in the WORLD you'd ever imagine. Go on, have a guess".'

I looked up from my rummaging. I'd lost my iPod down the side of the front seat but was too stunned to continue the search. What the hell was I hearing? I tried to speak but only managed a small croak.

She continued, 'I knew immediately and said, "It's Lorena isn't it!" Without hesitation, I swear. Last person in the world, right?'

I remained a stunned statue, buzzing on the inside trying to comprehend this woman who was essentially ripping me to shreds. I managed to loosen my mouth up just enough to say, 'Oh, um. Great.' And returned to the business of iPod foraging.

It wasn't until much later that night that the sparks of anger set in. *Calm down, Lorena, you're reading way too much into it.* But I couldn't stop the feeling I'd been cruelly patronised just because I didn't have a partner or wasn't married. Was that the crux of her reaction?

I called an emergency coffee date with Alice the following day, blurting out the story, her face contorting with disbelief the more I went on.

She sighed, calming me with her composed empathy. 'People have their own way of computing your decision,' she said. 'You may have to get used to comments like that.' I knew she was right and was thankful for her advice to resist taking it to heart and avoid buying in.

Advice I counted on a few weeks later at work. As I've mentioned, very few work people knew of my pregnancy aspirations. This particular boss was nothing short of amazed. I think her actual words were, 'Pleasantly blindsided', before adding, 'Given you're single. Aren't you?' *Sigh*. Oh well. She tried. Thankfully, she softened the blow with, 'Oh my goodness, I would have supported you the whole way, Lorena. Why didn't you say anything?'

I looked down the corridor at the entrance of the filthy public toilet where I once injected myself mid-class during an IVF round, then glanced back at her. 'It was just easier on my own.'

She nodded sympathetically as my mind whirled with questions of why I always felt such a strong tendency for secrecy. There was the time I was bleeding in that very same toilet cubicle after one of my failed rounds. How much easier would that have been if I'd just exited the loo and told her, 'My period came. I'm not pregnant. Again. Can I please go home?'

She looked at me and smiled, flushing a warmth of acceptance through the room. I leaned into my chair, feeling all was well in the universe. Then one of my male colleagues, Jeff, trampled in. My boss jumped up from her seat. 'Can I tell him?'

I nodded.

'Lorena's pregnant, Jeff. Isn't it marvellous?'

He looked me over and smiled, a cold whoosh darting from his eyes. 'Who's the sperm donor?'

My boss and I exchanged looks of dismay. She knew I'd

used a sperm donor. But this man had only just heard my news. He was guessing, being overtly rude, severely over-stepping. My boss, thankfully, overcame the awkwardness by shaking her head and muttering, 'Oh, Jeff. It's class time, I think.'

Upon reflection, it's not the sperm donor comment that bothered me. I did use a sperm donor. And an egg donor. It was more Jeff's unsolicited comment on the conception of my daughter. Like if he fathered a child, it was okay for me to ask, 'So was it the missionary position you conceived him in, or one of your Saturday night swinging from the bedhead in handcuffs sessions?' And let's be real, I'd never cross that line.

Though I rarely discussed my marriage status at work, it was pretty obvious I was single. Whether ill-meaning or ignorant, the fact that Jeff deemed it okay to make presumptuous assumptions on my pregnancy just because I was single upset me to no end. Because to me, it perpetuates narratives such as: 'you're less of a person if you're single', 'you're unlovable', 'no one wants you', and the real corker, 'using a sperm donor is pathetic'.

These comments are myths, founded on no one. I knew I had to remain armoured to cope with anything else like this that would edge toward me again in the future.

32

Easing Into Pregnancy

April 2019, 18 weeks pregnant, age 45

Mum and Dad continued to demonstrate their unrelenting support for me. I often wondered, now that the IVF dust had settled a bit and we were all breathing again, whether they felt quietly disappointed I ended up doing this on my own. We hadn't spoken about it. Well, not since the very beginning when I 'came out' with my decision. It wasn't just the fact that I hadn't found a man to partner up with and father my child. Something else was becoming increasingly obvious: there was clearly no immediacy for me to find someone.

I wasn't missing that 'other half', even during major pregnancy milestones. I know of some solo mums by choice who have felt loneliness in these moments. But to be quite blunt, I simply didn't. I never once laid there, looking at my baby's heartbeat on an ultrasound screen, and thought to myself *if only I had a partner to share this with.*

Perhaps I'm weird like that, I don't know. The far more likely 'perhaps' is that I was born this way. Made for the solo life. I think I've always known it, but being pregnant made it clearer.

I wasn't scared of parenting alone. If I did hold any fears, they were more about the continued viability of my pregnancy. Once I got through that and had a baby in my arms, I wasn't afraid of the future. I mean, yes, that's a sweeping statement. Of course there were things I was worried about. The usual things like: 'How will I cope with a newborn?', 'What if my baby gets sick?', 'How will we survive financially?' But the fear of being a solo parent, and the question of whether I'd cope with that never came up. I knew that this was the way for me, and even better, I felt proud. Proud of my choices. Proud of my journey. And more than ever, proud to call myself a solo mum by choice. Someone, please get this girl a rooftop so she can do some shouting!

If my parents had any inkling of disappointment, well, they never showed it. Perhaps the word 'disappointment' is too strong. I think, given their own thousand-year happy marriage, they must be a little sad I haven't found love for myself. And even I admit there have been moments where I get the 'what ifs', wondering what may have been if I'd managed to meet some better men along the way.

But my life was full. I had everything I needed, so there was no looking back. With my parents wholly by my side every step of the way, I was content. And still quite amazed by how open-minded they'd been throughout the process.

I really loved witnessing the different ways they both expressed their support for me and my venture into motherhood.

Mum, for instance, was the highly motivated one; smothered in endless layers of love and excitement for her future grandchild, and her grandchild-bearing daughter. A total lovefest. She was bursting to meet her granddaughter and put her hand up for every single task that needed doing, no matter how menial. Number one was the baby room.

I still lived in the same two-bedroom (sort of) granny flat underneath a house. The 'second' bedroom didn't have any windows. Three doors (I know!), including one that didn't open, but no windows. So, there was no way to let the light in. I didn't know the long-term solution to this, but I knew for now, for a baby and even into childhood, it'd be fine.

Mum and I headed to Bunnings to choose a colour scheme to paint ('refresh') the walls and built-ins. If there wasn't a way to let in natural light, we'd create our own sense of vibrancy.

'What do you think of this one?' I plucked out a banana-yellow sample card from the myriad options before us.

Mum squinted a little. 'A bit much, maybe?'

Damn. I'd wanted to go for it, but she was right. There's a (not very) fine line between painting the sunshine into a room and turning it into an indoor pineapple. I looked around again. 'This?'

Mum nodded. 'But remember, it usually dries darker.'

I grabbed the shade lighter, a lovely creamy yellow, and wandered over toward the pinks. Now, I'm not a pinky girlie girl. But I thought a nice subtle marshmallow pink seemed soothing and pretty. We chose a light shade that would warm the room without overpowering it and then raced back to my place where Mum excitedly painted as I brought in cups of coffee, turned up the radio, and generally just stayed out of the way. Mum's an excellent painter. Plus, I think she actually enjoys it. A totally foreign concept to me.

In the end, the room looked great. Better than great – bloody amazing. My baby's room! Mum and I took a step back, slurped on cool non-alcoholic beers, and took a minute. The fresh vitality of my girl's room was symbolic. All those times I'd been too scared to jinx myself by making baby preparations. I was now inching forward in miniscule baby steps (pun intended), to the timing I thought was in line with the growing baby inside me.

In the days after, I searched Gumtree where I found a cot. I also sourced a breastfeeding rocking chair for fifty bucks, which to this day I still can't believe I fit into the closed boot of my not-very-big Toyota Corolla.

Mum and I had ample fun shopping for baby clothes. Mum made the first purchase: a tiny, 0000, Bonds grey terry-towelling onesie. So cute! I lay it over the cot so each time I walked past I could pick it up, study it, press it to my chest, and imagine one day soon cuddling my baby inside it.

Meanwhile, Dad was helping out in very practical, subtle, but gargantuan ways. He would tend to the garden without me even knowing it – often while I was at work, ensuring it was always trimmed, spotless and neat. 'Have the garden pixies been again?' I'd email later on with a wink and a thank you emoji.

Dad's toolbox temporarily lived at my place too, because my rickety old rental property was all but falling apart. Dad was happy to help, fixing broken hinges, cracked steps, gluing down floor vinyl that had curled up becoming a trip hazard. He put up baby gates and created little safe zones for my future toddler. He hammered, drilled, puttied, painted. You name it, I was living in a castle by the time my parents had spread their love and hard work across the place.

I was so grateful. And, you know, I never even had to ask. Not for a thing – they'd both volunteer before I even drew breath. I knew I'd won the parent lottery! Sometimes in those moments after a long day of work, I'd lie on the couch, feel the nausea lift, and float in gratitude for a while.

Then, one day this daily ritual heightened.

Something inside my stomach began to tickle! I jumped up at the new sensation, eyes bulging, heart thumping. This caused the tickling to stop. But I knew what it was: my baby girl. I'd just felt her kick for the first time.

I lay on the couch, letting Fonzi take his place across my lap. The tickling soon resumed as small droplets of joy trickled down my cheeks. Suddenly, all the years of trying to conceive didn't matter anymore. I was here. In love and happiness.

July 2019, 25 weeks pregnant

Morning sickness decided to reappear, and I was gutted. Just like way back in my first trimester I was beginning to feel that nonstop carsick feeling again. I'd cut my work hours down a little by this stage but was undoubtedly working too much.

My baby was now the size of a rock melon, and I was showing in a way that was still a bit 'has she eaten too many donuts, or is she…?'

I was attending regular antenatal medical appointments at the local hospital by this stage. It's funny because I think I was expecting some sort of 'special' treatment, because not only was I deemed a *geriatric* mum (an appalling term used for women who give birth over the age of thirty-five), I was also very, very sure I was the oldest person to ever *be* pregnant. Wasn't I?

One of the midwives soon put me straight on my first appointment at the clinic. 'Oh no, we have women over forty in here all the time.'

My eyebrows shot up. 'But…' She must have misunderstood me. 'But I'm now forty-*six*!' That seemed extremely geriatric to me if thirty-five was the cut-off.

'Oh, no, you're still well within our regular range.' The

midwife angled my pregnant carcass onto the scales – the part of the appointment I always dreaded and was glad for the distraction of our conversation. 'We had two women over fifty giving birth just last week.'

I nearly bowled myself over with shock. 'Really?' Wow! I'm not sure what I'd been expecting. A brass band to announce my imminent, old-aged pregnancy?

And this one goes out to: Lorena Otes. The woman who has seen it all. Thirteen rounds of IVF, you know. Make way, for here she comes at the ripe old age of (drum roll), forty-six. Hopefully she doesn't trip over and crack a hip.

But seriously. None of the midwives ever had the slightest qualm about my age.

'You're fit and healthy,' one said. 'We'll monitor you as we would any other pregnant woman.' That was it.

None of them questioned my status as a solo mum by choice either. They didn't judge or comment. In fact, I was deemed blatantly, unashamedly 'normal'. After all the time I'd spent being treated as a 'special' one who 'needed' to get pregnant soon because her biological clock was threatening to implode. Now, I was just one of the dozens of mothers-to-be in the waiting room. Finally, one of the boring old crowd. And I have never been happier to be so vanilla in my life.

33

Baby Shower Time (Or not...?)

September 2019, 34 weeks pregnant, age 46

'No, no, no! I promise you, I really, REALLY don't want a baby shower!'

I was trying to convince Nicole I'd never been to a baby shower I enjoyed, and that I was fine without one. No, not fine: ecstatic! Relieved to dodge the whole thing.

I'm going to tell you why, but at the same time, I'm mindful of insulting the very few women whose showers I have attended. Including Nicole's. I really do apologise to you fabulous girls, who loved your own event.

But baby showers just aren't for me. The chocolate 'poo' inside the nappies where you have to guess which type of chocolate it is by eating the 'poo'? Nope! The competitive present-giving? Nuh. Perhaps, if it could be a bunch of friends hanging out with no fuss, I'd be keener. Besides, many of my friends my age had already been there and passed the exit of their baby-shower-attendance phase.

Despite my reluctance, I ended up having three baby showers.

And they weren't so bad.

The first one was a very quiet surprise celebration as Nicole's way of honouring my 'no baby shower' request

"

(mandate!), just me and her. We'd scheduled a morning coffee catch-up at my place, and I could hear her struggling down my side footpath. I craned my neck at the screen door to see a massive green trunk (yes, trunk) bobbing along with Nicole staggering behind it. It was that big and heavy, filled to the brim with presents.

She sighed as she heaved the thing onto my loungeroom floor. 'Well, if you won't have a baby shower, then the baby shower will have you!'

I shook my head and smiled. Typical Nicole. I sat there marvelling at the thoughtful gifts she had bought. Many of them I had no idea I needed which, in hindsight, could be a big reason for the baby shower frenzy of gift-giving. Not so much to out-present one another? Maybe.

But none of that mattered. This was perfect.

'Too much!' I kept telling Nicole as my couch slowly filled with gorgeous baby clothes, shoes, bottles, silicone plates, rattles, and contraptions I'd never seen. There were things for me too, like relaxing face masks and moisturisers.

All that aside, I had an enormous question to ask Nicole. I was a bit nervous, prompting her to say, 'It's okay, Loz. Just spit it out.'

'Well, I'm not married. And there's no one else—' Nicole nodded her head. She'd been there the whole time and knew my story better than anyone. I exhaled and continued, 'You can say "no" if you want.'

Nicole continued to nod.

'It's just that. Well, I have family who can take over if something, well, happens to me. If I… you know. If I'm suddenly not around anymore.' Nicole smiled, her eyes glistening as she waited for the rest. 'I wondered if you would be my baby's godmother. It may be for real, because it's just, um, me.'

Nicole's face crumpled into a joyous, teary mess as she nodded her head. We sat in a prolonged hug, absorbing the enormity of my request. I'm not religious, so the 'godparent' thing isn't about that. It was more about putting something in place in case my own family – Mum, Dad, or my brother – were unable to take care of my daughter.

All parents and parents-to-be need to prepare for the 'who will look after my kid/s if I fall off the perch' scenario. It's just that if you halve the number of parents involved, well, that gives it a distinct sense of urgency.

And that was how baby shower number one ended. I'd say a raging success!

Baby shower number two was another surprise affair, and this one also blew my socks off. I was walking into work the same way I did every Saturday morning, when I heard a quiet scuffle from behind the studio door. Normally, my Saturday kids are vocal and vibrant. But on this day, all I could hear was a few whispers and the teacher, my colleague and friend, calling out, 'Um, Miss Lorena. Can you come in here for a sec? I need you to look at something.'

I walked in to the students' collective, joyful calls of, 'SURPRISE!'

I looked over at my teacher friend who threw her hands into the air. 'It was their idea.'

What sweet, kind-hearted kids to organise an entire baby shower themselves, including pitching in for party food, a present, and decorations. There were more tears of joy as I made my way around the room hugging and thanking each girl.

They played music, we ate party food, we even did a 'gender reveal' – another previous hard 'no' for me. The students who thought I was having a girl stood stage right, and those on team 'boy' went stage left. I walked down the middle slowly edging toward the stage right congregation to the tune of excited squeals of, 'IT'S A GIRRRRRRRRL!' across the studio. Just divine, and a memory I'll cherish forever.

Then there was my third baby shower. A final unintended hurrah! Not bad for someone who didn't want even one, right? This time wasn't a surprise and was organised by a different boss. By this stage, my baby shower experience had been pretty good, so when she asked me if I wanted one, I surrendered and declared, 'Well, why not?'

What a fabulous afternoon. Our local café filled with excited dance teachers as they gathered to celebrate my long-awaited pregnancy. Very few of them knew of my desire to become a mum. But every one of them supported me, inspired by my story, celebrating with true delight.

When I looked around at the smiling faces there for me and my baby, I again wondered why I'd always felt so compelled to secrecy through my IVF experience. Now I was out in the light I could see so much more. There was no judgement. Not from the cohort, anyway. Just support and best wishes. It was a mind-shift, and something I'll always treasure.

Because I like to be organised and on top of things, I decided I would do an eight-week antenatal course. These classes prepare you for the birth, as well as the time leading up to it. I knew I could Google 'childbirth' and get answers, but I wanted a deeper knowledge of what was coming and what my options were.

Excitement filled me as I entered the clinic, wondering who else would be there. Perhaps I'd meet future mum friends. Maybe there would be another solo mum by choice! Or another donor-recipient family like a same-sex couple.

First to arrive, I scanned the info-packs for the one with my name on it, placed a sticky nametag on my chest, and padded across the carpet to take my place somewhere in the middle of the semicircle of plastic chairs.

I looked around the room. The walls were covered in medical posters. Mostly of the prenatal kind giving information on mental health, immunisation, and breastfeeding. An aroma of instant coffee, probably Moccona, the muddy office granule stuff, filled the room from the nearby kitchenette.

A midwife down the front was organising her presentation, sorting out props (including spooky life-like dolls), straightening papers, and penning last-minute information onto a poorly cleaned whiteboard.

Two-by-two, the other attendees walked in. My heart sank a little when the midwife closed the door after the last couple. A wash of embarrassment flooded me when I realised I'd taken up too much space, needing to shift over one seat so they could sit together.

I remained stoic. So what if I was the only one there alone? Mum had offered to come. Alice too. But as I so often did, I wanted – no, insisted! – I'd go alone. No discussion. Given I also had plans to give birth alone (more on that later), I was very happy to do this course without dragging along an accomplice.

Big mistake? Well, that's how it felt after the first session. There was a lot of talk about how 'your husband' would be the primary advocate for your decision making throughout the birthing process. Because you'll be in so much pain, you'll be delirious.

'Husband'. Not 'partner', or 'birthing partner'.

Husband.

I wondered whether I'd popped back a century to the early 1900s when it was illegal to procreate without a marriage certificate in your hand. When the midwife heard my conception story (we went around the circle one-by-one saying our names and giving a bit of background), she flinched a bit as if she'd never had a solo parent in her class before.

Maybe she hadn't. I didn't ask.

I told her about the thirteen rounds it had taken me to get pregnant and how jubilant I was to be a lucky solo mum-to-be. She replied, 'Well, thank you, Lorena. I'll try and tailor the course to fit you as best I can.'

I really hoped so. But somehow as the class went on, I felt her sense of inclusivity slip. So much so, I started skipping sessions. The ongoing narrative about husbands supporting you broke me. The midwife simply didn't make the effort to fathom my determination to give birth without a husband. Or anyone else, for that matter. She made all sorts of lovely, but ultimately 'no', recommendations. It went a little bit like this:

Midwife: 'Would you consider having your mum in the birthing suite with you?'

Me: 'I love my mum to pieces, but I do not want to put her through the ordeal of watching her daughter puffing and panting, semi-delusional, giving birth.'

Midwife: 'Have you considered a doula?'

Me: 'Yes, I have. But I don't feel comfortable with the idea of a paid alternative therapist encouraging me to squeeze a watermelon out my wazoo, when, in all honesty, I can do it by myself.' (I didn't really say that, but it's what I was thinking. I ended at the word 'idea'.)

Midwife: 'How about a good, trusted friend?'

Me: 'Definitely not, thank you.'

Truth is, I was terrified of childbirth and the pain. The midwife furrowed her brow when I annunciated this in class, telling me I mustn't have been paying close enough attention because the antenatal classes were supposed to demystify the process and reassure the birth-giver. Unbearable contractions preventing me from lucid decision making? Total loss of control? My mind spiraled, not at all comforted by the 'knowledge' (and onscreen visuals of somebody's baby emerging) I'd supposedly attained.

I didn't want anybody I knew witnessing me in that state!

But. Who would advocate for my baby if I passed out or became incoherent? Who would advocate for me? Someone (not a midwife) suggested I'd be putting unnecessary pressure on the midwives by not having a birthing partner.

I couldn't help thinking – wasn't that their job? Surely my way was also a valid option. Don't get me wrong. This midwife's caution and hesitation certainly rang alarm bells. But once I pored a little deeper into the subject, even asking about it at one of my following hospital appointments, I felt assured that I wasn't so wacky. And that plenty of women give birth without a loved one in the room.

So yes. I am going to rely on the trained midwives. I'm going to write out a birth plan. They're then going to pretend to acknowledge it, as they do with all birth plans, before casting it aside, because nothing ever goes to plan in the birthing suite.

Then, I'm going to come out the other end. As is my beautiful baby. Pun intended!

So, now you understand why I didn't graduate prenatal class. I had no choice really, and was far better prepared without it.

34

Here She Comes

October 2019, 38 weeks pregnant, age 46

Birth stories.

No one wants to hear them really, do they? Women love to tell them, though. Pretty much everyone I knew was excited to describe how their vagina tore so much they needed four stitches post-partum to sew it up again. Or something equally as harrowing.

Given the regaling of these stories was usually around the time my tummy was the size of a small planet, I didn't really appreciate the unsolicited insight.

Therefore, I'm more than aware that you, the reader, don't want or need any of the gory details of what went down on the day (days) my child emerged from me either. So, I'll spare you most of it.

You're welcome.

'This one's a special one,' a midwife told me.

I'd heard midwives say that many times before because of my intense conception story. I wasn't sure how comfortable I was with it. My usual response was to quell it with something like, 'Aww, all babies are special.'

But I knew what they meant.

I've mentioned how throughout my pregnancy, at all my appointments, I was semi-waiting for the midwives to realise how old I was and freak out. Well, eventually, this happened.

I was having bub's heartbeat monitored after she'd gone a bit quiet one afternoon at home. I was thirty-eight weeks along and had just begun maternity leave. In fact, I'd been working hard right until the end, preparing seven classes for their school concert. It was an often-hilarious challenge. Like we were speaking two different languages. I'd say, 'Can you roll on your bottom, end with both palms on the floor, and snap your legs in beside your hands.' And they'd look at me like I was speaking Martian. The sight of me and my extra-pregnant belly down on the floor trying to demonstrate, but looking more like a deranged, bulbous, duck made us all chuckle.

Finally, with all that done, I was set for a quiet week or so before my baby's arrival. Or so I thought.

Sitting with the heart monitor belt strapped around my stomach, bub's heartbeat was present and healthy. I relaxed, expecting to be sent home any minute. Suddenly, the flurry of an anxious obstetrician soared in from behind.

'No one told me you were forty-six!'

'Oh, it's on my card,' I replied.

'Well, we've got to get this baby out of you! You did IVF. And at your age? It's a huge risk to go beyond thirty-eight weeks.'

I breathed a sigh of relief. 'Well, I'm only just thirty-eight weeks today.'

That wasn't enough. The doctor kept shaking her head. 'I don't know why none of the midwives flagged this.' Then she thundered off.

I was left wondering whether my instinct had been right all along. Perhaps the midwives had been too casual about my age. What now?

I never saw that doctor again. She disappeared through an invisible time-warp somewhere in the maternity ward, replaced by an angelic midwife who gently advised me that I could, 'Go home. For now.' But I needed to be back the following day for an induction at 5pm. My baby was coming. I was going to meet her. Tomorrow!

There was suddenly so much to do. I knew due dates were estimates, but I thought I had at least another week. I needed to pack. Write my birth plan out. There were two piles of washing that needed doing, and a stack of washing up on the kitchen bench. Groceries.

But first things first, I needed to call my parents. Mum cooked a fabulous dinner that night at their place. 'The Last Supper' before meeting the little miracle that was about to catapult my life into the next realm of my dreams. Later, I lay in bed imagining, like I'd done so many times before, what life was going to be like with a baby in the house. Imagining the bliss. The hard times. How I'd cope. Imagining the four stitches I was absolutely, undoubtedly, going to end up getting in my downstairs region post-partum, and whether I'd ever be able to sit down properly again.

I couldn't sleep. Tomorrow I was going to become a mum. Tomorrow I would hold my newborn.

Tomorrow was the day I had been waiting for. For more than ten years.

I didn't meet my baby 'tomorrow'. Or the day after. Oh no, she

239

was *way* too comfortable to come out and stake her place earthside. If she'd had it her way, she would have snuggled in there for another century.

The midwives had other ideas.

I was given two doses of induction medicine, some sort of gel, as well as a kind of physical 'let's get the baby out' finger in the clacker procedure that still makes me wince when I think about it. I'd vomited everything clean from my stomach and was placed on a drip to replenish depleted fluids.

The pain was intense and constant. Luckily, I'd bought a *TENS* machine from Gumtree that I attached to my lower back. It sent soothing vibrations through the pain, acting as a sort of barrier. I paced the room for thirty-eight hours; one for each week of my pregnancy. Strangely, it was a quiet time in the birthing ward, so the midwives hung around a lot. One bade me farewell on the Saturday afternoon, went partying that night, and returned on Sunday morning to tell me all about the fabulous guy she'd met.

Eventually, a very, very (too) good-looking obstetrician came in with an ultimatum. 'You can either go home for a bit, because you're still not dilating at all, and there's no imminent baby emerging concerns…'

What? Go home? But—

'… Or. We can do a Caesarean.'

Oh.

I didn't need to think about it for long. I was tired. I'd been in an absolute shitload of pain for nearly two days. I sighed, resigned to the Caesarean. I'd hoped for a natural birth and had really, I think, done my best to achieve it. But bub was just too snug in there. Plus, this meant I could invite Mum into the operating theatre. I knew she'd love that.

Lying in the surgery, having just endured a scary anaesthetic needle that went straight into the outer membrane of my lower spinal cord, I was clammy and nervous. Mum stood behind me as midwives scurried about in preparation. Coincidentally, it was grand final footie day, so I hoped they were thinking about me and not the game. Why was my mind on fucking football? I couldn't focus on anything much, so my head was everywhere. What if something went wrong? Last time I was in surgery was for my final egg pick-up. That certainly hadn't gone to plan.

What if my baby doesn't cry?

I didn't realise they'd already made the incision. Suddenly, out of nowhere, the doctor told Mum to look over the curtain if she wanted to see him pull my baby out. Did she ever! A midwife clicked my phone camera, forever capturing the arrival of my precious girl. The doctor held her up for me to see, *Lion King* style. She was perfect. Eyes open, blinking, looking. He carried her to a nearby table as I lay in silence, waiting for the cries. Those first cries every mother holds her breath for.

Where are they?

Mum was over at the table, and I searched her face. A smile! My baby must be okay. There were some small gurgles, and then the crying. THE CRYING! The sound that would no doubt cost me sleep and sanity in the very near future, but for now it was all I wanted to hear.

It was around that moment the doctor asked Mum to cut the umbilical cord. What a moment for her.

Then my baby was brought to me.

I looked at her through hazy tears.

Did I love her yet? Was she actually mine? I'd used a donor egg. How did I feel about that in this moment?

I felt that I was absolutely, one-hundred gazillion percent, her mother from the moment my eyes absorbed her. I loved her immediately, immeasurably. She was mine, mine, mine! Donor egg, or not. Didn't matter. I looked at my baby, this newborn I'd been waiting for, for so long, and I held her close, telling her 'I love you,' over, and over again. That little hatching embryo was now the reason for my existence. My everything.

My life was hers, now. From that moment on, I would not stop loving her and living for her. My quest to become a solo mum by choice was complete. The love of my life had finally arrived.

35

The Life I'd Dreamed Of

October 2019, Bub is a few hours old

I never wanted to let go of her. I'd search her face for clues as to who she was. Who she'd grow up to be. She seemed so wise already, with her long 'piano hands', her button nose, and eyes that were taking in everything.

I already knew her name. I think everyone knew what I was going to call her. I just had one thing to ask Mum before I made the announcement.

My parents had been in and out during the hour or two after my baby's arrival. But they were pretty exhausted, ready to head home and chill. I was due to spend a few days in hospital to recover, so they'd be back to visit their granddaughter soon enough.

'Oh, before you go, I have something I want to ask you, Mum.'

She scooped bub out of my arms as I gently propped myself up in the bed. I was lucky enough to have been allocated a private room due to the unusually quiet patch. A miracle in a public hospital.

Mum and Dad were poised for my question.

'You guys have probably guessed I'm calling her Tyler.' I paused for the expected nods and smiles. 'But I was wondering,

Mum… And you can say no if it's too weird, but could her second name be Kathleen? After you?'

Well, Mum jumped up. 'Of course. That's lovely, sweetie.' She leaned down and gave me a big hug, with Tyler Kathleen Otes gently squeezed in between. 'Thank you,' she said kissing my forehead. Dad got up and rubbed my arm, a huge grin on his face. His surname would also be a part of his granddaughter's legacy. The three of us, all included.

They left walking on air and I, for the first time, was alone with my baby girl.

Midwives came in and out. They told me to holler if I needed help. Tyler seemed to be the loudest in the ward, crying all night. Granted, there weren't many babies there because it was so quiet, but I thought a midwife might come in and give me a hand to soothe her. Even after I rang the bell, no one hung around much.

I assumed this was what 'on my own' meant – that first night in hospital. I'm sure in hindsight, when the midwives offered to help, they didn't mean rocking my newborn to sleep. But still, I was confused. If I held her, she was alright. We were getting the hang of breastfeeding, though I felt like I had no idea what I was doing. Each midwife had a different method.

'No. Like this,' a hefty Amazonian woman said, slamming her hands onto my shoulders. 'Relax!' Then she whipped my boob out and attached Tyler to it. Any scrap of dignity I had was cast out the window. I wasn't allowed to sleep with Tyler on me in case, heaven forbid, she dropped off the bed. I was instructed to put her in her crib at my bedside so we could both rest.

Truth be told, I was ready to go home. It's just that my body wasn't. Far from it. You know me by now; I don't like to get graphic. But I want to touch on something here that I wasn't prepared for, that nobody talks about. I'd noticed the size of the maternity pads in the birthing suite during my induction ordeal. They were sleeping bags! Sleeping bags that were supposed to go inside your undies. 'They must be for emergencies,' I thought to myself.

Oh, no. Not for emergencies. Since giving birth, I'd lost so much blood down there, I'd soaked through one of those sleeping bags every couple of hours. Yes, through my vagina. It has nothing to do with whether you've had a Caesarean or not, that blood cometh. And cometh. And floweth in copious amounteth. And because of my Caesarean, I was still unable to walk around, so the poor midwives had the arduous task of changing those sleeping bags on my behalf.

Eventually after twenty-four hours of giving birth when I was finally able to stand up and shower, the gushes of blood made my head spin, causing me to grip on to the railings for fear I was going to end up in a crimson heap on the floor.

I just wasn't prepared for it. Nor was I prepared for the immense swelling of my downstairs area to the point I could barely walk, but that's a story for another time.

Back to my first night with my Tyler. Who I had already nicknamed 'Tylo'. It hadn't even been a day, and I was dealing out bogan Aussie nicknames. I had to put a kibosh on that because, Tylo? Really? No, Lorena.

I made it through the first night by staying awake for most of it, cuddling and chatting to my girl. She mostly slept on me, and in teeny tiny snippets in the bassinet. She made cute gargly noises and loud gaspy sounds. I'd been told that newborns were noisy sleepers but had somehow pictured it differently.

Friends and family turned up over the coming days. I was

glad to see them, but it was exhausting too. Many of them held off for a home visit later which I appreciated. Then, after three days, it was home time!

I dressed Tyler in her 'homecoming outfit', a tiny pink onesie and knitted hat that barely stayed on her head it was so big for her. I folded her tightly into a muslin cloth before dressing myself, pulling on a pair of leggings, a jumper and a hat – the first non-sleepwear I'd donned in almost a week. I felt a smidgen like 'me' again which was momentarily nice.

Placing Tyler in her car seat felt a little bit like dangling her over a balcony. She was so tiny, all I could think of was the danger I was putting her in. I kissed her forehead and sat in the back seat beside her, my hand across her chest the whole time, eyes never averting from her divine face. So in love with this little creature I'd made.

Dad was a careful driver at the best of times, and I'm sure he didn't exceed forty kilometres per hour the whole five-kilometre back-road drive home. We made it, and I handed Tyler to Mum to carry across the threshold for the first time.

We popped a bottle of champers, raising a glass to my new arrival. Fonzi joined the celebration with feline caution and an element of *who the hell have you brought home?*

Yes, I was a solo mum by choice, but I knew I was not alone. My parents shared the joy of the arrival of this stupendously precious child in a way I could only have imagined. They already loved her beyond words. And they planned on being there for us both, no matter what.

Eventually, as all things must end, they headed home. 'I can stay the night if you'd like,' Mum insisted.

But I counter-insisted that we'd be fine. 'This is what it's all about.'

'Well, just let me know if you need anything,' Mum added, as they closed the screen door and headed up the footpath, blowing kisses back at us on their way.

Leaving me, for the first time, all alone with my newborn.

36

The Fourth Trimester

October 2019, Tyler is home

Fonzi had always been 'man of the house'. Now, even more so – though I wasn't convinced he thought having Tyler there to stay was necessarily a good thing. After all, before her arrival, it had just been him and me having nightly winter snuggles and lap time on the couch. Suddenly, I was somewhat preoccupied with an exceedingly noisy intruder in the house. Worse still, she appeared to be staying.

Those first moments with Tyler were intriguing. So much was running through my head as I sat in what would become our regular spot on the couch for breastfeeding. For hours she'd guzzle and sleep. Fonzi tried to crawl up and share some lap too, succeeding for a while, sniffing Tyler and trying to work out whether she was a threat.

Many people anticipate they'll be scared or in a state of worry during those first few days bringing a newborn home. But I was neither. I had inklings of worry that something might go wrong. But given that I pretty much never let go of her, I knew she was safe.

Of course, never letting go of a tiny human poses plenty of problems. How was I going to get anything done? Well, of course, I found ways. I could hold her in one arm as I microwaved one of the freezer meals Mum had prepared for me. (I had a freezer full of them.) I could have a thirty-second shower before Tyler's crying became incessant, no longer content to lie alone on her little bouncer. I could wipe kitchen surfaces with her in my arms, popping washing in the machine as she lay gargling for twenty-five seconds on a soft blanket on the floor.

Bedtime always made me nervous, though.

I needed sleep. I hadn't had much in the hospital, and knew that as a newborn, Tyler would sleep more than ever. I just had to find a way to match her pattern.

It didn't work. On that first night, she'd howl whenever I attempted to put her down. Well, of course she did. Why wouldn't she? I was her warm, snuggly, milk-producing mummy. But my eyes were drooping like a Dali clock, and I couldn't figure out a way forward. I decided to put her bassinet in my bedroom by the bed. Surely I could get her to snooze in there if I set her down softly-softly, a little milk-drunk.

Anyone who's looked after a newborn knows that usually doesn't happen. I scooped her up and tried again. It was around midnight by this stage, though the concept of time mostly alluded me.

I'd been advised not to co-sleep for myriad reasons, number one being it can be fatal. Tiny babies can be accidently smothered in bedding, or by other people in the bed, with devastating consequences. Having weighed everything up, and putting all the recommended measures in place, including not having any bedclothes on Tyler's side (summer was coming, so that was increasingly easy), never drinking alcohol (I hadn't been anyway) and a bunch of other things, I cautiously entered the bed-sharing domain.

I am not advocating or recommending this. Seriously, each parent must make their own informed decision. Especially if there's more than one adult in the bed! But for me, it evolved into a nightly thing, and even at the time of writing, my five-year-old has never, not one night, slept anywhere but by my side. Bit of a spoiler there, sorry. It's just that I've always surprised myself by how much of the attachment parenting philosophy I've inadvertently applied to my role as Tyler's mum. I used to scoff at parents who bought bigger beds to accommodate their entire brood. Pah, what did I know?

I lay on my side – and I'll never forget this feeling, it makes me teary every time I think of it. After a few attempts, I felt the gentle latch of my little girl as she fed herself to sleep. Those tiny tugs as she drew comfort from her mummy were moments of heaven for me as I lay motionless for fear of disturbing her. The beating of my augmented, jubilant heart, the only movement in my body.

I continued attempting to put Tyler down in her bassinet but now she knew how great she could have it sleeping next to her mummy, why would she settle for anything else? I didn't blame her! Perhaps if I'd had a partner he could have shared the load a little. Who knows? It's not something I thought about very often.

The baby blues kicked in, as predicted, around a week after Tyler was born. I thought I was doing alright. Correction: I *was* doing alright. But that didn't make me immune to the anecdotal hormone shifts that happen after giving birth.

I was tired. So bloody tired. Yes, I'd figured out a plan that enabled me to get a bit of light sleep. And Mum and Dad were over every other day to help out. Mum would put on a load of washing, clear the washing up, or bring food. Or they'd hold Tyler so I could get a few things done.

On around day seven, a midwife turned up for one of Tyler's checks. It was a home visit where they check us both, and family life in general. On this day I was having more trouble than usual getting Tyler to sleep.

I'd been pacing the room with her in my arms, rocking, singing. Even on me, she was restless. I understood why – she'd just spent nine months snuggled up in my uterus. Earthside, the breathing air thing alone would have been a pain in the arse, much less all the other stuff she was learning and enduring.

I didn't stand a chance on this day, the threat of my own erupting tears imminent. When the midwife popped Tyler on the scales, she appeared to have lost a chunk of weight. My head hammered with the narrative I was failing as a mum. *I can't even feed her enough. There must have been a reason the universe made it so hard for me to become a mother, because I clearly suck at it.*

The midwife tilted her head. 'Hmm, that's odd. Tyler looks healthy enough. Here, hold her for a sec and I'll check the scales are working properly.'

I sobbed openly as she carefully lowered my 'malnourished' baby into my arms, fiddling with the mechanics of the scales, then placing Tyler back on. 'Four-hundred grams!' The midwife did a little happy dance. 'Tyler's *gained* weight, Lorena. These scales play up sometimes. But even if she hadn't gained anything, it's completely normal for her to fluctuate in these early stages.'

She put her arm around me as I picked up my girl, pressing her to my chest. 'You're doing great, Mum. Have a little cry, it's okay.'

I told her I didn't think I'd get the baby blues, because I'd been waiting so long to become a mum. She shook her head. 'It makes no difference. I've almost never visited a mother who didn't have the baby blues in some form.' I felt immediately at ease. 'Now, you're a solo parent. Do you have anyone to help you?'

'Yes. My parents.'

'Well, rely on them. Accept their help. It's okay to ask.'

My sobs increased as the midwife somehow managed to press the exact button I was most fearful of, the *asking for help* button. I'd started using it but still felt guilty putting people out. Even my parents, who had clearly demonstrated time and time again that it was never an issue. 'I'll see how I go, but yes, I'll try.'

The midwife gave me a look that suggested she knew exactly what I was thinking, and repeated, 'It's okay to ask for help, Lorena.' She paused. 'Now, is there anything else you need?'

I mentioned I was having a hard time getting Tyler to sleep. She looked around the room and saw a little rocker thing someone had given us from their own baby phase. 'Here, this could work.'

She took Tyler into her arms and gently placed her in the rocker. 'She can camp out here for a bit. You don't have to have her in her bassinet to sleep.'

'Really?'

'Of course not. Have her out here where she can be near you. Amid the noise of the day.' And sure enough, Tyler lay there, quite happily for the time being at least, wriggling in that way newborns do.

The midwife left and I breathed. For approximately forty-two seconds. Then Tyler's gargles deteriorated to mournful sobs. Oh well, it was a quick respite, but at least I'd had one. Using that little rocker for Tyler's day sleeps became a life saver. And as the baby blues waned, the life of our tiny, beautiful family began to take on some sort of idyllic regularity. Don't get me wrong, things weren't *Brady Bunch* perfect, but life was beginning to feel sweet and harmonious.

37

The Rites of Passage of Motherhood

October 2019, Tyler is two weeks old

Hordes of visitors came and went in those first weeks which was lovely. Friends and family were all dying to meet the little bundle I'd finally created. There was a plethora of cuddles, a squillion photos, many, many gifts, and general adoration. The extended family I'd always dared to hope for.

One of our highlight visits was from my brother and his family. My brother lives a three-hour drive away, so I knew we wouldn't get to see him all that often. But I'd always had a special bond with his son, my nephew, when he was little, so I had a feeling my brother would naturally reciprocate that with his niece. And boy, did he! From the moment he first held her, sparks flew. I felt emotional as I saw him introduce himself to her, knowing he was going to be a key male figure in Tyler's life.

Mum and Dad's frequent presence continued. Mum kept my freezer loaded with precooked dinners. 'It's easy, sweetie. I just cook a bit more when I'm making dinner for us.' She'd rearrange my freezer to squeeze the tubs of her culinary creations inside. My favourite was her chicken risotto. Warming, filling, and yum!

At around four weeks I was due to attend my first mothers'

group. This was a funny one, because there was a time I loathed the idea of sitting around in a circle with a bunch of new mums discussing their baby's faecal consistency while sipping take-away lattes. But then, more recently, I'd changed my tune a little, thinking of mothers' groups more as a rite of passage. Maybe I'd bond with some of the other mums and Tyler and I would end up with lifelong friends.

I still wasn't supposed to drive after my Caesarean and wasn't willing to risk it. So, I wrapped Tyler up, put her in her pram, and walked up to the village community hall where the first few mothers' group sessions took place. I laugh when I think back at those walks. I'd stopped to breastfeed her three times in twenty minutes. Every time she cried, I'd pick her up, perch myself on someone's low boundary brick wall and whip out a boob.

Eventually I arrived, taking a seat among the group of convening soon-perhaps-friends. It was like going to a new high school. Who would end up my bestie? A great metaphor for what my mothers' group experience turned out to be.

At first it seemed okay. Around twenty-five mums in various states of fatigue and disarray. No fellow solo mums, but I'd prepared myself for that after the antenatal two-by-two demographic. Over time, I broke off with a small contingent who were blunt, funny, and dare I say it, a little bitchy. I often refer to them as the 'Cool Mums of mothers' group.' But they weren't, really. Smug, more like. And off-limits to the larger part of the group who would be discussed incessantly.

'Did you notice how much of a diva Maree's baby is already?' one would say. At the time I was just happy to be accepted. And relieved that the finger wasn't being pointed at me and my own newborn, who was not shy to put on an Oscar-winning performance of her own.

Another Cool Mum added, 'I heard Helena's baby already sleeps through the night! She must be control-crying already. Tut-tut.'

Really, everyone was just trying to do their best. Our little chit-chat sessions reassured us that our own babies were doing 'better' than everyone else's. When one mum's son dared to start walking at just eight months, fractures of envy flashed through us as we secretly jibed about how 'she must be training him'.

I mean, really?

I started unravelling myself from these women after that. The way some of them spoke about their husbands was a low blow too. To me, a new friendship circle isn't the place to reveal that your husband is 'lazy and does nothing to help'. I'd made my choice not to have an 'adult child' in my life and discussing it felt cruel. And if anything, it put another notch in the belt of my solo mum life choice.

Don't get me wrong. These women had their moments of gloriousness. They were younger than me by at least a decade, quick off the mark, and could hold a speed-gif texting conversation like no one I've met since. I miss that part. Eventually one left the group, one moved interstate, and well, I paddled away. Perhaps Tyler and I would make lifelong friends further downstream.

If one thing was going well for Tyler and me, it was breastfeeding. She fed on demand, so I never scheduled, or made notes of 'right boob', 'left boob'. If Tyler was hungry, and she always was, it was one boob or the other. And endless couch time.

I kept a food stash on a small coffee table for emergencies. I couldn't just holler, 'Darling, would you mind making me a cup of tea?' And there were certainly no offers of, 'Sure, would you like a sandwich, too?'

I had fruit, breakfast bickies, and muesli bars that I'd set up on the coffee table each night before bed. I also tried to avoid using my phone while Tyler fed, choosing to read instead. Of course, I'm not a saint. Facebook called! Often. But I didn't want the phone radiation close to Tyler's head for hours each day, so I hammered through some great novels and memoirs instead. They also acted as little portals that gave me a sense of the bigger world around my blissful microcosm.

The days were slow and sometimes long, and I relished Tyler's small milestones. Her first smile (fart, I know); her eyes studying my face, recognising me as Mum; her strength building up every day, and the diminishing newborn look.

Some things were hard, though.

Despite the baby bath being a godsend, it was awkward to empty. I set it up in the laundry where a pipe connected from the taps made it easy to fill. Tyler loved her baths and it was part of our nightly ritual. Sometimes Fonzi would jump up to see what was going on, almost toppling into the water and giving us all a fright.

Emptying the tub sucked. It was heavy! And I'd had major surgery, so I wasn't supposed to lift anything. I'd found a way to crane the tub over the sink to empty the water. But one day it threatened to topple, so I had to heave it back into place.

I felt a sharp agonising stab across my Caesarean scar which continued to pulsate. What had I done? Tyler was safely in her bouncer as I assessed the damage. Nothing had burst, my scar seemed intact. For the following days I winced whenever I lifted Tyler. It took a week for my scar to feel right again, and perhaps I should have seen a doctor. (Lorena, you SHOULD have seen a doctor!)

It was moments like these where I could have done with another person around. Things are bound to happen. And it could just as easily have occurred when a partner was at work. But I knew I had the lower hand with physical stuff, especially heavy lifting.

Another time I felt alone was when I decided I'd give control-crying a go. I didn't call it that, though. The manual I was going by gave it the guise of 'sleep training'. Anyway, it's all the same thing, where you basically hang around your child's bedroom for a certain (often alarmingly specific) amount of time, then creep out when they become quiet (in theory, asleep). Then, if they wake and cry, you're supposed to leave them for, in my case, twenty-two minutes.

Twenty-two minutes? More like the longest one-thousand-three-hundred-and-twenty seconds of my night-after-night life. Pure hell. Tyler would cry, then scream. I'd try to keep busy by doing the washing up, my own tears flooding the soapy water. I still think of it when I wash up today, it was so distressing.

But, over time – say, a fortnight – Tyler worked out that Mummy was not coming and she needed to stop crying and go to sleep by herself. My heart breaks thinking about her being all alone in her room, scared, exhausted, and out of tears.

The relief that washed over me when the crying stopped, and the house went silent was so palpable it was physical. I'd collapse on the couch, throw the television on and have a cup of tea. Those moments lasted an hour or so, but were a savoured respite. Did they counterbalance the painful way we got there? I'm still not sure. Did I feel guilty as hell? Yes. Would it have been easier with a partner? Perhaps. But in some ways, it was good not to be comforted. To be able to feel the rawness that pulsed through me at the sound of my daughter's heightened distress. With no one there to dull that down, it became ingrained.

So, when one of those notorious 'sleep regressions' the baby books tell you about kicked in a few weeks later, and all the control-crying work fell to the wayside, there was no way I was going there again. Tyler always ended up in my bed anyway. Now, I'd just feed her to sleep then and there.

No one judged me. Even old-school folk like my parents smiled and said, 'Well if it works for you, then that's what you should do.'

And that's what I have continued to do, unashamedly, willingly, and happily.

38

This Section of the Birth Certificate
Will Remain Blank

December 2019, Tyler is 10 weeks old

Filling out a birth certificate application should be straight-forward. But not for us. I needed to collect evidence. Because apparently, you can't just put a blank space in the 'father' section without jumping through a bunch of circus hoops.

I decided the easiest first step was to call the issuing office. Sitting on hold for the usual four decades was okay because I was nap-trapped under a baby and a cat.

Eventually, a lifeform emerged from the other end of the line. 'How can I help you today?'

'I need to find out the required documentation for my daughter's birth certificate when there is no father, please.'

'Pardon?'

I repeated the question, slowly, sans patronising tone.

'So, the father is absent?'

'There is no father. There is a donor.'

'Then the donor is listed on the certificate.'

Tyler roused on my lap, possibly sensing the tension building in my chest. I exhaled. 'The donor is anonymous, therefore not the father.'

'Well, then you need to list the name of the person who IS the father.'

The conversation went round and around like this for a good few minutes. I was becoming increasingly uncomfortable having the 'there is no father' phrase on repeat. It was a fact of our lives, yes, and one that I was more than fine with. But having to say the words continually was beginning to feel like a knife in the groundhog gut. That somehow as a family who didn't fit the mould, we were rendered as 'too difficult' to create an accurate record of my daughter's birth and status.

I articulated our situation again, finally getting some form of recognition from the other end. 'So, you won't be claiming child support from this donor?'

Is this what it came down to? Whether I intended to claim child support? I was put on hold while the assistant chatted to her supervisor, returning shortly with the information I needed – written evidence of Tyler's conception from my fertility doctor. Great. Easy! I was relieved to hang up, knowing I was one step closer to getting Tyler's official documentation.

Still nap-trapped, I immediately emailed our overseas fertility clinic. Within hours they sent me a reference confirming I'd used a donor, who was neither the 'intended parent', or Tyler's father in any sense.

It was quite confronting. I pictured Tyler, ten years from now, asking me why the 'father' section of her birth certificate was blank. We'd already started reading books on donor conception at bedtime. Silly as it sometimes felt reading to a newborn who didn't understand a word I was saying, I persisted every night. Usually, they were books that explained donor conception in very simple terms. I wanted to ensure I gave my daughter a sense of self from the beginning.

I was very consistent with this because I'd read time and time again that full early disclosure is the recommended practice. If the truth isn't part of Tyler's life story from day one, we risk an identity crisis when she finds out later in life.

Tyler will always know how she was made. Well, as a baby she doesn't 'know', but through reading, I'd already started forming the language I planned to use in the future. Tweaking words until they began to flow and feel right.

In the early newborn stage, when Tyler slept in my arms, I would sit in her room in the rocking chair, feed her, and tell her everything I knew about her creation.

Tyler, you know, Mummy really wanted you. In fact, you were the most wanted baby in the world — no, the universe! There's nothing bigger than the universe. And it is just the tiniest part of how much I love you!

But Mummy had trouble finding you. There wasn't anyone I knew who would make a great daddy for our family. I wanted you so much though, I came up with another idea.

I asked a special doctor for some help, and you know what? He said, "Yes." That made Mummy super excited, and I jumped for joy!

The doctor said I needed extra help, so I asked a man and a woman to donate some tiny little cells so I could make you. It took ages. Years. Forever!

I was getting impatient. I just wanted to meet you. So, I kept trying.

I even got on a plane and went far away to a new doctor, and you know what? It worked! Here you are, my sweet. In my arms. The most beautiful, precious child in the entire universe and beyond.

And remember — I'll always be your mummy. Even if sometimes, when you're older, things might feel confusing. And if you ever have any questions. Or worries. I'm always, always, here.'

Something along those lines. It changed every time and still does. Now, at five years old, we have *The Book of Tyler*. A blank notebook that I 'read' to my daughter all about her conception story. I make up the words on the spot, but the plot stays the same. She loves it, asking for it regularly.

We also have an actual *Book of Tyler*. This one contains pictures of both donors and the words our family uses to describe them. For example, the female donor could be referred to as just that, or the genetic parent, or the genetic mother. I'm Tyler's biological mother (because I carried her – though there are different points of view on this). I'm also Mum, Mama, Mummy, and so on. And in our house, the sperm donor is either referred to as just that, or the male donor, or genetic father. There may also be 'donor siblings' – other children born using one of my donors.

These are the words that are natural and comfortable for us at the moment. But they're still 'my' words. Tyler can choose her own when she's older if she wants. Or maybe she'll be happy with the ones we have. I'll let her lead the way when she's ready, when she's starting to grasp the concept of her creation and what it means for her in the bigger picture.

There are many differing views on donor conception, especially where the donors are anonymous. In Australia, at the time of writing, gamete donation falls under the banner of 'ID release at eighteen years old'. This means that when a child turns eighteen, they can legally have access to the donor's information. This doesn't mean the sperm donor becomes their father. Far from it. It means they can know his identity and make contact.

Our family is slightly different as both my donors were anonymous. This doesn't mean Tyler will never know her genetic origins. It's just going to be harder. We have stacks of information from our clinic on both donor's medical backgrounds, traits, and details I know will help Tyler better understand her genetic lineage. And hopefully we'll connect with donor siblings along the way as well.

39

Epic Mum-Fails
and Flirtations with Mum-Rage

January 2020, Tyler is 4 months old

For a long while, I was in the deep trenches of the early baby phase. I didn't know what day it was half the time. Or even what hour it was. None of it mattered. I had my Tyler. And it felt natural to allow life to slow down a little.

I was so in love with the little creature I'd created. Her cute squishy face, her ever-inquisitive eyes. The unfolding of her world each day with tiny milestones like being able to roll over, reacting to my voice, and giggling to the sound of my laughter. She also held a somewhat dangerous fascination with her furry brother, Fonzi. He was still quite cautious and unsure who this tiny, noisy, often smelly new house guest was, probably hoping she'd be making her departure sometime soon. *Oh, Fonz, if only you knew.*

He knew. And one day, at just four months, Tyler grabbed onto his ear and gave it a tug. He returned the gesture with a swipe across the face, missing her eye by millimetres! This happened to be the very same day Tyler rolled over and off the bed, landing splat on the (thankfully cushion-covered) ground. I was just a step away, engaged in the three-ringed-circus act of getting dressed at lightning-speed before Tyler rolled over and, well, risked going kaput.

Fail.

Hearing the gentle 'thump', followed by the not-so-gentle cries of my baby, I launched over to her, inspecting every inch until I was sure she was okay. We'd both had a big fright. Lesson learned for Mummy: don't bother getting dressed. Stay in your pyjamas all day. Never leave the house. Then at least nobody gets hurt.

It really was an exhausting and emotional time. Unexpected incidents like this hit hard, making me question this 'natural mothering ability' others claimed I had. People say those things when you're in your best form. You're in a café, discretely breastfeeding your baby and your best friend leans over and says, 'Loz – you were born to be a mum.'

But that best friend didn't just witness your baby fall off your bed while you were wrangling yourself into a maternity bra. They didn't see your baby get swiped by the family cat, with a deep enough cut under her eye for it to bleed out into a bruise that made her look like she'd had two rounds with Ali.

Half the time, I was winging motherhood. Making it up as I went along. One thing I can be sure of, though – I was damned relieved to not have another opinion in the house. The 'you should do it this way' narrative would have driven me nuts.

Which brings me to the subject of mum-rage. Have I had it? Hmm, I've flirted with it every now and then. I've been known to throw a hairbrush or two in my time, and prone to a massive door slam more than once in my life, mostly as a teenager. And there's one thing teenagers have in common with mothers of little babies: hormones. The dreaded hormones that control our lives, our ups, our downs, the rush, the crash, the *I fucking hate myself right now, this world sux, and I'm a terrible mother/friend/human.*

I went through a bit of that in the early days. Ha, who am I kidding? I can be a moody-as-hell mum even now. Especially when I'm furious with my daughter for something (usually trivial) like spilling chocolate milk on the couch for the trillionth time after I specifically asked her not to drink it on there. And. I. Lose. My. Shit.

Way back at the mostly useless antenatal course I attended, a few helpful things were discussed. Like what to do when your newborn cries and you become triggered. Of course, the midwife's first advice was always, 'Hand your baby to your husband.' Yeah, great. Even the women in the group with husbands did a surreptitious eyeroll at that one. Because when does a baby ever unleash frenzied crying fits when help is actually at hand? *Murphy's Law* Number One.

I needed a plan for my own family dynamic. The midwife suggested that if the baby cries and you're feeling your anger boiling up, the best thing to do is put the baby in a safe place (their bassinet or cot) and walk away. For up to fifteen minutes.

FIFTEEN MINUTES! 'Make yourself a cup of tea,' she said. A cup of tea? With an inconsolable baby left all alone in a dark room? I could never.

Could I?

Within three weeks of the newborn fog, I'd put that advice into practice at least twice. Maybe more. I never walked away for as long as fifteen minutes. Usually barely two. But the permission that midwife granted to do this very simple act was an absolute godsend. I could regain my composure and breathe a little. Probably enough reason alone to have made that antenatal course worth it.

My biggest trigger was the constant crying. Plain old incessant crying. There were times I couldn't get Tyler to stop. Textbook early mum concerns, but at the time it felt like I was the only human in the world. I tried everything. Putting her in a papoose-style carrier, walking her in a pram (which worked, but how long can you do that for?), feeding her (which also worked, but I refer back to my previous point).

I had ample help from Mum and Dad, but it was still a twenty-four/seven affair as the sole parent. There was no 'partner' to pass Tyler to when I needed a spontaneous three-minute breakdown to shake off my frustration and resume my role as Mother Mary.

Yes, I have shouted at my daughter. Not often. In fact, very rarely. I wish I hadn't, but I'm not one of those always calm, always controlled parents. Any triggers I have are my own personal issues, not my child's and I'm mindful not to inflict them onto her. Now she's five, if she's 'misbehaving', and I find myself getting increasingly wound up about it, sometimes it only takes the smallest thing for the scales to tip. That can be confusing for Tyler as her mum storms off, slams the bedroom door and demands five minutes.

We always talk about these incidents afterward. Because usually it isn't just me. Tyler, along with all small children, can really push buttons. She is very determined (familiar), persistent (gawd), stubborn (here we go!), and is definitely still learning her manners. But as I'm the adult in the house, and as there's no buffer zone in the form of another adult, I must work twice as hard to recognise and take hold of my triggers well before they take hold of me.

It ain't easy. And I sometimes disparagingly ask myself, *Why did you work so hard to bring this child into the world if you're going to allow your own rage to strangle your happiness?* We can't be 'happy' all the time. But we can work through our moments. I may have chosen the solo mum path, but that doesn't mean I'm not allowed to say there are hard days. It's okay to acknowledge them, drown in them a little, then resurface and do better.

I continue to strive for this every day. And while Tyler keeps her cheeky, boundary-pushing sassiness, she's also a thriving, funny, caring, understanding little girl who expresses her love and emotions right out on the tip of each eyelash. In the exact spot where I place gentle kisses each night while she sleeps.

40

Time to Earn Some Money

February 2020, Tyler is 5 months old

I was most definitely NOT ready to go back to work! I wanted much more time with my baby and wasn't a mum who 'needed' work as part of her identity. Not anymore, anyway. My desire to revel in motherhood was all consuming. I wanted to stay at home with my girl endlessly.

But I had to go back. I couldn't risk losing the positions that had been held open for me. Also, I needed the money. Luckily, I love my job!

My dance teacher work was seasonal, which meant during the school holidays, regular classes stopped. This was handy for the timing of Tyler's arrival, because it enabled me to take off term four, the summer holidays, and then return to work in what originally seemed like 'forever-later' the following year. Tyler was still only five months old when term one, 2020, began. Practically a newborn, or so it felt. But my bosses wanted me back. So, I chose carefully how I would distribute these golden, precious hours.

My heart ached. We hadn't spent a single minute apart since the day Tyler was born. Yes, other people held her while I ducked to the loo or something. But we'd always been under the same roof.

Now I was going to have to gear up and drive to another building in another suburb, away from my daughter, tugging the invisible string that connected us, changing our immediacy in ways I wasn't ready for.

I had to prepare us both.

In the hour or so I had at night where Tyler lay sleeping, and I drank tea and snuck in a *Married at First Sight* episode (oh my God, am I putting this into print? Only one season, I swear!), I would attach the breast pump and express milk into little plastic bags. This was so Mum could bottle-feed my milk to Tyler when I was at work. A great plan, right?

Nope. Tyler just wouldn't take a bottle. Of course, whenever I tried, I could see her, five months old, looking up at me with a smirk on her face as if to say, 'You're kidding me, right?' Well, I had the real thing: two engorged sources of deliciousness dangling right there between us, so why would she want a bottle? When Mum tried the bottle and Tyler refused it in the same steadfast way, we knew we were in a fix. We'd given it a few futile goes in the lead-up to my ever-looming first day back.

A quick paragraph here on why I decided not to send Tyler to daycare, opting instead for my parents to take care of her. Number one is because as a family, that's what we all wanted. My parents relished the opportunity to spend time with their granddaughter, so in that way it was perfect. Number two, is that my hours were often late and out of daycare time. I didn't need to work long hours to make decent money so I wouldn't have to work that much.

'But how will she socialise?' people asked. Strangers in the playground, friends, or other mums. Seriously, she's five months old. Socialise? For me, that was the last reason to send her to daycare.

So, I kept my daughter home. Not one other person I know did that. Not one! That's not to give a dig to the parents who put their kiddos into daycare, especially the ones who have no choice. Daycare's a great invention and a necessity for society. It's also vital for a lot of solo mums by choice who don't have the options afforded to me. And believe me, I know women who cried a deluge of tears having to leave their kids because it's the only way they could work. I consider myself exceptionally lucky I had the opportunity to choose. Yes, we were skint. Yes, I was burning through my savings. But the biggest *yes* was that I had my girl with family all the time. And that mattered to me.

My first day back had arrived. I could hear Mum and Dad's footsteps nearing as they walked down our footpath toward the front door. Dread rose in my throat like the death knell of the attachment I'd worked so hard to forge with my daughter.

It often struck me as strange that a person like me, so independent, such a solo traveller in life, came to be so attached to my tiny human. Me, the one who craved solitude like it was my only lifeline, who needed 'alone' time constantly and consistently. How could that have changed so much?

It's simple. I just loved Tyler more than I could fathom. She was my superstar, with me her biggest fan. I wanted her next to me, sleeping on me, cuddles, floor play, walks in the pram. I never craved for someone to come over and look after her while I popped out for a massage or dinner with a friend. None of that was on the cards, and to be honest even now she's older, I'd still take her everywhere with me if I could. I'd never holiday without her, and the idea of a holiday nanny, or 'kids club' just isn't on our dance card.

My parents were also like that with my brother and me. In fact, our first family holiday was to Fiji when I was nine. Then China at eleven. One in, all in. No kids club or staying home with relatives. And I value that. Of course, good on you if you can head off to scale Everest for a week and leave your kids back home with Auntie Florence. I realise for mental health these away times can be necessary. But for me, I'd prefer to jet-set with Tyler in tow, attempting Everest with her in a papoose on my back.

But I digress.

I also had an innate fear (psychologists, prepare; you're going to have a field day with this one) of going back to life before Tyler. Not the life in my twenties and early thirties when I was partying and having fun. I'm talking about the life of a single woman trying to conceive. You've read the pages. It was tough. I couldn't fully let go of the very concrete fear that I'd somehow end up back there again. Whenever I've been out without Tyler – especially, at first – I'd often become inundated with the dread of what life would be like if my quest to be a mother had failed. Whenever I was out alone, I wondered, *Is she a dream? Do I really have her?* To this day that haunts me. Though now she's at school, I'm getting more used to it.

Mum and Dad had arrived. 'We'll be alright, sweetie,' Mum assured me as she entered our place, gently taking Tyler into her arms. 'If she's hungry, she'll eat.' We were all very stressed about my potentially famished daughter. The reality was that nobody was going to starve. Tyler may get a bit hungry and grumbly, but I was only gone a few hours (though centuries in my mind). And her deliciously chubby little body had plenty of reserve to keep her well and truly alive for that time.

I dug my face into Tyler's sweet, biscuity tufts of hair, my eyes squeezing shut to numb the sting as I told her, 'I love you.' Then I swung around and walked out the door.

I must have sat in my car gathering my wits for a good five minutes after I left the house. *Breathe,* I told myself. *You can do this.* She just seemed so young. Too young to be apart from her mummy. I scrunched my eyes again as tears pushed their way through. I knew I just had to go.

I don't recall the drive to work. Normally it took around fifteen minutes, but I was in a trance, thinking of Tyler, wondering how everything was going. My insidious attempts to focus on the task at hand – the class I was about to teach – went by the wayside as anxiety hammered every nerve in my body.

Lumbering into the all too familiar dance studio had a finality to it. The termination of my 'indefinite maternity leave'. The reward I'd earned for achieving motherhood felt cut short, and somehow disparaged, diminished.

Stop being a spoiled brat, I told myself. *You're so damn lucky. You're a mother now. You did it! Now get to fucking work.*

I greeted the receptionist, who, on recognising my distress, closed me into an enormous hug that gave me permission to set off the waterworks once again. Why I felt okay to cry in front of my colleagues now, where I never would have in a trillion years during my IVF days, continues to baffle me.

Perhaps it's because motherhood is universal, but somehow IVF as a solo woman carries an element of 'shame'. In motherhood, everyone 'gets it'. You're away from your baby which is heartbreaking. But with IVF as a solo mum? Well, it's your choice, for one. So, you don't get the right to splash emotion all over the workplace about it. Or maybe it's the 'shame' of choosing to be partnerless and being embarrassed about the reaction. Did I ever even feel that? Perhaps it was so locked up inside I was unable to see it.

I managed to make it through the afternoon albeit a little teary and emotional. On the floor, having a stretch between classes, I felt the rush of energy that was my intermediate contemporary class thundering in.

'Miss Lorena. You're back!' one of the students piped up. 'How's your baby?'

I executed a weird hiccuppy thing to hold in my emotion. 'Tyler's doing great! Thank you.'

'When are you bringing her in?' another student asked.

The whole class chimed in, 'Yeah, we wanna meet her!' Like she was some sort of celebrity. I promised to bring Tyler to see them in the coming weeks, then got into the business of teaching.

The hours went faster than I'd anticipated. And guess what? Tyler survived my absence! So did Mum and Dad. Pretty easily, too. Apparently Tyler cried a lot, refused her bottle, and was quite restless, eventually collapsing into a warm, cuddly mound in mum's arms where I found her on my return.

She was hungry and had missed her mummy, yes. But I knew she was in the best hands with my parents. So, for both of my twice-a-week work shifts, I was able to leave with a clear conscience that my family would be more than okay.

41

You Chose to be A Solo Mum, So…

April 2020, Tyler is 6 months old

Many times, I've seen online trolls comment on the posts of solo mums by choice in negative ways. It's often blokes. Or profiles that appear to be men. Comments like: 'She's too ugly to get a man' or 'Give her a night with me, she'll change her mind'. There's also the 'she's selfish doing it alone' narrative.

Solo mums by choice aren't in the business of taking too much crap, so the power of 'no response' is the strongest default. I don't know whether these callous condemnations are a reflection of an individual who fears a woman who doesn't 'need' a man? Perhaps strong women with autonomy who live by their own rules is a scary thing to someone hiding behind a keyboard. Perhaps it's a resentful reflection of someone's failure to satisfy a woman in his life. Or perhaps these people are just goddamn bullies.

Sometimes the comments are more unambiguous. Resentment over the fact that solo mums by choice in Australia are entitled to the government's Single Parenting Payment is one of them. 'You chose to be a solo mum by choice, so you don't *deserve* Centrelink assistance.'

Let me clarify here. Firstly, most solo mums and dads by

choice are intelligent, hard-working individuals. It takes a hell of a lot of planning, determination, and money to make babies this way. Most of us work. And pay taxes. I've done so my whole adult life.

Secondly, none of us go into this lightly. You don't 'accidently fall pregnant' as a solo parent by choice. Many of us go back to work. The financial back-up of Centrelink is there to protect our kids. It's nigh-on impossible to live on.

Lastly, we're almost always the sole income of the household. And unlike non-donor solo parent families, we're not claiming child support or needing legal assistance, so we don't burden the system. Similar family structure, yes. But bureaucratically separate.

It's hard when people who know little about the solo parent by choice community make nasty comments online. It's one time I feel the need to defend my choice. Apart from that, I feel the acceptance of solo parenthood as a choice is growing. Back when I started, I knew almost no one becoming a parent this way. Now we have celebrities including Natalie Imbruglia, Charlize Theron, Sandra Bullock, Fifi Box, and Rachel Corbett, all well-known solo mums by choice.

What's also interesting is that the younger generation are looking at this as an option much earlier in life these days. With medical technology improving at lightspeed, allowing early diagnosis around fertility, many young women find themselves faced with the reality of their conception limitations much earlier in life. What a great and accessible way for empowered, informed women to become mums on their own terms, whether partnered up or not.

I was beginning to notice some changes in my friendships.

Well, as a new mum, I was running with a different crowd. It wasn't like I was setting out to make friends – it just happened. My mothers' group was long gone, severed by an odd conversation we'd had about something so trivial I can't even remember.

Things were more complex with some of my single friends who didn't have kids. One was a solo mum by choice in the making who was never able to conceive. That's a tough one, and I'm loath to allow my head to drift into that territory. What would I have done if Tyler hadn't… nope. Too hard. So, I could see why our friendship faded.

My beautiful motorbike friend, Monica, came back into my life in wonderful circumstances. We'd drifted apart over the years, as friends often do. After offering her eggs to me all that time ago because she was 'never going to need them', she ended up becoming a mum after all. A solo mum, in fact. Her beautiful child is just eight months younger than Tyler. They adore each other and we hang out whenever we can.

Many of my old friends remain steadfast presences in our lives. Alice, Nicole, Cass, as well as numerous ex-colleagues-now-mates. But, as a single mum, I think people are sometimes still a bit unsure how to take me. *Is she dating?* (No!) *Does Tyler know there's no father in the house?* (Yes! And we talk about it openly.) *Are they just going to stay like that forever?* (Maybe. Forever is a mighty long time, though.)

Sometimes it feels like I'm caught between the world of childless single friends who still want to catch up 'like we used to', and partnered acquaintances who have barbecues, but only invite 'couples', because a single person would create an uneven number, and how would that work? Plus, will she hit on my hubby? (No, I will not, nothing's changed.) So, what do I do?

I seek out my own people.

The solo mum by choice community is a tight one and I've discovered many, many beautiful women there. I can't believe there are so many of us. When I first started out, I felt like the only one in the world going it alone, but the rising number of women becoming solo mums by choice is astonishing. And like all minorities, we find solace in one another. There's no talk of child-support, of the 'bastard father who ran off with the secretary'. There's the common thread of our kids having one parent who loves them to the end of the universe and wanted them even more.

I haven't quite found my solid solo mum 'tribe' yet. Perhaps one day. But I do love the women I speak to regularly from here, there, and across the country. I'd also like for Tyler to have mates who share her family structure. I keep open to all opportunities because Tyler deserves a solid group of donor-conceived friends. Not just one here and there. It's up to me to do better with this, and I have every intention of getting there.

The solo mum by choice community itself has very specific criteria regarding who 'qualifies' to call themselves one. It's not elitist or intended to create exclusion. I'll explain why.

A 'solo mum by choice' is someone who goes into motherhood with the intention to conceive and parent alone. That isn't to say they can't still meet someone and fall in love at some point. Conception is mostly via sperm donation, sometimes egg donation too. The donor/s can be known, anonymous, or a friend – just not an intended parent.

Another way is solo adoption. A hard one unless you're a

celebrity (with money, I presume), or a younger person. In Australia, it's virtually impossible to do, though some women and men manage it. I have a solo mum friend who fostered a newborn and ended up adopting him officially when he was two. An amazing outcome for them both.

There are other methods of becoming a solo parent by choice including surrogacy and embryo donation, as well as combinations of any of the above for men who naturally find it more of a challenge to follow the solo parent by choice route. They're out there, though!

One thing about solo parents by choice is that we don't have to worry about exes chasing us for custody. There aren't any child-support payments because there's simply no one to chase. A woman who falls pregnant to someone they don't end up with, even if they split before the child is born, is not considered a solo mum by choice, even though technically she is choosing solo motherhood. It's a fine line, but it's there. There are plenty of queer solo parents by choice as well. Sexuality doesn't define the desire to become a parent or how you choose to do it!

One last thing to flag before I move away from the politics of the solo mum by choice world. We (and I think I can speak for most solo mums by choice here) are not man-haters. Most of us just didn't manage to find the right partner to go down the parenting road with.

Many of us have had a terrible time dating-wise. And remarkably, many still haven't given up. That takes guts. At any given time on the solo mum by choice forums, there's a very busy sticky thread on dating life and how everybody's doing. Certainly not my cup of tea for now, but something very few of us would ever totally rule out.

We have dads, brothers, uncles, and male friends. I know I'm always ensuring Tyler has great male role models to help guide her. I'm lucky we have my dad, brother, uncle, and some special male friends who all play a vital role in Tyler's life.

I hadn't even been back to work a whole term when Covid landed and changed everything. I couldn't believe it. Each time I left Tyler to go to work in the lead-up, I dreaded it, spending time psyching myself that we weren't all going to get sick and die.

Then, suddenly everything closed down. Society shut up shop.

I no longer had to leave my girl to go to work.

Lockdown meant I could stay at home, teach my dance lessons on Zoom, and be with Tyler all the time. I set up a 'bubble' with Mum and Dad so they could babysit at their place while I was upstairs in their bedroom teaching classes. It worked brilliantly.

I would never say Covid was a good thing. It was a sad, uncertain time, and people died. But if a global pandemic was going to arrive at any point in my life, this was the time for it to happen. Our lives slowed down. We went for daily walks up to the park where a little café had just opened. We had everything we needed, including my daily flat white.

Part of me feels selfish talking like this. And I was terrified for the future, despondent for the people suffering. No one knew how the pandemic was going to play out, and I had a vulnerable baby at home as well as two elderly parents to worry about. So, we took it day-by-day. I watched my daughter in slow motion as she grew, said her first words, and took her first steps. By the time her first birthday rolled around in October, we were allowed twenty people over to celebrate. So, we did.

My choice to be a solo parent landed me in a fortunate place during those lockdown periods. I seriously would have gone nuts spending twenty-four/seven with another adult in the house. For some solo parents it may have been a lonely time. Not me! As long as my daughter, my cat, and a few good books were nearby, I was more than happy.

42

An Unexpected Predicament

Autumn 2022, Tyler is 2

Something wasn't right. Like I'd just swallowed a golf ball or something, forcibly hiccupping in the way you do when you've been crying hysterically. Except I hadn't been crying, nor had I been guzzling anything from the local putt-putt range.

I padded through the familiar darkness of my bedroom. My daughter's gentle sleepy breaths filling the silence.

What was that? My heart seemed to be skipping beats. I eased onto the edge of the bed, plunging my fingers into the side of my neck searching for a pulse.

Bah-boom. Bah-boom. Then a tinkly feeling in my throat followed by a quick cough and *Bah*-pause-*Bah-bah-boom*. My heart had paused for a second, before pumping two successive quick beats in a row. Like an improvised percussion solo in the concert hall of my bedroom.

I looked across at my sleeping daughter as she shifted onto her side, reaching for her favourite narwhal plush toy. The one with two tiny toy narwhal pups in its Velcro-rimmed, pregnant tummy. 'How did they get in there?' I'd quizzed Tyler earlier that night.

'Well, the doctor put donor sperm with a donor egg and then put them in Narwhal's tummy to grow.' I smiled at the memory,

283

my erratic heart easing back to some semblance of calm.

Ba-boom. Bah-pause-*Bah-bah-boom*. Another quick, hiccuppy breath caught in my throat, growing the golf ball to tennis ball size. *Breathe slowly. Stay calm.* But it was relentless.

Sweat beaded on my forehead as my involuntary coughs stirred my daughter's peaceful slumber. Whisps of butterflies cascaded through my windpipe and I struggled to sit still. I jumped up and headed for the kitchen. A drink of water and I'd be fine. Must be stress. Work was picking up after Covid, and Tyler had entered the notorious 'terrible-two' phase. Things were trying, but not impossible. Perhaps I was having a mild anxiety attack.

You'll be fine.

I went back to the bedroom and lay down, my daughter's arm flinging across me as it always does in her sleep. I felt instantly comforted.

You WILL be fine!

Lying there, my mind jumped into the elevator of irrational thought. *What if I'm having a heart attack? These weird palpitations. Coughing. Aren't those the symptoms? What if I die right here tonight?*

I hadn't yet taught Tyler how to phone the emergency services. How would she get help? I never thought I'd need that level of precaution. I hadn't envisioned a scenario like this. There are apps where kids can contact 000 if their carers are indisposed. There I was, the only adult in the house, with a toddler who would be utterly hysterical if she woke to find me lying lifeless beside her. Who would find her and help? How long would our windows and doors remain locked before anyone would notice our absence? How would my daughter survive?

The black of the night crowded my head. *More deep breaths.*

Sleep was still a long way off, so I sat up in bed and lit up my phone. 11:36pm. Shit! I typed, 'Heart attack symptoms in women' into Google. The results didn't wholly match my symptoms. Yet still, there was nothing to tell me I was going to 'for sure' survive the night.

As a solo parent, I'd expected to handle things alone. 'Par for the course', as they say. I didn't have to cook for another adult, or clean up after them. I didn't have to share parenting decisions or compromise when parenting styles clashed. It was me and my girl against the world. I was ready for pretty much anything.

Until now. This was something I'd pushed far down into the depths of my mind. No one wants to think about the possibility of dying. We realise it'll happen one day, but not in the middle of the night, lying beside the two-year-old you did thirteen rounds of IVF to create, who you love more than life itself.

I'd pushed thoughts of death and loss away. Loss, I'd experienced enough of. Death? Well, that's for when I'm much older. Right? Not tonight. I had day-to-day stuff to get on with. Washing. Cleaning. Will I dress my daughter in her dinosaur trackies tomorrow, or that gorgeous new unicorn dress her grandparents bought for her? Those things were far more important than a slightly shonky palpitating heart, and whether those skipping heartbeats of mine were going to lead me to my untimely demise.

The more I thought about it, the worse the palpitations became. With increasing distress, I checked my pulse every minute. Still that strange, infrequent rhythm. The tennis ball in my throat expanded to basketball size and I was certain my heart would explode any second.

You need to do something.

For a second, I considered phoning my parents. Mum could come over to look after Tyler while Dad took me to the hospital.

No. You can do it alone. Go to emergency. Just as a precaution. You'll be home within the hour.

I fumbled through drawers searching for a pair of comfy jeans. Making the decision to go calmed me down, and I was lucid enough to know I didn't want to leave the house looking like a vagrant. Stumbling through the kitchen, I packed snacks for my daughter. Then I crept back into the bedroom, sat down beside her, and paused for a minute.

Did I really want to disturb her? Making the decision to go had made me feel better, but what about her? Perhaps I was okay now. Testing my theory, I lay down for a moment.

Aah. Yes. Maybe we can just stay home. I'm fine.

Bah-boom. Bah-pause-*Bah-bah-boom.*

Fuck.

I gently tickled my daughter's cheeks. She twitched her nose, lazily flopping my hand away with a swipe her arm.

'Mummy,' she groaned.

'Sweetie. Mummy's not feeling very well. We need to pop to the hospital.'

Tyler's eyes blinked open. 'Mummy?'

'It's okay, sweet. Mummy's okay. We won't be long.'

I leaned over to switch on the bedside lamp, flooding Tyler's eyes with a cruel waking jolt.

'Mummy, I don't want to.'

'Neither do I, sweetie, but I'm a bit worried. We'll be quick.'

I watched as she rubbed her eyes, trying to figure out what was going on. 'How about we put on your favourite dinosaur trackies.'

Her face scrunched up and small tears began to eject from the insides of her eyes. Waves of guilt flooded me as my mind raced to find a better way. 'Darling, come here.' I enveloped her quivering body into my arms. 'We won't be long, I promise. I just need the doctor to have a quick look.'

'Mummy,' she wailed into the '*Bah*-pause-*Bah-boom-boom*' of my still-not-right chest. With a sudden wave of urgency, I scooped her up and carried her to the car. Her cries echoed through our snoozing street, her sadness cutting through my soul as we drove the four kilometre trip to our local hospital, not knowing for sure whether I would have enough gusto in my ticker to make it.

It would have been easier if I could have parked in the '15 Minutes Only' area by the doors of the Emergency Department. But I knew we'd be more than fifteen minutes, and I had no one to move the car for me and I'd end up with a ticket. So, we drove to the visitors' carpark and walked back, my daughter now calmly in her pram, checking I was alright and telling me a thousand times how much she loved me.

By the time we bundled into the triage area, I felt more at ease. At least now if anything happened there was a medical team and a host of adults who could take care of me and my girl. And I had a feeling we were both going to be alright.

43

Asking for Help is Hard!

Winter 2022, Tyler is 2

That scare shook me! We were in emergency all night with my heart monitored, checked, and re-checked. Tyler was a superstar, clearly worried about her mummy, quietly playing, looking at books, eating, and half-dozing. Eventually I signed an early release form. Once I knew there was no urgency, I just needed to get us both home.

I was back in day surgery in the following weeks having some in-depth tests on my heart. The diagnosis was: ventricular ectopic heartbeats – a reasonably dangerous condition where extra heartbeats occur in the ventricle chamber, disrupting my normal heartbeat rhythm and putting strain on my heart. Yikes!

The first question I asked my cardiologist was, 'Why?' Actually – that was the second question. The first was, 'Am I going to die?' The answer to which was, 'Not anytime soon, but we'll keep a close eye on you.'

As for 'Why?' This answer was hazy. Stress was an option. But was I stressed? The going back to work thing certainly hadn't lowered my stress levels. The uncertainty of Covid as well. Could parenting alone be unknowingly stressing me out? Who knew. Slowly over time the ectopic beats seemed to lesson. I tried not to stress. Not to worry about Tyler, money, work, the state of the world.

Then, not long after, I found myself in the emergency department again.

It was a bitterly cold winter's night at the end of our second term back after the Covid lockdowns. My students were still relishing the joys of being back in the studio, including the things we'd once taken for granted, like having space! So many of them had been doing class in their loungerooms, or even on the cold concrete surfaces of their garages. To be able to move again was a level of heaven we'd never again take for granted.

At the end of each term, we had 'watching week', where parents were invited to come in and view their kids doing class. It's quite lovely having parents proudly watch on.

I was demonstrating an inversion exercise – yes, that is what it sounds like, handstands, cartwheels, and headstands. I can still do a mean cartwheel and had executed a few of them on this occasion. The parents spontaneously applauded, making comments like, 'Miss Lorena, we didn't know you could do that!'

I looked at them with feigned confusion. 'Well, I am a contemporary dance teacher, folks!'

The students stood back, cringing slightly at the 'older person' exchange. After all, they just saw me as 'Miss Lorena'. Not the forty-nine-year-old middle-aged person that I was. Bloody amazing I could still cartwheel, really!

That night, locking up the studio, I headed out into the cold, crossing the street and walking down a quiet backroad where my car was parked. The same road where I'd sat in the gutter all those years ago crying after my first negative pregnancy test. That jagged memory still stabbed every time I parked there.

Tonight, the street felt eerie. Too dark, too silent. No one was around and the cold air gave me a chill. The streetlights seemed to illuminate the road, so I decided it was safer to leave the footpath and walk there. Fumbling down a small hill, my eyes were useless, it was so dark.

I thought I was stepping onto the edge of the gutter, but it was a grassy overhang.

My foot slipped. Folded.

CRACK!

The sound of my foot breaking echoed in my ears. My breath tightened and small whimpering sounds escaped as I squeezed my eyes shut and prayed it was just a sprain.

I sat in the gutter. Almost the exact same spot as on the pregnancy test day.

Get home. You need to get home.

My left ankle was screaming. Pleading for me to do something. I began to shake. Nausea filled my gut, threatening to erupt into something more unpleasant. I had to get home to my baby. Then deal with whatever this was. Just. Had to. Get. Home.

My foot was an inferno. I couldn't put any weight on it, and all movement caused lightning bolts of agony to surge. With gritted teeth and a scrunched-up face, I hopped four car-lengths to my vehicle. Unlocking the door, I carefully inched myself into the driver's seat as waves of nausea continued to crash in tidal waves over me.

Call Mum and Dad. They can come and get you.

No. I had to get home. Ten minutes along the main road and I'd be there. My driving foot was unhurt.

With a new wave of energy, I turned on the ignition. Indicated. Eased the car out onto the road. *You can do it*, I assured myself on repeat. *Get back to Tyler. Deal with the foot later.*

I drove home clinging so hard to the steering wheel it nearly cracked. As though the harder I gripped, the less pain there'd be. Adrenalin must have switched on after the initial shock because by the time I got home, the nausea had dissipated, and I felt suddenly stronger.

I arrived simultaneously with my parents. 'How did it go?' Mum asked.

'Good.' (Good? Huh? What was wrong with me?) 'I, uh, hurt my foot. It's quite bad.'

'Oh no, sweetie.' Mum looked at me hopping and carried Tyler down to the house.

Dad looked concerned. 'Do you need a doctor?'

I shook my head. 'Let's go downstairs and I'll have a look. It could be broken.'

First things first, Tyler needed feeding. Yes, she was two, and yes, I was still breastfeeding. Very, very much so.

Instinctively she knew something wasn't right. The waves of our mutual dopamine hit, once attached, comforted us both in ways I can barely describe. Now, I could think properly.

I had to figure out the extent of the damage.

Boy had I done a number on myself! The torture of removing my shoe was almost faint worthy. The golf ball of swelling on the outside mid-section of my foot indicated that yes, I'd definitely broken it. The amethyst-coloured bruising that had materialised was beyond impressive.

Dad stood up quickly. 'That's it. I'm taking you to the hospital.'

'No, no. Let me see how it is tonight. Please. We'll go tomorrow.' I didn't want another night in emergency. And there was no way I was parting with Tyler. 'I'll take some Nurofen, ice it, and sleep carefully.'

At 'ice it', Mum jumped up and extracted a bag of peas from the freezer. Dad sourced the Nurofen, and Tyler dozed contentedly in the warmth of my embrace. The only way I could get my parents to be okay about leaving me was to assure them I'd go to emergency the following morning.

At 7am, and with very little sleep because they were both worried sick, my dutiful, loving Mum and Dad appeared at my door ready to share the burden. Dad drove me to emergency while Mum looked after Tyler. I had student assessments at work later on, so I needed to be there by 1pm. Talk about everything at once.

I was away from Tyler for longer than I'd ever been by far. Over ten hours! I've never felt more guilty. Mum-guilt is a real bitch, popping up all over the place. On this day I felt helpless, useless, an utter failure. Like I'd been catapulted back to childhood again. Is that what asking for help is? When you can't manage something yourself, so you need someone to step in and look after you?

In hindsight, of course not. But on that day? Absolutely, yes, without a doubt. As if the post-Caesarean Mum and Dad taxi service hadn't been enough, this was a whole new level of dependence.

My parents wouldn't have had it any other way. Mum, relishing the extra precious one-on-one time with her granddaughter. Dad, the superhero without a cape, doing the equally hard yards on the front line at the hospital.

I wasn't surprised to learn I'd indeed shattered my foot. The doctor held up the x-ray image and confirmed after only a few hours of waiting in triage. 'Fractured cuboid. You'll need a moonboot and crutches for four weeks.'

I hobbled from the hospital into work with ten minutes to spare to choruses of, 'Ooh, are you alright, Miss Lorena?' My students performed the movement phrases I'd set with artistry, strength, and the impeccable contemporary technique we'd spent lesson after lesson working on. I was proud and relieved on all fronts.

Then finally, time for my most important part of the day. Dad drove me home to Tyler, where we found her in her highchair, giggling with Mum. The two of them so enraptured with one another they barely noticed our entrance. I cuddled my girl, both of us exhausted. My own emotional overload set to burst at any moment.

Mum and Dad staggered out the door an hour and a coffee later, relieved everything was now essentially okay.

As I lay in bed that night, Tyler sleeping gently beside me, I reflected on how the day had upended a whole stack of values and concerns I never really knew I had. My inability to ask for help is a well-known fact. But the helpless, childlike feeling that came along with it had taken me by surprise.

And then, finally, after multitudes of over-contemplation, I began to laugh out loud. I tried to mute my chuckles so I didn't wake Tyler, but the ludicrousness of my broken foot suddenly hit me. After impressing my students' parents with my cartwheeling ability, then exiting the building only to break my foot falling down a gutter? You couldn't write it!

What a huge relief I could finally see the funny side.

44

The Ways We Support One Another

October 2022, Tyler is 3 years old

Life plodded on – and I limped right alongside it. Feeling one minute like a complete schmuck for my recent shortcomings, and the next, immensely humble and grateful for the help I wasn't having to request, ever, in the form of my parents being there whenever Tyler and I needed them.

Dad continued to drive me into work for two weeks following my accident. What a pain in the proverbial for him. He never said anything like that, and to be honest I think he quite liked being able to help. I, of course, struggled with depending on anyone, but accepted it with grace because it kept us functioning.

Mum, ever the steadfast support, wore her love for her granddaughter right on her sleeve. When she and Tyler were together, she didn't hear a thing. Not least for the first ten minutes or so. From day one, right to the present, it's been a running together in a field moment each time they're reunited. And now that Tyler's older, the reciprocation of this is beautiful to see.

Dad is much the same, but he tends to be more of a slow burn; often drawing, reading, or playing on the computer with his granddaughter. What a lucky girl Tyler is to have these two legends in her life. It's almost as if Tyler's only set of grandparents are instinctively giving twice the love.

Still, I was desperate to regain my independence. One night, carrying the laundry basket downstairs to fold our clean clothes, I slipped on a step and went down. I didn't have my moonboot on, so to protect my broken foot, I did a weird twisty movement that would sit beautifully in any innovative contemporary dance piece. I thundered down, still holding the laundry basket and yelling, 'FUUUCK,' quite oblivious to the three-year-old watching *Octonauts* in the next room. One of the few times I've used a 'big four' word in Tyler's vicinity.

I managed to crack the cartilage of two ribs, confirmed by my GP a few days later. I kept soldiering on. Only just, and with no one to bounce off or hand my daughter over to for some physical and mental relief, life was beginning to feel heavy. I won't say I was nearing rock bottom. I know what rock bottom looks like, and this wasn't it. But I was having a fuck of a time and needed to pull myself out of it.

I needed to start giving myself some credit for all the solo mumming. Sure, I was receiving ample help. But this was essentially still my own gig. Things weren't perfect, and my mind was about as fuzzy as a mum's can get. But regarding the act of mothering, I began to feel more comfortable acknowledging that I was doing a pretty good job. Tyler was thriving. Outgoing, clever, playing nicely with the other kids in the playground. I had a kind giving girl with a huge capacity for affection and love.

We were winning!

Until the *next* thing happened that shook my apparently brittle bones to the core.

We were out at the local village precinct. I was limping

around, still in the shackle that was the moonboot, perhaps just a week or so until I could finally get rid of it. The spring sun was shining, wonderfully pungent wafts of jasmine filled the air, mixed with the delicious toasty coffee aroma from the flat white I was sipping. Tyler was playing in the playground.

Or was she?

I turned around for five seconds to greet a mum from Tyler's gymnastics class. By the time I turned back, Tyler was gone.

My first instinct was, 'She must be here. Somewhere!' Walking around, I searched tunnels, caves and in between equipment. Nothing. *Where the hell is she?*

My search became frantic. 'Tyler? TYLER! Where are you? TYLER!!!' I couldn't find her. Tears streaked my face as I pictured all the things that go through every mother's mind when her child vanishes in public. Only, I had one extra horror: Tyler and I didn't share the same DNA. *What if she's lost and something happens? How will they find her?*

In hindsight, this is crazy. A strand of hair from her hairbrush would solve that problem just like for any other child. So why did my mind rush to that place? Was I harbouring some sort of deep-grained insecurity about our connection?

A group of women, including the gymnastics mum, gathered to help me. 'What's she wearing?' one asked. 'How old is she?' 'What colour is her hair?'

The questions blended into one as my head compressed to the size of a pea. The knot in my stomach so tight I could barely breathe. Five long minutes passed.

'Is this her?'

I fell to my knees, grabbing hold of my girl, sobbing and

swearing never to let go. Eventually, I loosened my grip and looked at her. 'Where were you?'

Without a care in the world, she pointed in a direction up the hill and said, 'I was chasing a tissue over there. It looked like a bunny.'

Turns out she was running after a restaurant serviette that was dancing along the footpath in the wind. And as the playground wasn't fenced, she'd gone a lot further than I thought possible in almost no time.

I was shaken for days, but you won't believe it... there's more. This last story is quite amusing, really. And kiboshes any undercurrent of worry I've ever had about the connection between Tyler and me.

When I was a kid, around Tyler's age, I stuck a music box ballerina up my nose. Oh yes, folks, I stuck it so far up there it broke, and I ended up in the hospital emergency room.

So, you can imagine my surprise when, like mother, like daughter, Tyler announced one evening that she'd broken off a piece of apple and wedged it up her nose. I shone a torch into her nostril but couldn't see a thing. 'Are you sure it's still there, sweet?'

'Yes, Mama.'

Oh, gawd.

So, off to the good ol' emergency department we went. Again. This time, backwards and forwards for days due to staffing shortages before an ENT doctor finally managed to suck the thing out with the world's tiniest vacuum.

I don't know whether it was coincidence. A crazy result of epigenetics? Nurture over nature? But the similarities between my double-donor daughter and I never ceased to amaze. And though this instant was by no means solid proof of anything, it certainly came as immense comfort that Tyler and I were, indeed, every inch birds of a feather.

45

Exciting Adventures

November 2022, Tyler is 3 years old

One day on a whim, I decided to buy tickets to go to Fiji. Well, why not? Covid seemed far behind us, and I found an amazing deal I could afford. It'd be a small, safe adventure, just the two of us.

I've done a fair bit of travelling in my time and I've never been afraid to go alone. In fact, I'd say a lot of times I preferred it. Doing what I wanted, exploring new places not confined by another person. I know. How could I have not seen the 'solo life' signs, even back then?

Yet the thought of taking my daughter away scared me. What if something happened? Eventually, a reality check inside my head piped up. *Um, it's a package deal in a Fijian resort, you doofus. You're not trekking up Everest!*

I followed my instinct and booked the tickets. We were set to go in ten weeks. All I needed now was to get Tyler's passport. Easy, right?

Not easy.

Since I'm Tyler's only parent, there were some hoops to jump through. Of course there were. But I'd left ample time for that, surely.

With Tyler restless in her pram, I queued up at our local post office with her passport form filled out and ready to go. I knew there was an extra form I needed to declare I was her sole parent, but felt confident we'd be done within the hour.

Finally, we reached the front of the queue and the assistant beckoned us over. A lovely lady who grabbed the extra form and started setting Tyler up for her photo. A difficult task in itself for a three-year-old who is not allowed to smile, just look straight at the camera. No blinking, no screaming, just stillness while waiting for the tell-tale 'click'.

The blessed assistant spent fifteen minutes trying for the money-shot. But the longer Tyler was there, the more restless she became. Little kids don't understand how to do a neutral expression and we weren't getting anywhere. The assistant was understanding. 'Happens all the time. Just bring her back tomorrow.'

I nodded, handing the extra form to her. 'How long do you think this will take?'

'Probably around twelve to fourteen weeks,' she said. 'They're frantic now everyone's travelling again after Covid.'

Twelve to fourteen weeks? My skin prickled. 'We leave in ten weeks. Can I please fast-track the application?'

She shook her head. 'No. I'm afraid you can't with this extra form.'

'But I've already bought the tickets. I need her passport in ten weeks. Nine, really.'

The assistant was already looking over my shoulder to cajole the next customer. 'So sorry.'

I walked out to the street clutching Tyler's passport forms. In a trance, I popped her into her car seat. She was happily chewing a biscuit, blissfully unaware of the big dilemma. I was going to lose my non-refundable, non-transferable money if I didn't get this sorted. I'd only just scraped up the money, and what a bloody idiot for not checking first.

I went home and did some research a-la-Facebook. I logged on to a trusty solo mum by choice group and searched 'passport applications'.

There it was. Countless threads of solo mums in my exact predicament. Matched by a plethora of advice on why it happens and what to do.

Apparently, and very strangely, solo mums by choice are lumped into the same category as all other single parent families. The reason for the extra form is to declare there is no other existing parent in the child's life. Perhaps someone might be planning on fleeing the country with their kid, but without the consent of the other parent. It's murky territory. And not fair that donor conceived families also get caught in the red tape.

There was a solo mum on the forum who insisted we, as donor families, didn't have to wait and that we could still fast-track our kid's passport. It was just a matter of finding a post office clerk who knew this and was willing to do it.

Mission accepted!

Mum and I wrapped Tyler in a rainproof jacket, snuggled her into her pram and jumped onto a citybound train. I figured if we went from post office to post office, one of the busy city ones would hopefully 'deal with this stuff all the time', and we'd get it done. Facing torrents of rain, we pressed forward.

Stop one: The Sydney GPO.

Nope. No way. And even worse, the clerk hollered at the top of his voice for the whole post office to hear that, 'Because your child doesn't have a father, you are not qualified to fast-track her passport.' Case closed. Nothing would alter his or his supervisor's viewpoint.

Mum was fuming. 'That's your personal business. How dare he yell it like that,' she said through gritted teeth. She was right. It was also discrimination. The fact that solo parents by choice were not recognised as separate to those who, for whatever reason, decided not to include a second parent on their kid's birth certificate. Two very different things!

Stop two: Much the same, but with a little less volume.

Stop three: 'Yes, I think that's possible.' My face lit up as the smiling assistant disappeared out the back with Tyler's forms for what felt like forever. I swung my head around to Mum who was playing a distracted version of peekaboo with Tyler. I gave her a fingers-crossed/thumbs up sign. Then the assistant returned, took Tyler's photo in a single shot (was this woman an angel?), stamped forms, took my (extortionate amount of) money and sent us on our way.

I couldn't believe it. 'It'll be delivered within 48 hours,' she said. That easy. We were set! I was immeasurably grateful to the solo mum by choice community for their help, advice, and proactive stance. I wouldn't have had the confidence to ask if not for them. What a determined, robust bunch of women.

The day of our trip soon arrived. I was nervous, but excited. There would be so many firsts for Tyler; first time on a plane, first time overseas, first time away from her beloved grandparents and Fonzi. Huge!

The flight went well – with take-off and landing the obvious highlights. I'd crammed a backpack full of activities, so we had plenty to do. I don't think Tyler quite understood that we were actually flying. 'Like a bird,' I tried to explain. Or that we couldn't just 'pop' home. We landed safely and had a two-hour taxi ride to our hotel. Thank goodness they provided a (shonky) car seat for Tyler. I sat in the back next to her as the driver hurtled along the twisty roads of the south main island.

Tyler was overtired. I could feel her breathing begin to quicken as tears erupted. 'Mummy, why is this man taking us away from our home?'

My heart caught in my throat as I nuzzled over and hugged her tight, not having a clue what to say. What *do* you say to that? And what had I done? Dragging my three-year-old to a foreign country on our own. This taxi driver could be an axe murderer for all I knew, and here we were in the middle of nowhere with him. I cursed myself for being such a fool and hugged my now sobbing daughter, careful not to let her see the tears that had also begun sneaking across my face.

Of course, we arrived at our hotel safely to the tunes of '*Bula!*' as the beautiful staff greeted us and fussed over Tyler. I breathed for the first time since leaving the airport. Perhaps we'd survive this holiday after all.

And we did! Apart from the time a local Fijian came into our room with a machete. Turns out he was just there to open coconuts, but it certainly gave me a shock when he strode in. Again, big man; small woman and toddler. One fleeting second. That's all it takes, and that's just how we feel as women.

In the end, I didn't have a concern in the world; we were safe and well taken care of. There were mocktails by the pool; copious amounts of delicious food; swimming. Tyler experienced her very first breakfast buffet where her eyes lit up knowing she could choose anything she wanted. 'Even the chocolate muffins, Mummy?'

'Yes, even the chocolate muffins, Ty-Ty.'

She met a girl her age and both our families hung out, often eating meals together if we all happened to be there at the same time. We were privy to a drumming fire-dance display and a full concert of Fijian music and dance where the audience jumped up on stage and joined in. There's video evidence somewhere of me in a conga-line. A previous hard 'no' for me (in the same category as karaoke – 'I'll never do it!'). But we were on holiday. Together. Anything felt possible.

46

Time to Cut the Cord

February 2024, Tyler is 4 years old

Time was flying by. My career as a dance teacher was satisfying. And I'd started delving into the possibility of being a writer as well. I was entering writing competitions and winning prizes, writing for *Mamamia*, and had articles being published in various literary journals. It wasn't a money-making venture (yet), but my ambition was set in that direction. Above all this, my calling as a mother was still stronger than ever. Always number one.

Sometimes juggling everything was bloody hard. To get any writing done, I'd often pop Tyler in front of the television for an hour or so. I'm not a parent who allows 'screen time' apart from TV, and I've had some major guilt trips relying on this form of 'babysitting'. But how else was I going to write? I only needed a couple of hours a day. Surely with a bit of scrounging I could find that time. Sometimes Tyler would sit in her pink and yellow bedroom for ages, playing. I could hear little giggles as she'd role play with her toys and dolls, guiding them through various scenarios. This made my writing time blissful because I knew we were both immersed 'together' in the separate worlds of our imaginations.

Occasionally, I'd ask Mum and Dad to take Tyler so I could squeeze in some writing. I also wrote while she slept, sometimes way into the morning hours. I was loving it, a new form of expression that was exciting my brain and satisfying my creativity. Plus, I relished the idea that as a middle-aged, new mum, I was forging a dual career path.

At this point I was still breastfeeding Tyler – mostly just before bed as she fell asleep. I didn't talk about it much, as it really wasn't anyone else's concern. Besides, no one was more surprised than me that we'd gone beyond a year of nursing. I'd always thought of long-term breastfeeding as a bit weird: 'They'll be feeding through the school gate, will they?' It's funny, because that line has actually been used on me. Acquaintances suggesting it's okay to breastfeed, just not at school age.

Well, we still had over a year before school. And I'd long decided we'd stop when we were both ready. Not before. Though that's not exactly how it happened. I ended up being 'ready' and Tyler was not! Far from it. For her, it was a sad time saying goodbye to 'milky milk'. I do hope she has a memory of it when she's older. It was a lovely time and one of my proudest achievements as a mother.

The 'attachment' parenting style was never something I thought I'd subscribe to. But I ended up being about as attached to my daughter as it gets. Long-term breastfeeding; co-sleeping; no daycare. I'm a disciplined dancer, so I thought I'd be a rule-follower rearing my child. I was constantly surprised by how often I went with my instinct instead. The narratives of, *dinner at 5pm; bottle at 6:30pm; bed at 7pm; wake early, get on with the day; sleep in your own room;* were never a thing in our house.

I was lucky to have Tyler in bed by 10pm, and dinner was rarely before eight. She'll probably be in my bed with me until she's ten, but either way I'll always let her be the guide. I'm certainly in no hurry to throw her into a 'big girl bed' in her own room. I love having her in with me. Fonzi's there too, our own little bedsharing family. Sometimes I can't move for limbs and fur, but we have a bed full of love, and that is a beautiful thing. And much easier without a partner in there too.

When I reflect on our home life, there have been plenty of ups and downs. Mostly we're a fun, silly, content little family. I can be a grumble bum at times; that's part of what a family is. The overworked, under-rested, never-stopping parent. But generally, our day-to-day lives are enjoyable, playing silly games, chasing dinosaurs, reading. Just being together.

Daily, Tyler will crouch under the breakfast table. 'Which Octonaut are you, Mummy?' I know this is the cue, our breakfast ritual, where Tyler launches into the character of 'every scary creature in the universe on top of the Octopod', and I need to sound the Octo-alert and save the day.

We have our own little love language fortified by the beauty of Tyler's vivid imagination. I'm not gonna lie – it can be a challenge at times for an adult to do the imagination thing over long stretches of time. But I know these days are short-lived. And that they're everything I dreamed of. So, I continue through Tyler's childhood to be an Octonaut, dinosaur, the tickle-monster. Whatever she wants. Because these days are priceless and beautiful.

The time inevitably arrived to send Tyler to preschool. I'd been dreading this in the way I'd dreaded returning to work nearly four years earlier. I'd remained resolute in my decision not to send her to daycare. She hadn't 'needed' it the way people suggested she would. She was thriving. Social. Confident.

I chose a sweet little preschool that had a lovely feel. We did a few orientation sessions and then Tyler was ready to go.

Me? Not so much.

She was only going twice a week, but that was two whole days away, and the first time she'd ever been separated from family. My baby was beginning to flee the nest, if only for a few hours a week. I felt sick thinking about it.

The first day rolled around. Tyler was apprehensively excited. I was holding my shit together, but only just. Distracting myself by taking photos of Tyler at our front door, then out the front of the preschool. She had her favourite dinosaur, Spino, (as in Spinosaurus) in her arms, and with her backpack on her shoulders, she looked like she was about ten years old.

We walked into the preschool hand-in-hand before she broke free, running to the dress-up area, so excited she didn't even remove her backpack. My heart melted with relief as, right on cue, one of the lovely teachers put her hand on my shoulder and said, 'She'll be fine.'

I nodded in response, and in the name of ripping-off-the-Band-Aid, I pecked Tyler on the cheek, bade her farewell, and legged it out before the waterworks began.

And boy, did they begin. I made it to the car where I sat and shook for ten minutes, our lives together flashing before me. How could we be here already? Where did the time go? We'll never have those baby days again. Nor the toddler days. We'd never get another 'first day of preschool', and bloody hell, Tyler would be going to school next year. What was with that? The best piece of advice I'd ever been given as a new mum had been: 'Make the most of every day because time goes so fast.' I'd been trying to do that, yet here we were.

Although we were the only solo mum by choice family at Tyler's preschool, the other parents were generally lovely. We made some beautiful connections. One afternoon at pick-up time, one of the sweetest mums 'tried' to put herself in my shoes.

'Hey Lorena, how's it going?'

I told her life was pretty good and commenced with the small talk.

'Well, I'm going to have a taste of life in your shoes next week,' she said. 'Hubby's off on a work retreat so I'll be a solo mum.'

I gasped. If there's one thing to be wary of when talking to a solo mum by choice, it's saying this kind of thing. I usually shake it off. Like when people tell me I'm 'brave' for going it alone. I think these comments come in the form of admiration and empathy. But the way it lands is more like naïve ignorance. I say that with kindness and due diligence.

You are not a solo mum for the weekend. You have a partner who has an income. Solo mums have a solo income. Just because a partner is away doesn't mean every part of them has dissipated. You can still call them for support. And you know they'll be back.

Some solo mums by choice get quite fired up about this. My comment is usually something on the lines of, 'Well, I bet you'll be glad when he's back.' That's what I said on this day, because the mum meant well.

We were very accepted by the other families at Tyler's preschool. I'm grateful for that, because I wasn't sure how it would be. I think people have way too much to worry about than gossip about our take on family diversity. I hope for Tyler it stays that way. I'll continue to keep her teachers and educators informed of our family structure, and the language we use around it.

Here's one: what do we do on Father's Day?

There are a few options for us. The main one is celebrating Tyler's grandpa, her Papa. We make a card for him, buy him a tasteless present in the name of attempted humour, and have heaps of fun. Tyler loves to take the lead, especially when choosing cards and presents.

More recently, we've learned about *FUDGE* Day, an acronym for 'Friends, Uncles, Donors, Grandfathers, Everyone'. We make, or buy (usually buy) some delicious fudge, and celebrate all the men in Tyler's life. It's a great concept. *MADGE* day for Mother's Day is similar.

So far, Tyler hasn't had too many 'why don't you have a father?' type questions. Kids of course aren't afraid to ask. And when they do, her usual response is, 'I just don't.' Sometimes she may use the term 'donor', or even 'sperm donor', because I've been very literal in the language I use around this.

It's a bit controversial that a two/three/four/five-year-old drops the word 'sperm' in the school playground. But evidence-based research indicates that full disclosure, and the use of correct terms at a young age, is the recommended best practice. It's not wholly unlike using the correct terms for private parts. And Tyler's teachers have been prewarned about it, so no one will be shocked if it happens.

Tyler doesn't yet know in explicit detail what sperm or eggs are. All she knows is that you need both to make a baby. I'm hoping she continues to tell her story with confidence and that it's just so normal, everyday, to her that it becomes a bit 'meh'. Because the reality is, it's only a small part of her as a person.

And the place she has on this planet is viable, deserved, and treasured.

Not to mention she is loved beyond ridiculousness, but that is, of course, a given.

February 2025, Tyler is 5 years old

Tyler never seemed too upset that she didn't have a dad. She never said anything much, and with all the love in her life, including that of her grandparents, I knew her cup was full.

Until.

One night at bedtime, she'd chosen *The Book of Tyler* for me to 'read'. That's the blank folder where I'd tell her creation story to her improvisation-style.

On this night, we got to the '… and Mummy searched and searched but could not find a daddy' part.

Tyler looked up at me. 'I wish I had a daddy.'

I gulped. I'd been anticipating this moment since the day she was born. Many solo mum friends had mentioned their own experiences, and I was starting to wonder if perhaps Tyler would skip this phase.

No matter how 'ready' you are, and how much you 'prepare' yourself, your heart still breaks a bit. Mine did, anyway. I went into my, 'Well, you have so many people who love you,' speech but that barely touched the surface. Then I said, 'What is it about not having a daddy that makes you sad, Ty?'

'All the other kids at school have one.'

Again, my heart leaped into my throat. 'Well, you have a wonderful Papa.'

'Yes, but I don't have a daddy to play with.'

I kept grappling. 'But Mummy plays with you.'

'It's not the same. Daddies play differently.'

I was floored. I gave Tyler a big hug, rocking her, telling her how much I love her. I listed all the people who love her and held her tight for a few minutes. Then, as quickly as she went into it, she came out again. 'Mummy, why aren't we reading?'

We finished *The Book of Tyler* and read a couple more of her favourites before I tucked her in, kissed her forehead and lay with her until she slept.

The following night, I brought it up again. I'd been thinking about Tyler's very specific line of sadness and wanted to try a new tactic. 'Ty, do you know that Mummy never had a papa?'

Her eyes lit up. 'Literally? What the?!' (One of her favourite phrases.)

'I know! I never had a grandpa in my life. Can you imagine not having Papa?'

She shook her head. 'Nope.' Then, in the way I'd taken her into my arms the previous night to console her sense of loss, she did the same.

'It's okay,' I said. 'Both my papas died before I was born. I did sometimes wonder what it'd be like, though. To have one.'

Tyler held me tight. 'It's really great, Mummy!' I'd finally reached her. I'm under no illusion that not having a dad is on the same scale as not having a grandpa. But at least after this revelation, my girl was reminded that all families are *not* the same. And that even if it feels like something is missing, life can still be great.

I know this will come up again. And I'll probably be equally as taken aback. But I figure all I can do is be prepared, transparent, open, and honest.

47

A Silent Revelation

April 2025, Tyler is 5 years old

I didn't think I'd find myself back at the exact same climbing gym I used to frequent thirteen years ago. The one where I first met Richie.

When a birthday invitation landed in our school WhatsApp chat, I immediately responded, 'Yes, Tyler would love to attend.' Then I put my glasses on and had a closer look.

Oh, shit.

My initial instinct was to write back and apologise, I had my days mixed up and we couldn't come after all. But that wasn't fair on Tyler.

On the day of the party, we pulled into the business park that housed the climbing gym, parking the car in the same spot I used to swing my motorbike into all those years ago. My stomach churned. My heart had been beating properly since the palpitation debacle, but today it threatened to stop altogether.

What if Richie was in there? Why was I trembling? Perhaps I secretly wanted to see him, prove to him that my life had moved on, and that he was just some loser left behind. Truth is, I hadn't given him a single thought in a decade. Why was revisiting our old haunt grappling me like this?

Tyler's hand reached for mine as we entered the building.

We stood at the door looking around. Me, searching for ghosts of the past; Tyler, a little unicorn looking for her herd. 'There they are!'

'Where?' I asked, clicking back to the present. A long table at the side of the entrance was filled with unicorn partyware, a rainbow cake, masses of presents, and a congregation of five-year-olds chattering about how high they were going to climb.

An instructor showed the adults how to belay their children. Tyler displayed a real love for the sport, not necessarily going high, but using her strong legs and unyielding coordination to get up the walls. 'It's a bit scary, Mummy.' The kids' area was filled with colourful imaginative walls. Tyler's favourite was, of course, the dinosaur maze.

We're not a sporting family. I can't catch a ball to save myself, and I'm even worse at throwing. Give me a frisbee, and you'd better hope I don't lop your head off. But somehow, we both enjoyed climbing. Especially when dinosaurs were involved. Tyler loves playing with dolls at home, but not nearly as much as her immense plastic insect and dino collection.

After their initial climb, the kids settled at the party table to refuel and chatter. I took the opportunity to duck up to the bouldering area for a step into memory lane. 'I'll just be a minute, sweetie,' I whispered to Tyler as I slipped away.

Entranced, and with a thumping heart, I ascended the shabby worn carpet stairs that hadn't changed since the last time I'd been there. Unsure of what I'd find, I peered over the edge to scan the area before stepping out. There were only two men there, one with longish wavy surfer hair like Richie's. He was bouldering across one of the toughest overhangs, holding on by a thread. His mate was sitting below, spotting him and mansplaining some guidance and advice.

'Match your feet and reach with your left arm, mate.'

I studied 'mate'. He seemed shorter, stockier than Richie. Then again, it had been over twelve years since I'd last seen the man. Twelve! The one who treated me so badly. Stole my confidence. Robbed me of hope and tricked me into thinking he was one of the good ones.

When I really stopped to think about it, Richie had been the catalyst awakening my need to become a mother. If he hadn't been such an indescribable arsehole for so long, I would have perhaps settled for second best. If he'd decided to 'give it a go' with me, perhaps I'd have ended up on a very different trajectory.

Perhaps I would have had a kid with him. Perhaps I'd never have discovered the solo mum by choice life! Perhaps I'd never have known Tyler.

Whoah! What a revelation.

How lucky I was that Richie was a chauvinistic cheat who had a lowlife dickhead as a best friend. In some ways I owe them a handshake and a beer down the pub to say, 'thank you.' Because through their maltreatment, I discovered the life that was meant for me.

'Come on, Steve, you've got this!' The bouldering climber was still dangling, arms shaking from exertion, under the trickiest part of the overhang.

Steve. No one I knew. I breathed a sigh of relief and watched Steve collapse in a heap of frustration below his failed attempt. He yelled a profanity so loudly, I was sure it was in earshot of the kids below. Masculine toxicity oozing as he began to pace the area, his failure consuming him. Embarrassed? He caught my eye as he marched past, and I flinched a little.

'Mummy?' A small face peered around the corner where the staircase met the bouldering platform. 'Mummy, I couldn't find you.'

'I'm here, sweetie. Mummy just popped away for a sec to see where she used to climb.'

Tyler's eyes widened. 'You've climbed *here*?'

'Yes, sweet. A long time ago.'

'Can you show me, Mummy?'

'Not now, sweetie. That's a part of Mummy's life that's finished.'

Tyler looked at me, searching my eyes. I stretched my arms out wide for a hug. She melted into my embrace like a tiny hummingbird under its mother's wing. I picked her up and carried her toward the stairs, taking one final look over my shoulder at a place I'd never need to see again. Steve was shaking his arms out ready to re-attempt his climb. And though I was sure he was a perfectly lovely man, as they often are, I was thankful I didn't have him, or anyone like him, in my life anymore.

Tyler looked up at me as I put her down to descend the stairs. 'Mummy, when I couldn't find you, I thought you were gone.'

'Never gone, Tyler. Mummy is here for you. Always.'

Epilogue

You've read my story.

If it were a more viable option for me to have searched for an Australian egg donor, I may have. Realistically, after twelve own-egg rounds, I'd run out of time long before I made the decision to go with a donor egg. And, in hindsight, with Covid approaching, that time would have stretched out so long my baby may never have happened. I always say, if things hadn't worked out as they did, I wouldn't have my darling girl. It really comes down to that.

With today's technology, and the shrinking of our world in terms of global communication, it's only a matter of time before Tyler finds the genetic connections she will likely crave. I'll be sitting at the sideline ready to jump in to ensure she gets what is a very basic, fundamental, human right – to know her origins.

Sometimes, when she was brand new (and I still do this today, but she doesn't often sit still long enough), I'd gaze into her eyes, search her face, to find familiarity. I made her, after all, and if you've ever heard of the power of epigenetics, you'll know that a woman's body can make some major genetic decisions on behalf of her baby in utero.

You can't alter DNA. But the way genes are expressed can be decided by the host body (me!). Even post birth endeavors such as breastfeeding can have an epigenetic effect. The Google rabbit-hole for this is quite something!

Plus, and this is really cool, fingerprints are created during various interchanges of genetics and environmental factors in utero. If a baby's finger presses against the amniotic sac, pressure on the sac plays a role in creating the ridges of the baby's fingerprint. So, I essentially played a role in crafting the unique swirls on some, if not all of Tyler's fingerprints. I love that!

When I look at my daughter it's like I'm looking into a mirror. She looks like me! And, bloody hell, she looks like her cousin too. It's quite spooky how similar their facial features are. She may have come from a different blueprint, but some sort of universal magic has played its hand in creating a girl who is very much our kin.

I love nothing more than for a stranger to tell me how similar my daughter is to me. She is the living, breathing reflection of the dream I've had for so long. It wasn't just a 'selfish' desire for motherhood, I wanted her. Tyler. This one right here, the one that I got.

All the IVF rounds were worth it. I bow down to every single one of them for leading us to where we've landed.

The End

ACKNOWLEDGEMENTS

This was a hard book to write. It began way back in 2014, where I persisted, even though I didn't know how it was going to end. All I knew was I had a story I needed to tell. When I was unable to face my computer, or show up on the page, I made detailed notes. Writing and re-living everything at every stage of this book's development felt, at times, impossible.

Thank you to my early readers for their encouragement, insight, gentle feedback, and advice. Most of all, thank you – all of you – for believing in my story: Trish and Andy Otes, Rachel Jim, Heidi-Nicole Horn, Angela Jolie (name changed), Leanne Haines, Kirsty Koolloos, Craig Evers, Laura Hale, Shan Humphreys, Pam and Max Goldsmith, Athena Law, and Lindsay Bartels. Thank you to Nicole Webb for your invaluable feedback in the early writing group days.

Endless gratitude goes to my superstar editor, Andy Otes, who, as my father, had the somewhat odious and unenviable task of combing through 120,000 words of gibberish to help shape my memoir into what it is today. They say, 'Don't get a family member to edit your work.' But Dad, a professional editor, copywriter, and ghost-writer, armed himself with his customary yellow highlighter and went gently to town on my work. Thank you, Dad, for being tough on me, for giving me just the right kind of criticism, and for adapting to my many, often discordant, requests and retorts. I continue to learn so much every time we work together.

To all the medical professionals heavily disguised in the pages of this book. I wish I could shout out and name you all. Without you, I wouldn't have become a mum! A special shout-out to the nurses who work so hard behind the scenes, not only within the realms of their job description, but also so often going the extra mile with phone calls, shoulders to lean on, and encouraging rapport. These are the people who also have to deliver torrents of bad news to patients every day. I salute you all.

Big thanks to the writing tutors and mentors I've had along the way: Patti Miller, you inspired me right at the very start, particularly with structure and dialogue; Bernadette Foley, without you, there would be no Chapter One, and therefore no real backstory; Ashley Kalagian Blunt, you showed me how memoir, like fiction, can be written in scenes. Thank you all. I am inspired by each of you.

Gargantuan thanks to everyone at Hawkeye Publishing. I entered the 2024 Hawkeye Manuscript Development prize solely for the feedback. I never expected to come second! Thank you to the judges, Camille Booker, Gabrielle Davis, and Meesha Whittam for recognising my manuscript as a topical, necessary piece. Your comment, 'This book will change lives,' continues to blow me away. Your feedback propelled me forward, giving me the confidence and reassurance I needed to get it published. Thank you to Skye Martin for the gorgeous cover and to Anne Freeman for the inspiration and incredible base design.

To the incomparable Carolyn Martinez, my publisher. Thank you for championing strong, female voices, in this case (still pinching myself), mine! What you do for debut authors is beyond next level. I've felt the substance of your belief, encouragement, and support from the moment you posted your own book out to me all that time ago. Not only are you lovely, you're also knowledgeable, quick-thinking (thanks for the title change and Part Three inspiration!), professional, and I look forward to continuing to work with you. Thank you for this opportunity. It's one of the highlights of my life.

Immense gratitude to Isabelle Marot for your patience and tireless advice, particularly regarding Tik Tok – terrifying territory for me, but you have been wise, kind and always so very supportive. Thank you!

Thanks also to the Hawkeye editors who have read and given advice and suggestions that have made this book so much stronger.

Special thanks to my friends who stuck by me during the 'trying to conceive' days. You all appear in this book somewhere. I simply couldn't have done it without you.

To all the other solo mums by choice out there. You each have your story. But one thing I'm sure we all have in common is our fierce determination to become parents. To those who fought the good fight but didn't get their baby: may we walk in solidarity for the bloody hard journey it is in the throes of the IVF trenches. I see you all.

Thank you to my family. To Danny, Kell, and Monty for all the fun times during a very tough period. To Uncle Mike for your support.

To Mum and Dad: Thank you. THANK YOU! Words don't do justice to the tonnes of gratitude I have for you both. You always listened, understood, and stood right there next to me throughout every single up and down through the timeline of this book. You still do! I'm a lucky duck to have you as my parents. I love you both endlessly.

And lastly, to my Tyler, the happy ending of this story. You have shown me what motherhood is. And so much more. I suspected along the way that it would all be worth it, but you have truly blown the ups-and-downs out of the park. I couldn't love you more, my beautiful girl. You are my love, my joy, my everything. I will love you 'til the stars go black!

ABOUT THE AUTHOR

Born and bred on Sydney's Northern beaches, Lorena Otes is a long-time scribbler, professional writer, debut author and classical ballet/ contemporary dance teacher.

Her memoir, *Solo Mum by Choice*, placed runner-up in the 2024 Hawkeye Manuscript Development Prize. She is now a literary judge for the 2026 Hawkeye Prize.

Lorena has written for *Feels Blind Literary*, *The Brussels Review*, *Mamamia Online*, and *Bounty Parents*. Her humour articles have appeared in *Witcraft Magazine*, *Defenestration Literary Humour Magazine*, *Scalar Comet* and *Little Old Lady Comedy*.

Lorena is a flash-fiction-writing tragic. Her stories have longlisted in the Australian Writers' Centre's Furious Fiction competition, the Not Quite Write Prize, The Letter Review, and she received Highly Commended in the Writers Victoria's Best of Times Short Story competition 2024.

Lorena is a huge (HUGE!) Bonnie Tyler fan, and listens to her music with abnormal regularity. She is an avid reader, motorbike enthusiast, and a proud solo mum by choice to her fabulous, dinosaur-loving six-year-old daughter.

www.lorenaotes.com.au

Book reviews can make or break a book. If you liked what you read today, please do consider posting a review on Goodreads or your favourite forum.

Solo Mum by Choice is available at hawkeyebooks.com.au and all good bookstores and libraries.

If you enjoyed *Solo Mum by Choice*, you'll also enjoy:
The Beauty of Broken Things by Melissa Sharman
New Year's Eve by Sarah Todman
The Truth About My Daughter by Jo Skinner
A World of Silence by Jo Skinner